D1367440

THE OUT AMERICAN

George D. Stoddard

LOOK FOR
EDUCATION

Southern Illinois University Press
CARBONDALE AND EDWARDSVILLE

Feffer & Simons, Inc.
LONDON AND AMSTERDAM

Library of Congress Cataloging in Publication Data

Stoddard, George Dinsmore, 1897–
　　The outlook for American education.

　　Includes bibliographical references.
　　1.　Education—United States.　I.　Title.
LA210.S73　　　　370'.973　　　　74–11369
ISBN 0–8093–0681–6

11/28/74 Baker & Taylor 8.95

TO MARGARET

CONTENTS

PREFACE

This book brings into focus a wide range of educational problems, issues, and opportunities. It is designed to give the school or college executive, teacher, and advanced student something to vary from. It may arouse the latent spirit of school board members and concerned citizens. Neither a textbook nor a research report, the book is essentially one man's view of where and what the action is in American education.

It is pleasant to acknowledge the "tender loving care" of my editorial assistants, Dr. E. Frederic Knauth and my wife, Margaret T. Stoddard. To the initiate, their expertise is apparent on every page. Mr. Vernon Sternberg, Director of the Southern Illinois University Press, has been most helpful at all points.

I also wish to acknowledge with thanks permissions granted by the various copyright holders and publishers to quote from the following works:

Mathematics Education edited by Edward G. Bogle. Copyright © 1970 by Herman G. Richey, Secretary, The National Society for the Study of Education. Reprinted by permission of the University of Chicago Press.

The Education of American Teachers by James Bryant Conant. Copyright © 1963 by James Bryant Conant. Reprinted by permission of McGraw-Hill Book Company.

August 1973   *George D. Stoddard*
New York City

THE OUTLOOK FOR AMERICAN EDUCATION

1

JOHN DEWEY
AND AMERICAN EDUCATION

The social matrix of education in America cannot be understood without reference to the lifelong work of John Dewey. In assessing the place of Dewey's philosophy as applied to education we need to bring in other theories only by indirection. So much has been said by his critics and supporters, from Thomists to humanists, and in his name so much has been done or left undone that a writer today is unlikely to add anything new or significant. Considering my restricted purpose, which is to provide a setting for developments in American education, I can be selective.

First, a few direct quotations to set the stage.

Thinking includes all of these steps—the sense of a problem, the observation of conditions, the formation and rational elaboration of a suggested conclusion, and the active experimental testing. While all thinking results in knowledge, ultimately the value of knowledge is subordinate to its use in thinking. For we live not in a settled and finished world, but in one which is going on, and where our main task is prospective, and where retrospect—and all knowledge as distinct from thought is retrospect—is of value in the solidity, security, and fertility it affords our dealings with the future.[1]

Knowledge, as an abstract term, is a name for the product of competent inquiries. Apart from this relation its meaning is so empty that any content or filling may be arbitrarily poured in.

1

The general conception of knowledge, when formulated in terms of the outcome of inquiry, has something important to say regarding the meaning of inquiry itself. For it indicates that inquiry is a continuing process in every field with which it is engaged.[2]

Intellectual operations are foreshadowed in behavior of the biological kind, and the latter prepares the way for the former. But to foreshadow is not to exemplify and to prepare is not to fulfill. Any theory that rests upon a naturalistic postulate must face the problem of the extraordinary differences that mark off the activities and achievements of human beings from those of other biological forms. It is these differences that have led to the idea that man is completely separated from other animals by properties that come from a nonnatural source. The conception to be developed in the present chapter is that the development of language (in its widest sense) out of prior biological activities is, in its connection with wider cultural forces, the key to this transformation. The problem, so viewed, is not the problem of the transition of organic behavior into something wholly discontinuous with it—as is the case when, for example, Reason, Intuition, and the A *priori* are appealed to for explanation of the difference. It is a special form of the general problem of continuity of change and the emergence of new modes of activity—the problem of development at any level.[3]

John Dewey as Social Innovator

It is an error to identify "scientific" thought with all thought. In the flood of evolutionary theory loosed upon a Victorian society in which all things seemed possible to the elite, and anything disagreeable—war, disease, poverty, overpopulation, environmental spoilage—rarely intruded upon one's vision, the urge to preserve the *status quo* found expression in curricular and classroom rigidity. The best minds in the best of worlds had spoken their piece, and the teacher, however far down the social ladder, was to be the transmitter. John Dewey, above all others, saw through such pretensions and their insidious control of the mental and emotional habits of the young; he worked to free the mind from beliefs, right or wrong, that were presumed to be true without confirmation and therefore not allowed to be tested in the thought or experience of the learner. Dewey rightly sensed that the system was hostile to the full development of free and responsible persons under a democratic government. Method became important, as did the very atmosphere of the school or home. In essence, Dewey's reforms were more psychological and social than philosophical; they usually focused, not upon some abstract principle of logic, but upon actual, observable results in the learning and behavior of children—a legacy from his early Chicago attempts to maintain an experimental school. Few philosophers have ever had such down-to-earth preparation for their ideas.

The reader of Dewey has to dig for the idea, the experience, the principle buried in language that is sometimes opaque. Moreover, Dewey returned to the same argument so many times in so many ways that a backing of sorts could be discovered for wide variations in schoolroom practice. Still, Dewey never departed from his conviction that science was of such overriding importance to the future of the world that the schools would be compelled to include it in the curriculum. He looked upon science with appreciation and approbation; he played up, perhaps overplayed, its power to achieve good ends.

Nor was he ever shaken in his faith in government based on the free and informed minds of the people. Throughout his long life Dewey felt himself to be a citizen of the free world; to many foreign observers his was the voice of democracy. It takes no great exercise in extrapolation to imagine Dewey's reaction to the spectacle of the world's greatest democratic power rushing to the defense of politico-religious autocracies in Spain, Portugal, Greece, Vietnam, and Latin America. That this may be different from a necessary stance of coexistence with governments we deplore or distrust is the kind of mental exercise Dewey regarded as the right of every student and teacher to examine. Dewey simply would not accept the traditional view that such issues should not be brought within the circle of the students' understanding. World-shaking concepts and events were to be analyzed as a personal experience for each learner. Then perhaps, as Thorndike independently maintained, what was learned became capable of definition and evaluation, thus providing a base for new materials and new approaches. In Dewey's theory, there was always this preparatory ingredient of thought and action, but unlike some of his overenthusiastic followers, he did not thereby denigrate thought as such; it would be more accurate to say he wanted to ensure its soundness. Dewey bore a deep-seated grudge against persons who regarded the child as a passive creature to whom learning would be applied like a fresh coat of paint.

In presenting us with a new chart, Dewey did not set us adrift without rudder or compass in a sea of ethical choices. He stated over and over that as individuals or social bodies we are forced to make hard decisions. Any culture that can set up standards for its deities can do the same for itself. Any punishment dreamed of for the hereafter can be imagined—and has indeed been undergone—by those who live on earth. The new faith that Dewey proclaimed was a faith in man's ability to set goals, to grow toward them, and to improve in both aim and accomplishment. He had no need of an absolute faith that diminishes the power of people to think for themselves.

Dewey maintained that we must teach the child, knowing him for what he is and where he is, but also with reference to his future in a changing society. This future will contain his past. The way he tackles problems will condition his mental effectiveness in the years to come. Mental maturation, no less than physical, calls for environmental interplay. The growing mind seeks a new hold on old ideas or "verities." It craves events, experiences, and solutions not previously envisioned. Moreover, the process of education is complicated by an individual's unremitting effort to stitch together the fabric of memory, present awareness, and imagination, all emotionally tinged.

The Preprogressive Days and After

It is often said that in the preprogressive days of education, up to about 1920, emphasis was placed on content, on the intellectual aspects of school life. Plainly this is a confusion of intent with achievement. As we go through the textbooks, read the reports, and recall the almost complete lack of reliable measurements, we are safe in making a few statements about the "old days":

—There was little attention to individual differences in ability or interests, to personal growth or social significance, though moral precepts were not lacking.
—There was little attention to intellectual endeavors above the level of information and memorization, that is, to the vertical integration of learning.
—The arts in every medium were downgraded as trivial if not sinful.
—Science as a working principle was rarely found outside the best academies and colleges, and, thanks to Darwin, it was often suspect.
—The teaching of the classics was generally barren of literary appeal.

The public high school had been in existence only since the Civil War and the land-grant colleges for a like period. Few high school graduates found favor in the Ivy League colleges. Since the correlation between inherited wealth and intelligence was erroneously thought to be high, there was not as yet much demand for scholarships and loans in aid to the needy. The situation was not helped by adherence to the false doctrine of mental discipline or the transfer of training. This fallacy regards mind as a muscle that gains through exercise, especially if distasteful.

The rigidity of instruction in those not-so-far-off days has been well documented in words and pictures. What saved the schoolroom then saves many a situation today, namely, the intelligence and wit of the teachers themselves. The critical think-

ing that was frowned on by school authorities was aroused by
"radical" teachers who compensated for their low social status
by inducing a spirit of intellectual restlessness in the young.
(So it is today, especially at the college level.) Most teachers
under the sharp eyes of supervisors and school trustees settled
into the dreary business of passing along sterilized textbook
stuff of little contemporary appeal.

Small wonder that the new "progressive" textbooks, boldly
proclaiming the right of pupils to *think, question,* and *act*
raised the hackles of the conservatives. Whole communities
were caught off guard. A generation, soon to inherit a great
depression and a world war, was written off with distaste. As
it turned out, these cataclysmic events shut the door on a
scholastic past that was sufficiently dull in peace and dangerous
to national security in war. In World War II the fighting man
was dependent for his military effectiveness on the technical
achievement of persons far away in laboratories and proving
grounds. The young, briefly exposed to the rigidities of education, had managed to preserve their ability to adapt, to co-
ordinate, and to cooperate. Moreover the destruction of Hitler
was a goal deeply sensed and responded to by postadolescent
youth. (The young recruits of the 1960s, fed phony issues in an
atmosphere of political deceit, responded in a totally different
manner.)

Dewey, Kilpatrick, and Counts, among others, had accurately
predicted the turn of events. With the coming of a new spirit
in the schools, teachers were free to change the pace, to ex-
periment, to make adjustments in view of the well-documented
differences in individual ability. The slow learner was not to
be cast off as a social misfit. He was to be given assignments
that would yield a sense of progress and self-respect. After all,
one half the total pupil body in any school was, and is, below
the average. In progressive education, failure, a constant bug-
bear in school although smoothed over for adults in their
world, was regarded as a shoddy substitute for advancement at
a slower pace along less abstract lines for those who could not

otherwise keep up. This instructional tolerance was viewed as a rational concomitant of compulsory attendance up to a specified age.

Who Killed Cock Robin?

Well, then, what happened to such humane concepts as the whole child, the integrated curriculum, learning through thought and action, life adjustment, creativity, and respect for the individual? What was the weakness in the progressive education movement that finally led to its abandonment, at least in name? A brief recapitulation at this point will suffice, since I am not primarily concerned with recounting past mistakes or lost opportunities.

The usual gap between principle and practice was widened. It seems unlikely that many schools ever subscribed fully to progressive principles, while others carried them to absurdity. At this point a cautionary statement will mark me as a deviationist from pure progressive doctrine: I am not averse to the clock, to the concept of mental age, to organized subject matter, to the goal of intellectual maturation. As will be seen, I favor a system of instruction that distinguishes between cultural imperatives and cultural options. And now to a few flat statements on what happened:

First, teachers and school principals did not undertake a careful reading of John Dewey. As a result, they failed to achieve a synthesis of thought and action in the school's program. True, children were freed somewhat from physical restrictions; they talked and moved about more, and they joined in stimulating group activities. But it was easy to make a fetish of activities, group spirit, and projects. Most teachers had only a dim awareness of the intellectual demands of subject matter at stages beyond their own school grades. Classroom teachers were vague about the upsurge of science and technology in our society; they were strong on words but weak on other abstract symbols, laboratory setups, and experiments. Progressive educa-

tion, almost for the first time in our culture, did indeed encourage teachers and children to release some of the energy of
affection and friendship that hitherto had been in short supply.
This new understanding favored systematic learning under free
conditions, but the curriculum experts went astray; they failed
to replace outworn instructional units with new ones that
would express not only freedom of pace and approach but a
persistent, spiraling growth in the various structures of knowledge. These structures, as for instance in language, are sufficiently complicated to engage the full intellectual resources of
the brightest pupils from kindergarten to university. Central to
the principles of progressive education was the encouragement
of originality as manifested by a growing attention to the arts.
This aspect of the movement often deteriorated to a senti-
mental pottering; neglect was replaced by dilettantism, although a few outstanding schools did escape this outcome.

Second, in stressing adjustment and social significance,
teachers and principals failed to realize that most of the child's
life was spent outside the school. There are dozens of agencies
related to home, church, neighborhood, or city whose chief
concern is with character education, recreation, and social experience. Of course they teach conversation, reading, and the
social studies *incidentally*. Some progressive schools adopted
this point of view; subject matter became incidental to some
larger purpose and was subtly downgraded. Perhaps if language
had been viewed as "communication" its prime function in
learning and adjustment would have been acknowledged.
Through measurement—not a strong point in the progressive
movement—it could have been demonstrated that most parents,
in addition to neglecting the place of science and the arts in
child development, were also undependable as guides in language, literature, and normative behavior. Moreover, the significance of the child study movement was not appreciated by
either parents or teachers. The school and the home began to
look more like each other, and both more like a kindergarten.
Demonstrations and activities were piled up, and a jargon was

developed, but no premium was put on knowledge as a tool of thought and a precurser to intelligent action.

Third, it became fashionable—perhaps it still is—to deplore our clock-run daily life, our dependence on the calendar. Why not admit bright children to the first grade at the age of four and push them up and out of school at an early age? Why place reliance on classes, grades, promotions, certificates, degrees, or anything else that includes time as a silent partner? The answer is that we exemplify orderliness in the world of nature, and orderliness is a hedge against chaos. In this respect school people are not alone. Chronological age is a factor in sexual consent, marriage, citizenship, military service, eligibility for public office, insurance, employment, and retirement. Time is a factor in social responsibility, too; it reduces the frustrations we should face in its absence. An intuitive approach to the idea of the temporal uniformity of nature predated scientific observations. The sun did rise, quite regularly when one knew the rules; moon and stars, like the seasons, displayed an observable rhythm. Of course time can be a taskmaster and a tyrant, but this is an unlikely outcome in the lives of most children.

Time in Its Proper Place

By fixing *some* age as a requirement we get a needed stability for social operations. The thing to do is to fix a *right* age. Thus, long ago I advocated the lowering of the age for voting from twenty-one years of age to eighteen.[4]

> Now is a good time, too, to abandon the idea that at age twenty-one, and not before, the American citizen is entitled to full voting privileges. In the light of researches in child development and experience with in-school and out-of-school youth, *voting for all persons at age eighteen is clearly indicated.* By that age, most persons have finished school and are meeting real economic and social responsibilities. Their intelligence, energy, and sense of participation adequately counterbalance the wisdom and life experience of voting citizens in the later decades. Moreover by voting, they might learn what voting

means. Their interests, if specialized at all, would be attached to the needs and problems of youth, and that would be all to the good.

Now, in the early 1970s, most people seem to agree, and Congress has acted accordingly.

A person at any age can be legally declared incompetent to perform the duties or enjoy the privileges to which his age status alone would entitle him. Some children—I have known a few—should never go to school; to live at all (a doubtful privilege for the ones I have in mind), they must be tended constantly like fragile plants in a hothouse. Others clearly can learn to read at the age of three or four and will do so if mildly stimulated at home or in a nursery school. This is a better solution than a premature immersion in a group of six-year-olds, many of whom are already in deep water. At every age there is a spread of talent along some line. A schoolroom is more than a varied group of readers, computers, or reciters. Differentials in health, behavior pattern, and self-image, as well as in mental ability, are of importance. To some degree they affect the prognosis of scholastic achievement. The "progressives" were aware of this, but they scarcely knew what to do about it. For some of them resistance to the "shackles" of time did not parallel the child's frustration; it was largely their own response. Preschool children need some scheduling of events, other than meals; they respond well to plans that furnish starting and stopping points. Freedom and anarchy are no more equivalent in school than elsewhere. In essence, the progressive school movement caused pupils to turn from "Look, I can write!" to "Look, what fun I'm having!" That so many children nevertheless grew into mature and imaginative adults is not only a tribute to the sagacity of their teachers and parents but also to the inherent resilience of the children themselves.

Appraising John Dewey's Writings

In the decades since John Dewey died there have been many reappraisals of his work, ranging from the malicious to the laudatory. Although I once worked with him on a nine-author book, I was not one of his students and certainly am not a disciple; I just happen to agree with his basic tenets.

The public image of those who belittle Dewey, even to the point of hatred and ridicule, has been widely disseminated in popular magazines. Still, "nobody but nobody" seems to have read Dewey in the original. From secondary sources he is maligned as one who drove learning out of the public schools and led progressive education down the primrose path! Thus the mild, scholarly Vermonter, John Dewey, a man who worked three quarters of a century to remove from the eyes of youth the blinders inherited from medieval scholasticism and super-stition, is made to assume devilish powers. The truth is that Dewey held no brief for doing-without-thinking, for "life ad-justment" devoid of abstract learning. He was himself one of the great abstractionists of modern times. But there are many who cannot forgive him for holding fast to *action* as a con-ditioner, concomitant, and result of *thought*. Dewey was for life in the living, not simply the having lived; he sought a fresh solution to the great issues in education, a solution congenial to free men.

We still hear much about "Dewey's world." Where is it? Surely it does not characterize American life today, in or out of school, although the schools that are closest to it successfully compete for honors in science, art, and literature and are per-haps our best examples of democracy in action. It is clear that some of Dewey's critics have no use for public schools of *any* type, and that what they really fear is the freedom to think, to differ, to create.

What are the basic principles expounded by Dewey, in some cases originating among the ancient Greeks? To save time, I shall pull out from Dewey's writings (they come to thirty-six books and eight hundred articles) a few clear concepts. They follow, mostly in my own words:

(1) Thought and action must be combined, if only to test the validity of thought. Action includes invention, problem-

solving, applications, decision-making, evaluation, productivity, services.

(2) Interest is a crucial factor in learning.

(3) Change is a rule of life; education is a continuing reconstruction of experience.

(4) Persons develop best in a dynamic societal structure.

(5) Concepts of the *absolute* in human affairs are alien to a maturing intelligence. No benefits derive from postulating the absolute in authority, virtue, or the meaning of life.

(6) Life fulfillment is not achieved through ignorance, frivolity, or superstition; it can be reached only through learning and the creative process.

(7) Immediate enjoyment is not the all-in-all of life; there are problems to be solved, and the consequences of acts and decisions are to be faced.

(8) Wisdom is based on knowledge and on the processes of thinking; we should discover and use effective methods of analysis.

(9) In all human affairs the domain of the arts should be taken into account.

(10) Metaphysics and magic now serve no useful social purpose.

Do these concepts portray a man who tries to escape from thought? No, the reverse is true. To some critics the fearful thing about Dewey is that he represents, above all other Americans of our day, *man thinking*. The golden rule in thinking is to think straight. Thought, if it is to be effective, must be at once free and informed—a difficult pairing. Freedom as modified by a liberal education leads to more freedom; through education new levels of human endeavor can be reached.

Reductionism Will Not Serve

Following Dewey, we should not try to reduce complex social concepts to lower or prior conditions. We know better than to look for creativity in some particular combination of brain cells. Organic continuity in nature permits seeming discontinuities in function, intent, and performance. As far as we know, man has changed but little genetically in fifty thousand years—a short span, but long enough to permit the rise of speech, writing, crafts, science, art, and social structure. If we must push man back to his natural beginnings, to the essence, we cannot stop with even a hundred thousand years, though our ancestors were sufficiently repulsive at that time. We should back up at least a half-million years to a period when the man-ape began to look and act like no other animal.

The great explosion that all previous development must have *permitted* (since it came about) was in the brain and especially in the cerebral cortex. That such a path should be taken by one species and to a lesser extent by other mammals is startling, but it calls for no magic from on high. Reptiles developed armor, claws, teeth, and a fierce temper. Fish, with a few notable exceptions (else we humans would not be here), stayed in the sea. Man's choice, beginning with tools and weapons and relying heavily on technics of differentiated yelling, led to an upright posture, to the freeing of the hands, to eyes at the front and a forebrain above. It also allowed some physical weaknesses to evolve, but they were overcome by the use of fire, shelter, and clothing, and especially by group solidarity. Language became the key to all human progress.

The Meaning in Life

But from what matrix is education supposed to emerge? If précis are needed, several come to mind, and all are Dewey-inspired:

(1) Through science, a further penetration into the structure of matter, life, and the universe.

(2) The foreshortened past as a prologue to an undefined future.

(3) Nothing from fear, superstition, or magic.

(4) Life fulfillment, not as an end point but as a series of actions interspersed with thought.

(5) An approach to philosophy that embraces all science, social structure, and human aspiration.

(6) The resolution of the mind-body-soul problem through the acceptance of man as a uniquely evolved species—the one

animal that conceives of a past and a future; that speaks, hopes, and despairs; that explores the universe; that cannot bear to die like other animals and, seeking gods, finds them at last in the power and beauty of his own creations.

This brings us to the meaning in a person's life and down through the lives to come. For me, it is to transmit, on an ever-ascending scale of wisdom, beauty, and love, the unique biological resources that we inherit and the exciting forms of civilization of which we are capable. Morality and justice, no absolutes, are functional derivatives of experience and good will. Our highest involvement in this enterprise, all within the realm of the natural, rises to the rank of the *spiritual* as a figure of speech. We are moved and mystified as science pushes outward the study of natural phenomena. Beyond science it is a rewarding experience to embrace humanism. This line of thought and action runs clearly through American history—through the strong, new world of Jefferson, Emerson, Horace Mann, Abraham Lincoln, and John Dewey. It is not enough to *return* to such a world; rather, in the midst of much confusion and clamor, we should get on with it. And that is where education comes in.

Dewey and Today's Reactionaries

The great opposition to Dewey, climaxing in paranoid responses, is found in those who perceive his intentions and find them hateful. A member of the John Birch Society, a neo-fascist, a religious fundamentalist conditioned to the epithet "godless," all will find much to criticize in John Dewey. At times such critics apply organized pressure upon school boards, school executives, and officeholders. The last especially are a "soft touch." Now, as I write this, a majority of the members of the House of Representatives have voted to rescind by constitutional amendment the United States Supreme Court's recent ruling against the use of prayers in the public schools— a revealing display of public piety and political expediency.

Organized opposition to Dewey's pronouncements flared up following his death in 1952. Of course, much depended upon the climate of opinion. The United States, like the rest of the world, was badly shaken by World War II and found no sense of security in a nuclear bomb race with Communist powers. Korea, Cuba, Czechoslovakia, Santo Domingo, the Middle East, South Asia, and Southeast Asia introduced a bewildering tangle of postwar crises that a bypassed United Nations seemed impotent to resolve. The schools were in a quandary with respect to the content of teaching in the social studies. The search was on for simplistic solutions to complex problems, and "Deweyism," as propounded in the progressive education movement, was an easy target. Humanism, with which Dewey was identified over a fifty-year stretch, had given way to "realism," that is, to power plays, armaments, space competition—and to "containing" communism, even though it controlled nearly half the world's population. In all this Dewey was a disturbing voice of conscience and therefore suspect. His long quest for certainty had served only to highlight the factor of insecurity in all human affairs.

Yet I feel that Dewey would prefer today's turbulence to yesterday's submissiveness. He opted for channeling energy into rewarding activities. He sensed that the arts, like science properly conceived, would extend the range and the quality of personal experience. In accompanying cognition by action and allowing it to be transformed in the process, Dewey overcame the ancient mind-body dichotomy. Still, Dewey did not stress the fact that there may be distance and a time lag between thought and its application, either in the person or in society as a whole. Deferred action is common in any complex situation; it finally may carry a measure of serendipity. In fact, I hold that an original thought, however inapplicable and useless it may seem to be, runs the risk of being utilized in a new climate of opinion. There is no such thing as a permanently wayward thought; if science ignores it, there is always art to give it life and form.

The Permanence of Change

Of course, no philosopher can speak for all time, and Dewey knew this. A central part of his philosophy is the concept of change, of hypothesizing, testing, revising, evolving. It is Dewey's *method* of arriving at observable and applicable truth that keeps his thought alive and will assure its periodic revival. Dewey's idea of freedom bore no relation to license; he simply wanted to remove the blocks to freedom of thought. This called for more action than had hitherto been the lot of children and youth, but not absurd action, not violence or delinquency. He was for enthusiasm and camaraderie, for a reaching out in the process of learning. Since Dewey, like Whitehead, was not enamored of the overstuffed mind, some critics jumped to the utterly false conclusion that he was anti-intellectual. Stressing the interaction between the organism and the environment, he insisted upon improving the environmental conditions of learning, including such workaday items as attractive classrooms, adequate teaching facilities, and motivation through projects. In Dewey's elementary school of his Chicago days, the children displayed a natural freedom totally different from the stiff alignment elsewhere that smothered creativity. He extended the coverage of the term *democracy* to school children and thereby lessened the tight control of the teacher over all happenings. By carrying this principle to an extreme, some "progressive" teachers became in practice the servants of their immature pupils; learning as a systematic, forward-moving venture was the first casualty. This same debilitating procedure is again cropping up in those versions of student-directed activity that are empty of responsible, productive, intellectual labor.

Are we then to assume that Dewey's philosophy of education was flawless? Was the decline of progressive education only a failure to abide by the principles of the master? I think the answer is *no* on both counts. While Dewey stressed doing as a needful element in thinking—a kind of governor—he did not stress the place of a structure of knowledge to which the learner must attend if he would advance not only his range of inquiry but the essence of the thought process. Science, for example, is a poor place for innocents abroad. As teachers we try to combine Dewey's sequence of thinking-doing-rethinking with its application, at first incipient, to recorded knowledge, not as a means of overwhelming the child but rather to set him above casual, repetitive bits of information. Apparently Dewey's defense of his own aphorism, "Education has no end beyond itself; it is its own end," did not clear up the intrinsic defect of circularity. Although he elaborated the underlying principle he had in mind, namely, that education is so broad and deep in its implications and adaptations that its ends are natural counterparts to the process itself, the lesson was lost on thousands of teachers and school authorities who took it to mean that *any* activity was proper, that *any* learned item was equal to any other, and therefore that education as a profession could divorce itself from all external intellectual infiltration; to the extremist, method became the all-in-all. To reach this scholastic perversion of one of Dewey's lesser remarks, exuberant but misled "followers" had to ignore the great thrust of his contributions to school and society.

Geiger sums up his centennial study of Dewey in these words: [5]

> Perhaps, then, it is not fair to John Dewey to place his ideas against the crazy background of a fugitive present. We may say instead that when men are finally ready to apply intelligent inquiry to the solving of their problems—and if they never are, nothing more need be said—the thought of John Dewey will be there.

Philosophy to the Aid of Education

It would be difficult to trace modern educational theory and practice to pronouncements in the fields of metaphysics, epistemology, or theology. Equally difficult would be a search among the philosophical "isms" that arise and have their day.

Philosophers differ among themselves, and few have applied themselves to a consideration of a philosophy *of education*. At the same time, educators have long turned to philosophers in the hope of filling a gap in their intellectual armament. Plato, Locke, Rousseau, James, Dewey, Russell, and Whitehead are rich sources of educational enlightenment, while Pestalozzi, Herbart, and Froebel supply working models. The converging point is found where the philosopher undertakes an analysis of *values*. A society's concept of the values to be inculcated and maintained will in theory determine what knowledge "is of most worth." Thence the pathway to schooling, from kindergarten to college, is discernible. The trouble is that "theory" is open to obfuscation and is often distorted by the pull of practical affairs. Anybody can teach anything and find a theory to fit.

If it were permissible to construct a mosaic of educational philosophy—that is, educational by implication—out of the views of a retinue of philosophers a few recurring but not identical patterns would be observed, as, for example,

—The importance, if not the primacy, of the intellect.
—The supporting role of feelings and emotions.
—The significance of character and personality.
—The role of practical experience in the learning process.
—The relinquishment of certain fundamental questions to physical science and psychology.
—The urge to seek values beyond self and society, often with religious overtones.

Doubtless we are on safer ground to infer a philosophy or theory of education from observed educational practice, with the "reasons" therefor, than to wend our way down from a system whose components are, like G. Stanley Hall's tome on adolescence, "more often referred to than read." In short, in place of the term philosophy *of* education we might better say philosophy *in* education. This usage would dramatize the difference in goals between the two professional fields. The philosopher is always thoughtful; the educator may or may not be, but he is always active. A philosopher like John Dewey, willing to test his ideas in the give-and-take of a schoolroom, gathers strength from both sides.

The American School System and Its Critics

If there is one social instrument in the United States that does not rate the appellation The Establishment, it is the public school system—that is to say, systems, for each of the fifty states has its own organization. The states, in turn, have delegated most of the power inherent in this gigantic enterprise to thousands of separate school districts. Moreover, the school directly supervises the child for only a half day for half the calendar year. Education on a quarter-time basis—that is the rule for the American school child. Yet in the minds of some critics the school's time, which is devoted to what is *not* being done in the home and neighborhood, should be shortened. These critics often deplore the difference between school and home; the latter is idealized and deemed immensely superior. When homes, that is to say farm homes, really had much to offer by way of firsthand experience and responsible duties, the necessity of public schooling was nevertheless apparent to the leading thinkers of the day; however, it took the incomparable Horace Mann to transform common yearnings into a national movement. Today many American homes do not provide meaningful tasks for children, are short on speech (not words), on reading beyond sports, comics, and ads, and on writing of any kind; they are at the same time long on gadgets, plastics, and commercial TV. Even so, the home is suddenly touted as a milieu for the instruction of children in language, social studies, science, and the arts—subjects that still form the basis of cultural maturation and of competence in numerous job classifications.

The school has a purpose not defined by itself but by evolving social patterns. It was not designed to imitate the home—even the good home—but to supplement and enrich it, to carry through on behalf of all children learning tasks that are beyond the grasp of most parents, all this in a milieu specially equipped to help children feel at ease in the immediate surroundings and unafraid of the future. This kind of life begins at school, and there is no true substitute for it. No longer do we look upon school as only a preparation for life; we sense it also as a life in itself. An adult world of work-for-pay is no more "real" than study-at-school, but different; at that changeover point, the worth of the years of schooling is given its first great test.

If the school is to become purposeful for all segments of the student body, it must take its aims more seriously. Learning only for the sake of learning, that is, to satisfy curiosity, is a valuable trait, but it needs reenforcement. The school's plan of marking, grading, testing, and promoting is often attacked on the wrong grounds. It is as if the score did not count. Tell *that* to a wage earner, a sportsman, a businessman! What is wrong with the assessment procedure is that it embodies too much fragmented memoriter learning. The drive for excellence that is best stimulated by parents and teachers who believe in it is regarded by the fuzzy-minded as undemocratic. The evidence is all about us that schooling strikes some children as a series of steep steps that lead nowhere. It should be easy to correct this perverse attitude in the case of English and the social studies and perhaps in the descriptive portions of science, for example, earth science. Various art forms, especially music, are also close to the child's inner self, but a long way from the prim once-a-week music supervisor, or the sterile arts assignment of a teacher ignorant of art.

School Time Cannot Be Postponed

Unlike most other social experiences, compulsory schooling has a fixed life expectancy. Starting from the kindergarten age it flourishes by law for about ten years. Once relinquished, the school infrequently permits a person to return to it. There is no intentional exclusion at the college level, but there, too, not many go back to finish what they may have left unfinished. Adult or continuing education is changing this situation somewhat, but its main appeal lies in a fresh start. Only an enthusiastic leader will hold adults to further systematic learning and perhaps to changes in their views and actions. Hence the school should treasure the small amount of time over a short span of years assigned to it as the chief, if not the only, organ of systematic learning. The heart of the school is in its curriculum. The school should indeed be linked to the community's cultural resources, but unless they are geared in to the school's program they will not carry much weight.

The Past Is Alive

An unhappy symptom of academic malaise in our times is the disparagement of learning, especially of learning that derives from past insights and achievements. Yet, though we call it by different names, much of what we study is history. How old must a child be before he realizes that few living artists can equal those of classical and Renaissance times? That no contemporary composer can replace the masters of the two preceding centuries? That science would be hopelessly in arrears without its foundation in the work of Euclid, Galileo, Harvey, Boyle, Newton, and a hundred others? That Chaucer, Shakespeare, and Cervantes have not only inspired people down through the centuries but have made permanent contributions to the structure of language? Of course it is not enough to stop with the past nor to be paralyzed by the splendor of its genius, but those are small dangers. Every teacher is obligated to expound the relevance of learning that has stood the test of time. If such learning, as a prelude to its counterparts on the contemporary scene, is derogated or abandoned by a weak teacher and a pliant administration, there will come a time when the most promising students will feel shortchanged.

Thus in retrospect it appears that teachers were unequal to

the task of proclaiming the vital messages of classical art and literature. The classics were first overlaid by pedantry and then allowed to fade away. Latin and Greek, when taught as "dead languages" with an emphasis on grammar and sentence structure, achieved irrelevance alike for student and curriculum maker. They could now be restored, not as intact languages but to provide a kind of thesaurus in the early study of English. By the time of high school and on into college, a program covering selected classics in translation would go far to preserve their unique contribution to Western philosophy, drama, and poetry. Of course, a school board might still be fearful of their power to influence the searching mind. The classics are *pagan*; they remind us of the thought and deeds of great men whose zest for life was not often shared by the late-arriving Christians. If now the humanities in general are entering a period of decline, it may be a matter of their attempt to find answers to questions that are still "disturbing" and "unsafe"—a role that should carry a special appeal to the rebellious student.

Abandon the Public School?

Some of the proposals for radical change in the public schools go beyond the extremes of "progressive education," but in which direction is not always clear. Thus the idea that compulsory education should be abandoned in favor of an elysian free-for-all is proclaimed as radical, futuristic, soul-saving. Of course it is nothing of the kind. It is a regression to the primitive conditions that characterized much of the human race up to World War I and is a conspicuous feature of some countries to this day. The outcome can be summed up in a single word: *hopelessness*.

Not all the eclogues of Vergil will entice the American city dweller back to the village or farm, nor return the youth population to a mastery of simple tools and crafts. We have plumped for a division of labor, for expertise in a thousand job clusters, and there is no turning back. Unskilled or semiskilled labor remains firmly at the bottom of the economic ladder. Educational systems have nothing to do with this rating; what is in plentiful supply and easy to learn tends to be downgraded. On the other hand, leaders in education, joining leaders in government, industry, and the labor movement, have helped this group to secure basic economic and civil rights. The well-documented "upward mobility" of American society is a by-product of the public school.

2
THEORIES AND PRINCIPLES OF LEARNING

Priorities

Education does not take all psychology for its province. There is a selective principle that bears upon the relevance of research to the practice of teaching. For psychological studies in support of educational principles and practices, we prefer

—Mice to birds or fish or bugs.

—Apes to dogs or cats or mice.

—Humans to subhumans.

—One sex to a composite sampling.

—Age-mates to a wide scattering of age.

—Speech-related behavior to nonspeech.

—Personal and social behavior to physiological events.

—The symbolic to the discrete.

—The normal to the abnormal.

Researches on subhuman species yield clues for human development and behavior, but the best generalizations in support of a professional decision are those based on identifiable samplings of children. The rule is, to understand the child, study the child.

The psychology of learning in children, youth, and adults is the principal supporting science for educational method. There are of course islands of support in general psychology and biology. Since teachers are less scientists than practitioners, they must be selective; for them much of the technical literature is irrelevant. An eclectic approach is justified, since no supporting science can produce a valid theory of education. All we can say is that, insofar as scientific branches impinge upon educational methods and programs, the measurable effects must be sought chiefly through psychology. For education, the scientific study of learning is the staff of life. Now, *learning* is no simple concept. In acquiring physical or motor skills the infant depends strongly on inherited mechanisms; for a time, special clues and incentives appear negligible. Under normal conditions, the infant breathes, sucks, excretes, yawns, blinks, stretches, burps, sneezes, wiggles, and cries, "quite naturally." His bodily efficiency improves, and soon—very soon, in the culture pattern of the Western world—he learns to govern his responses. According to Margaret Mead, primitive children are allowed to remain almost undisturbed for months or years as they slowly adjust to what is expected of them, but the typical mother in our culture has other ideas. A social pattern is imposed upon the child from birth, and success is measured by the speed and accuracy with which a child, even before speech, not only grows, responds, and coordinates but also meets prescribed standards.

The Power of Speech

With the advent of speech, learning becomes immensely complex; it is at this point that the apes drop back in competition with the human animal. True speech is the atomic energy burst of a nervous system and its attached organs. Now for the first time in the long animal chain a past and a future are discerned and recorded; the mind has acquired a tool of vast power. With human speech there is no longer any point-to-point comparison of child and animal behavior; a direct transfer from nonspeech to speech situations is impractical and may be misleading. The magnificent work of Köhler on chimpanzees gives only clues for the psychology of man, but when these clues are followed through in human situations we have a fruitful source of guidance in education. The changing complexity of tools, let us say from the ax to the alphabet to the moon rocket, is an index of intellectual potential, all without any observed improvement in genes or sensory functions. Following the acquisition of speech the dominance of the cerebral cortex in every problem-solving or creative act is assured.

The same considerations apply to any direct extension to man of the studies of conditioned responses. Of course my mouth waters when I think of ripe strawberries. The thought "rings a bell," and a bell can ring the thought. I can be tempted, satiated, or disillusioned at this salivary level. Unlike a hungry bear, I build up word-centered, value-centered responses to even this simple stimulus. I carry on an inner argument of for-and-against, now-or-later, this-or-that, good-or-bad. The theory of the conditioned reflex has been unable to rescue associationism from its eventual sterility in human affairs. We learn to take actions and decisions not based on the chain links of simple association—choices that combine the past (memory, habit) and the future (options, predictions, goals). Intelligence becomes intelligence-in-action, and the test lies in its efficacy. Similarly, today's runner runs with everything handed down to him in genes through countless generations; at the same time, he runs with his trained, motivated, competitive self—truly a unique mechanism. Since a general theory of learning must take account of physical performances as well as those of a more intellectual or creative type, we are forced to construct subtheories. Consequently, as we search for ways to improve teaching, it is always appropriate to ask, *What kind of learning do we have in mind?*

Items that are best not forgotten should be overlearned, that is, they should be stamped in by conscious repetition and interlaced with pattern-forming operations that either encompass or promise a reward. Otherwise the experience remains weak and susceptible to obliteration. The human nervous system is geared to forgetting, and there is no gainsaying this protective device. Since some things, such as logical formulations, basic concepts, and the structure of language, should be deeply in- grained, the first rule is that of selection, and the second, an insistence upon comprehension up to one's mental capacity.

The negation or destruction of the ability to learn is less complicated. Like arsenic, extreme brainwashing will poison anybody; unlike arsenic, which is harmful only if ingested, the mere absence of appropriate stimuli will defeat the mind's in- tent. Various drugs will suffice, or, in future, radiation. Nature has this in common with culture: progress is slow; annihilation, swift. Thus we arrive at the opposite pole of the learning proc- ess: the antilearning process, the learning not to learn. It is always abnormal, always an escape. It is like learning not to walk, or eat, or sleep, but more common. Teachers rightly look to clinical psychology to buttress their understanding of this phenomenon.

In short, for teacher education our researches and demon- strations in the supporting disciplines of psychology and soci- ology may safely be confined to *learning* and to the reverse process, *escape from learning*. For school-age populations, the former predominates. Teachers should therefore be true pro- fessionals in the art of teaching; in the concomitant art of practicing mental hygiene they must often call on others.

The Growing Child

The term "growing" is so characteristic of a child that to say "growing child" is redundant. Still, children do not start from the same base, do not grow at the same rate, do not exhibit the same pattern of special interests or aptitudes, and do not arrive at the same intellectual level. By the age of five or six, children are in fact widely diversified. They have inter- twined their learning habits with personal experience. Some children, nurtured in good homes by insightful parents, show a remarkable capacity to learn. Other children from equally good homes are defective, perhaps from birth; nevertheless, under skillful direction they may make progress and develop into well-adjusted persons. Few children at home or in school will come up to their full genetic promise. The art of rearing children, teaching children, loving children combines both knowledge and experience. Yet it is precisely in these directions that many parents and teachers are deficient. If I place teachers above parents with respect to educational impact, it is because teachers have undergone professional preparation that bears on what children need and how they learn.

In any culture children need to learn how to move about in the environment—at times to control it—with a minimum of frustration. Infants have certain clearly defined psychological needs—to taste food; to touch and be touched; to hear pleasing sounds; to win that mysterious, approving, mother's smile. They must learn to differentiate among the sounds people make. The world of childhood is not only one of hot-cold, light-dark, smooth-rough, and all that; it is also a world of yes-no, do-don't, good-bad, smile-frown, self-other. It is, in short, a social world in which values are imposed right from the start. These value judgments begin in the home, and they are never fully detached from the home.

The Man-made Part of the Environment

The term "culture pattern" is not a reference to some vague, teleological force. It is simply the man-made part of the environment. Our psychological mechanism tries to adapt itself to the basic demands of a culture, the process being initiated and stamped in by a program of learning. Before the invention of writing such programs were familial and tribal. Primitive survival demanded only "how-to-do-it" courses of instruction in which traditional ways predominated. Nevertheless, the observation of remote tribes and villages is not without relevance to modern education; their wise men often asked the right questions. There is in some obscure societies a reliance on

voodooistic practices that presage contemporary clinical practice. Primitive tribesmen act much and say little, but what
they do say, or have recited for them by a medicine man, has
a curious lack of guile; it strikes us as childlike. While Western
children are not primitive, they too ask questions about reality
that get to the root of things. In fact, their early questions,
uninhibited by cultural reticence in matters of race, sex, or
religion, may be more searching than the answers given. Home
and school both derive from the culture pattern laid down by
tradition, law, and fashion. We know what variations in heat,
water, soil, and sunlight will do to the growth of a plant, but
these variations are as nothing compared to the potential variations in a child's nervous system. Within genetic limits un-
determined except in an optimum environment, the human
organism matures in terms of what happens to it.

Scholastic Disciplines as Tools of Thought

Noting the basic difference in the pedagogical approach to
quantitative studies on the one hand and to the arts and
humanities on the other, we may define each discipline as a
tool of thought. Mathematics is the outstanding example of the
sui generis control over postulates, problems, and methods,
while the arts rely more heavily on intuition and imagination.
Only in general terms can we construe a psychology of learning that covers all mental activity. Avoiding the awkwardness
of such expressions as the "psychology of physics," or the
"psychology of art," we can at least promote a psychology of
instruction *in* physics, *in* art, and so on. We might say that
the orderliness of mathematics, physics, chemistry, and biology
comes to the student ready-made. In personal and social relationships he will be more on his own, but he will nevertheless seek to impose order, if only to keep sane.

The teaching of science illustrates the fruitfulness of collaboration among physical scientists, psychologists, and educationists in the development of specialized curricula. Lacking such
cooperative efforts we have short-changed pupils at the time

of their greatest potential interest in a subject, that is, before the high school years. From the standpoint of a theory of learning we have allowed the whole field of science to remain sterile. If science is what we should teach—or art, or history, or language—all the repetitious bother of teaching *about* and *about* a subject bears on neither a mental process worth sustaining nor an outcome worth recording. A whole new study of the teaching process is waiting to be born. It may well begin with the curricula developed at Harvard University and the Massachusetts Institute of Technology, among other centers, and put into practice by teachers who are themselves steeped in a discipline and therefore cognizant of its special power. The central theoretical issue is this: given a sound curricular structure combined with empirically effective teaching, what happens in the mind of the learner, and to what extent does it affect his developing personality?

A Comment on Skinner's Views

Learning theory derived from animal psychology has long been a stock-in-trade of teacher education. Stimulus and response, rewards and punishments, reinforcements—almost anything short-range—manage to get teacher and pupil through the day with a feeling of something accomplished. That the rewards are scholastically tinged and the punishments more mental than physical does not alter the basic situation. Recently, one of our "experimental" school systems has reverted to candy-bar prizes for bits of learning—a procedure long familiar to animal trainers. Doubtless these far-out teachers find comfort in Skinner's latest attempt to move from autonomous man to a creature caught in the meshes of his immediate environment but lacking the wit or the drive to set up counter controls. To quote: [1]

> The evidence for a crude environmentalism is clear enough. People are extraordinarily different in different places, and possibly just because of the places. The nomad on horseback in Outer Mongolia and the astronaut in outer space are different

people, but, as far as we know, if they had been exchanged at birth, they would have taken each other's place.

Well, yes and no! The astronauts were pulled into an orbit of expertise on the basis of successive waves of selection by a team of scientists who knew what they wanted to do and what kind of person could carry it out. My feeling is that highly skilled horsemen who have learned how to survive in wild, unfriendly regions have something in common with the astronauts; a space agency team sent to Mongolia for the purpose of recruiting candidates for rocket engineering would not come back empty-handed, provided at least one college there had done its spade work. The cowboy on the Texas plain is closer to the Asian nomad than to anybody who works at the Lyndon B. Johnson Space Center. In fact, the scientists, technicians, and astronauts in Houston and Cape Canaveral have *nothing* in common with 99 percent of the American population in terms of their work habits and expertise.

The oldest environments are the seacoasts, the jungle, the arid zones; their inhabitants, inevitably subservient to these conditions, nevertheless learned how to modify them in order to survive. Generally they had no place else to go. In the future, thanks to the ubiquitous airplane, distance will not be the great restrainer; political factors that have little to do with individual choice will set up the barriers. However, when Skinner states (p. 211) "a person does not act upon the world, the world acts upon him," he is defining a one-way line of force as if it were never reversed. Military and political revolutions, perhaps originating in the mind of one man, together with migrations in search of food, shelter, or religious freedom, do change the world. Bruner clarifies this point.[2]

Because our ultimate concern is with the emergence of human adaptation, our first concern must be the most distinctive feature of that adaptation. This feature is man's trait, typical of his species, of "culture using," with all of the intricate set of implications that follow. Man adapts (within limits) by changing the environment, by developing not only amplifiers and transformers for his sense organs, muscles, and reckoning powers, as well as banks for his memory, but also by changing literally the properties of his habitat. Man, so the truism goes, lives increasingly in a man-made environment. This circumstance places special burdens on human immaturity. For one thing, adaptation to such variable conditions depends heavily on opportunities for learning, in order to achieve knowledge and skills that are not stored in the gene pool. But not all that must be mastered can be learned by direct encounter. Much must be "read out" of the culture pool, things learned and remembered over several generations: knowledge about values and history, skills as varied as an obligatory natural language or an optional mathematical one, as mute as using levers or as articulate as myth telling.

On balance, a satisfactory theory of human learning does not emerge from Skinner's attempt to bring his views on behavioristic psychology into focus. We cannot ignore the cognitive processes, the feelings, the intentions, the inner speech of persons, for they too are a field of force, a world of their own, not to be reduced to observable, discrete events. Case studies in depth, à la Piaget, are necessary for the understanding of children, far beyond anything appropriate for the bird or the white rat. For example, it is largely through words alone that psychiatrists get an inner view of the person's "environment" as conceived and responded to. Feelings of guilt, remorse, or inferiority may establish an emotional climate, a pattern of life, incapable of being extracted from objective elements in one's surroundings. On the positive side, a scientist, an artist, a saint may succeed in overriding almost every environmental obstacle except death itself. In modern parlance, *I choose, therefore I am.* There is at least a trace of this drive in everyone, and it becomes a duty of the school to nourish it.

Piaget's Contribution

In two dozen major books covering a half century of observations of child learning and behavior [3] Jean Piaget, director of the Jean Jacques Rousseau Institute in Geneva, has developed theories on the way children learn. Of special interest to teachers is Piaget's concept of stages in a child's mental development that appear to dictate what he is able to understand at a given chronological age. In view of the disparity between mental age and chronological age, together with an observed continuity in learned behavior, we need not go as far as Piaget does in postulating a mind-set based on strict hierarchical progression. To say that a child can learn only what his physiological structure permits him to learn is somewhat circular. In any case, following the observations of Jerome Bruner, teachers no longer stress the concept of readiness as if there were a waiting period before the student could go further along a line of abstract learning. The normal brain does indeed mature, but not at the same rate nor by the same stepping stones for all children. The strength of Piaget's enormous contribution lies in his methods; he has painstakingly studied each child as a true psychological phenomenon not to be lost in a mass of statistical fragments. It is this approach to child behavior that has helped nursery-school teachers to exert more influence on child behavior than their counterparts in the elementary school. As school subject matter becomes more specialized and more intertwined with cultural experience, the observed priorities, stages, and hierarchies become less significant. Some dull children will go round and round instead of moving upward; on the other hand some bright ones will appear to "leapfrog" intellectually. To some extent Piaget's stages or plateaus are a product of scholastic and cultural conditions. Granted that the ability to make logical deductions of increasing complexity follows upon prior sensory experience and trial-and-error formulations, the language component comes in fast and is not easily bundled into temporal compartments. The factor of time may be compressed (as in brightness and genius) or elongated, depending not only on the brain as inherited but also on the total experience of the maturing child.

One great principle that emerges from Piaget's lifelong work is that nature and nurture continuously interact to form the character and quality of overt mental acts. Behavior is organismic. The prepared intellect is different from one deprived of the opportunity to solve problems; the ability to solve problems is no simple derivative of genetic constituents or of the nervous system of a child at birth.

We Work Together, but We Think Alone

The more we know about the learning process the more evident it is that some teachers and school systems give up too easily. It would be reassuring if these schools would prove that at least they do well by the average and bright pupils, but we lack such assurance. The child easily acquires more information at the same level of abstraction as his existing hoard. Embarking on excursions into new territory, he may not so much stop as be stopped. The blocking may characterize a group, but it is always sensed as personal. We work together, but we think alone. In abstract learning the step across may be the step up. At every point the student's persistent questions of *why* and *how* deserve attention, but most of all the child himself needs attention; to "earn" it, he will undertake learning tasks that at first seemed forbidding.

Kurt Lewin's Contribution

In Lewinian theory the emphasis is on topology. Forces are vectored, as it were, furnishing direction to the goal-seeking person. As the child matures, he is able to place himself more accurately in a field that offers pathways to the solution of problems. The child seeking his mother stops pushing against a frontal barrier and discovers possible ways around it, even though he must at first move away from her. If the mother quietly joins the child in the enclosure, his behavior is different. Now the child is where he wants to be; he stays there. This basic demonstration permits many variations that Kurt Lewin and others developed geometrically.

Lewinian formulations forced a reexamination of the relation between repetition and learning. Gestalt psychologists had already noted the phenomenon of sudden insight under certain conditions. An ape or a child could learn some things without overt trial-and-error. What observer of child behavior has not sensed this? Vocabulary may be acquired in a one-shot experience, provided past experience is linked to a fresh elucidation. I recall the way my son at the age of four learned the pronunciation and meaning of the word *schedule*. We were standing at a bus stop when he suddenly asked how I knew when the bus would arrive. I told him it always came by on the hour and the half hour, since the driver needed a half hour to cover the route and stop at various places. The driver was watching the time, just as we were. Furthermore, he was following a schedule that told him what stops to make at what time. The next day I overheard my son tell all this to his two-year-old brother, with clear insight and an emphasis on the word *schedule*. Such episodes cause one to question the validity of vocabulary counts that assign a fixed degree of difficulty to a word. In any culture, *pity* is a more difficult concept than *ear*, but it does not follow that *ear* is harder than *kneecap*. Selective learning at the same level of abstraction is a blessing if the brain is to be more than a warehouse.

Student teachers should be asked to set up experimental classrooms following Lewinian or other theories of group dynamics. Every teacher training institution should provide mockups, lofts, or stage settings for teaching *in situ*; it is one way to make the student and the class come alive. It will be recalled that Lewin set up three styles of classrooms: authoritarian, democratic, and laissez-faire. The authoritarian classroom resembled many an American classroom in the United States, teacher centered, disciplined, efficient. The democratic classroom followed Dewey's theories and anticipated the better school settings of the 1970s. The laissez-faire group was admittedly something of a caricature of progressive education, but its counterparts were to be found in actual practice. Authoritarian and democratic groups achieved equally well, but the laissez-faire group accomplished little and behaved badly. The test situation required that the teacher leave the pupils to themselves near the end of the project and, further, that they dispose of their handiwork (painted papier-mâché masks) as they saw fit. At once the dynamics of the three groups became apparent. While the laissez-faire group had not finished anything worthwhile, they had "had fun." The authoritarian group fought over what to do with the finished masks and destroyed them all. The democratic group in an orderly manner voted to give one mask to a favorite teacher, another to a classmate in the hospital, and the rest to the ongoing school exhibit of classroom work. Yes, it does sound almost too pretty!

The best way to get a sense of what really happens to children under different methods of classroom instruction is to engage in "live runs" in school systems. It is not too much to ask. Some teachers are habitually authoritarian. Others are too weary or overburdened to exercise leadership. Still other teachers feel left out, in fact *are* left out, as machines and electronic devices take over. But it remains difficult to find teachers who are fully aware of the potentialities of democratic teaching—that unique blend of firmness, kindliness, and *savoir-faire* that is guaranteed to raise the level of aspiration in the classic Lewinian sense. In the words of a contemporary psychologist: [4]

> Lewin left his mark on the thinking of a whole generation of social scientists. He put his stamp on a whole discipline, giving it a name (group dynamics), a scope (action research), and a purpose that transcended psychology itself by setting as its goal not only the study of man but the betterment of society. Indeed, in an age of Black Power, urban decay, campus turbulence, bitter political turmoil, and talk of "participatory democracy," today's change seekers have a great deal to learn from Lewin's concepts and experiments.

Educators will find comfort in Lewin's topological approach to the problem of motivation—in his emphasis on the dynamics of the here-and-now as against genetic control.

3

INTELLIGENCE AND
THE LEARNING PROCESS

Binet's Contribution

Learning, especially language learning, starts with the infant and reaches an intensive stage before kindergarten. The child's mind is no blank page to be written on. It changes, grows—or fails to grow properly—in terms of a constant interaction between the brain and its stimuli. The French psychologist, Alfred Binet, who in 1905 collaborated with Théodore Simon to produce the first successful test of intelligence, clearly stated the case more than a half century ago: [1]

> A child's mind is like a field for which a farmer has advised a change in the method of cultivation, with the result that in place of a desert we now have a harvest. It is in this practical sense, the only one available to us, that we say that the intelligence of children may be increased. One increases that which constitutes the intelligence of a school child, namely, the capacity to learn and to improve with instruction.

Admittedly, a brain may be so defective at birth that a child is doomed to permanent feeblemindedness. On a percentage basis such a condition is rather uncommon. On the other hand, some children seem to be irresistible in their ability to push toward high intellectual, artistic, or personal accomplishment.

A professor I know recently mentioned a boy named Edgar,

whose measured I.Q. fell below 70. His school counselors rec-
ommended that he be sent to an institution for retarded children, but his mother would not have it so. Instead he was
given tutorial attention in school and out. He was not assigned
obscure intellectual tasks. Slowly he went up the scholastic
ladder. He found satisfaction in handwriting and spelling and,
to everyone's astonishment, in the appreciation of art, music,
and the theater. Now grown up, he is a skilled worker and as
happy as anybody else. But we must beware of false hopes.
Not all children have the capacity to do what Edgar did. How
do we tell? There is only one way, and it is a hard one. Every
child must be given a real choice, not only to develop normally
as a well-mannered school child, but if need be to receive
special attention and tutoring. Given an early start, a few will
respond to an amazing degree, lifting their I.Q.'s from the so-
called feebleminded ratings to average or above-average levels.

Are There Sex Differences in Intelligence and Aptitudes?

A common question is, Are there sex differences in intelligence? We may recall the famous answer of Samuel Johnson
in the eighteenth century. Asked which was more intelligent,
man or woman, he fixed his interrogator with a cold stare and
said, "Tell me, sir, which man and which woman?" Dr. Johnson was ahead of his time. At any rate, the method of standard-
izing mental test items would obscure sex differences in I.Q.
if they existed. As I stated at a meeting held by the Educational Testing Service: [2]

> The young girl, further along physiologically and presumably
> mentally, learns to read sooner and better than the boy. For a
> time, she holds her own in mathematical and other abstrac-
> tions, but the boy catches up. He keeps growing for a longer
> time. It may be that the so-called genius rating—a precarious
> label—is achieved by a child who starts fast like a girl and
> perseveres like a boy. In any case, sex-related differences should
> be reexamined in relation to cognitive theory and test stand-

ardization. As long as scores are computed with chronological age as a denominator, we need separate male and female norms.

Other tests are needed to supplement tests of intelligence—for example, tests of mathematical, artistic, or musical aptitude, of personality, of vocational interests, and the like. They, too, are limited in their applicability. In fact, there is no good substitute for the evaluations placed on pupil progress by alert teachers and counselors. Some years ago the public schools of New York City dropped I.Q. tests. The New York experts believe they can better assess a child's capability by offering him a series of carefully contrived learning experiences. They strive to get the student *engaged* in learning.

The Brain Is Affected by Experience

In addition to congenital effects on the nervous system, deleterious events may take place at any age. Poisons can be ingested. Diseases and extreme malnutrition can make a direct and destructive attack. Not established but perhaps true is the theory that extreme frustration or emotion may damage brain cells and thus reduce mental power. A functional splitting of the brain into two hemispheres, from whatever cause, will allow two "minds" to develop in the person. Of course, everyone knows about persons suffering from neuroses (complexes) and psychoses (various forms of insanity); their deterioration in reasoning and judgment is a significant part of their peculiar behavior. While it may sometimes be true that "great wits are sure to madness near allied," a causal connection has not been established. For most persons, the more stable the personality the more effective the exercise of intelligence.

The work of Neal E. Miller and others discloses the brain to be a neural network whose parts communicate by chemical means. In recent years this interaction and its resultant mental processes have been intensively studied. These researches, based on animals, postulate both environmental enrichment and deprivation as factors in brain changes. Correlative researches on humans will permit only enrichment; the chief reliance will be on the observation of behavior patterns. In his approach to learning theory Miller asserts that the subject must want something, respond to selected cues, and get a reward.

After twenty years of research on the white rat, which is described as "a serious mammal, with a highly developed brain, not too different in complexity, in differentiation, and in organization from our own," Krech comes to this conclusion: [3]

> The brain from a rat from the enriched environment—and presumably, therefore, with many more stored memories—has a heavier and thicker cortex, a better blood supply, larger brain cells, more glia cells, and increased activity of two brain enzymes, acetylcholine-sterase and cholinesterase, than does the brain from an animal whose life has been less memorable. [P. 372]

Krech and his associates conclude that, in spite of the chemical nature of brain activity,

> manipulating the educational and psychological environment is a more effective way of inducing long-lasting brain changes than direct administration of drugs. Educators probably change brain structure and chemistry to a greater degree than any biochemist in the business. Another way of saying this is: *The educator can potentiate or undo the work of the brain biochemist.* [P. 373]

Still, there is a wide research gap between the brain of the rat and the brain of the child, a gap that can be closed only by an intensive study of those environmental forces conducive to the acquisition and development of speech. Krech holds that speech is not a gradual improvement over primate vocalization but a phenomenon based on new cortical tissue found only in the human brain. The human cerebral cortex is the only one in the whole animal kingdom formed by and for speech. Man's hand and tongue are likewise unique in that they enjoy a relationship favoring one cerebral hemisphere. A hypothetical corollary is that if we seek to improve children's intelligence we should provide infants with selected sensory experiences and relate each experience to words and sentences.

We Learn to Be Intelligent

Obviously I regard psychology as a science that cannot be reduced to more basic elements however influential they may be as limiting factors in behavior. To quote: [4]

> Men think in man-made symbols or they do not think at all. Intelligence, as an ability that grows through the interaction of nervous structures and mediated social events, may be regarded as our most purely psychological phenomenon. In studying early education that may be designated effective or good, we turn to the significance of images, concepts, formulations, and experiences rather than to actual changes in nervous tissue or in physiological function. . . . The brain is not a dead tool or chest of tools. It is not a machine. Its stores of remembered items are not lined up on a shelf or imbedded in an automatic circuit. They are chosen in the first place and once chosen, their quality depends upon their availability on demand for abstract thinking, problem solving, and creativity. That, in turn, depends upon a prior process of coding and integrating. Without the early intervention of speech this whole series of events would be encumbered [p. 6]. . . . Granted that each of us is a unique bundle of cellular units, we *learn* to be intelligent, or not to be, and some persons learn faster than others. In fact, for some children such learning is so hard to come by, even under conditions of expert instruction, that we are justified in applying a low I.Q. rating, and in retaining it if the learning difficulties persist, but not otherwise [p. 7].

Heredity Is Fixed; Environment Changes

Psychologists generally agree that the preschool years are the most important period for establishing a fruitful relation between a child's maturing intellectual structure and the environment. These are the most plastic years, and the most vulnerable, too. First impressions, first blockings, first mental habits combine to set the stage for attitudes toward learning. To quote again from the paper I read at the conference on testing problems: [5]

> Since the reliability of infant tests may reach $r = .90$, their failure to predict later or final mental standing is another way of saying that we do not know what the subsequent environmental encounters will consist of; in fact, we have poor measures of such influences at any stage of development. The studies of S. A. Kirk and others, comparing I.Q. changes in retarded children, indicate the fruitfulness of such an attack even when the precise forces at work are, to say the least, homogenized. Whatever the events, learnings, and situations may be, it appears that the essence of a fruitful interaction is to get beyond repetitions or aggregations to a spiraling integration. This means a putting away of childish things in the later portions of any mental test. Even to test the hereditary component as a *potential*, we need to give full play to hierarchical experiences and to relate them in time sequences to the intellectual demands of a particular growing child. So, let us stop worrying about how much of intelligence is due to heredity and how much to environment. It never was a good question. There can be a hereditary or congenital defect so severe as to make any environmental influence negligible. I have myself seen an adult inmate of an institution whose I.Q. might be placed at 1; she could smile, period. On the other hand, potential geniuses who "waste their sweetness on the desert air," for all we know may be rather numerous.

As of this writing there is nevertheless a renewed interest in the hereditability of group differences in the I.Q.—a question that, along with a dozen other issues, presumably came to rest with the extensive reports of the National Society for the Study of Education thirty years ago.[6] The controversy stems from a single paper published in 1969.[7] The paper might have been relegated to the archives of psychology had not Jensen claimed that blacks *by nature* rank significantly below whites in I.Q. True, untrue, or not proven, the claim that one race is inferior to another by genetic inheritance alone raises hackles, especially in the United States. If untrue, it is rightly viewed as the unfortunate error of a hastily contrived study. If not proven—and it has not been—it becomes a hypothesis of sufficient importance to be assigned to a research team of geneticists, psychologists, and sociologists.

Whatever the final outcome, it is clear we cannot rest the case on comparative analyses of variance. I.Q.'s have been raised—and are being raised—in numerous samplings of children whose early childhood environment has been enriched, even though as of today the particular ingredients that produce changes in mental ratings are elusive. It has been argued that the alleged inferiority of American samplings of nonwhite groups rests upon a massive negative selection: the less able persons were driven from their native lands, or, as in the case of the Negro, enslaved. The evidence in support of this hypothesis is lacking. Achievement based on inherited social rank and on the acceptance of the *status quo* would tend to skew the putative distribution of talent. At the other end of the curve, for Europeans as well as Negroes, enforced illiteracy overwhelmed genotypic scattering. From the emerging middle class in free societies has come the majority of gifted children and intellectually successful adults. Educability is not to be confused with social status at a given time.

Intelligence Is a Process

Intelligence is not like blue eyes or a Hapsburg lip; it is not a *thing* at all, but a process. The best way to tell how fast, how far, and in what directions a child may develop is to give him the opportunity. Until we have mental tests to fit the comprehensive definition to be cited presently, it will be better to assess environmental effects not in terms of I.Q. changes but in terms of observed progress in a child's all-around learning and behavior. For a long time to come researches will be needed on the components of the environment that are conducive to maturation, learning, and personal stability. Since the human race is irretrievably mixed genetically we should concentrate on society's impact on the quality of the child's mind from birth through adolescence. He will never exceed his unknown genetic potential (how can he?), but in this defective world he is unlikely to approach its limit. The general aim is to move the normal distribution of talent and fulfillment upward, skewing it away from its lower ranges, but unless fulfillment is defined so as to include goodwill, the resulting social benefit will be negligible.

Dobzhansky sums it up: [8]

> All bodily structures and functions, without exception, are products of heredity realized in some sequence of environments. So also are all forms of behavior, also without exception. Nothing can arise in any organism unless its potentiality is within the realm of possibilities of the genetic endowment. Lest I sound to you an extreme hereditarian, I hasten to add that the potentialities that are realized in a given sequence of environments are, especially in man, only a tiny fraction of the individual's total potentialities. If an individual with the same genotype would develop and be brought up in some different environment, he might develop quite differently.

In short, one can only be what one could have become.

A Comprehensive Definition of Intelligence

There are many compact definitions of intelligence, but they serve their shorthand purpose best after a more comprehensive statement has been formulated. One I submitted years ago appears to have held up well: [9]

> Intelligence is the ability to undertake activities that are characterized by (1) difficulty, (2) complexity, (3) abstractness, (4) economy, (5) adaptiveness to a goal, (6) social value, and (7) the emergence of originals, and to maintain such activities under conditions that demand a concentration of energy and a resistance to emotional forces.

Knowing that the parts, if separated, must be recombined into a functional whole, we may attempt a breakdown of the definition given above.

Difficulty refers to the percentage passing test items, provided this percentage increases with chronological age up to a point and is progressively related to the requirements of all the other attributes of intelligence. For example, success at levels that involve abstractions transcends the facility for memorizing.

Complexity refers to the multiple-track nature of abilities that combine to form general intelligence. The base is to be kept broad, so that intelligence, while undergirding specializations (scientific, artistic, literary), is not identified with them.

Abstractness is close to the core of intelligence; it is not the all-in-all of the concept but a necessary ingredient. In mental activity we deal with symbols, speech being the prime example. From language, scientific notations, and art forms the teacher is able to get an estimate of this ability for each pupil; mental testing helps in arriving at reliable judgments.

Economy is the same as speed. If the insight is sudden and not seen as immediately related to the task at hand (the problem may have been put "on the shelf") we call it *intuition*; even so the logical steps appear to have been taken unconsciously. While some psychologists question the appropriateness of "economy" as an attribute of intelligence, I believe it is better to retain it. Other things equal, a fast mental solution is better than a slow one; it permits the learner to keep more variables in mind, and to move on to other problems. Of course the term *slow learner* is often misunderstood. It is true that a slow learner, given a few more years of growth, will solve some of the problems solved earlier by bright children. But if he keeps to his role as a slow learner, as not all do, he will not catch up at all. The habitually slow learner is defective in mental power as well as in his rate of getting the right answers. That some outstanding persons were considered dull in school should not deceive us. Perhaps they were dull only as observed by teachers who tended to downgrade the uncooperative or offbeat pupil. Perhaps their greatness, like that of saints or military leaders, did not demand unusual intellectual gifts. We know, too, that neuroses that interfere with scholastic performance may be overcome at a later time; they may be transformed into a driving force.

Adaptiveness to a goal and *social value* shade into each other. The former is a common factor in measures of intelligence, if not in the definition. Aimlessness results in a low score. Thus if you try to solve the ball-and-field item in the Stanford Revision of the Binet-Simon Scale the way most golfers actually hunt for a lost ball, you will fail. (The task is not the same in the two situations. The child attacks this little problem in geometry without clues, and the empty field is enclosed. The golfer thinks he knows where the ball is, resisting the idea of its being lost at all; a systematic approach, perhaps instigated by the other players, is saved for the last.) The departure of the theoretical from the actual does not invalidate such items; aimlessness is a mark of failure to understand the problem. *Social value* reflects the importance of the culture pattern in tests of mental ability. Language, the following of verbal directions, and the solving of simple problems carry much of the weight. Excellence in speech (comprehensiveness and originality) indicates general ability, but stuttering caused by mechanical or emotional blocking has no bearing on the ability to learn.

The highest reach of intellectual achievement is found in the *emergence of originals*. In the common failure to emphasize this quality, both the mental tester and the teacher are vulnerable. It is not a question of searching for genius, desirable as such a step would be; more simply it is to extend to each child at any chronological or mental age opportunities to succeed in his own way. The child will cooperate; except to plague the teacher, a pupil does not want to say "two plus two equals five." Such an answer is wrong, but not original. But the child does want to describe *his* surroundings, findings, and feelings, and will often choose original combinations of words or images to do so. The approach may be inherently artistic. Teachers and parents, above all others, should encourage and applaud departures from the prosaic. There is no need to worry about intellectual anarchy; the rigidities of subject matter will prevent that. In scientific learning, variations are helpful chiefly in approaching the unknown; otherwise the solution is contained in the problem, and the problem itself is formulated in terms of logical modes. Since the crust that hardens over the structures of thought is not easily broken, there is all the more reason to reward originality.

Though mental tests are deficient in this respect, it is useful to retain the concept of a *concentration of energy* as a mark of intelligent behavior. Most test items are passed or failed in a few seconds or minutes. A teacher's questions that call for analysis, synthesis, and the ability to write are in some ways superior to intelligence testing. The ability to select, to put together things that belong together, to project careful thinking upon a problem, to proliferate, is foreign to most machine-scored test items; instead we are constantly shown snapshot pictures of where a pupil is at a given time. In my view, it is a mark of intelligence to stay with a problem, mobilizing data and concentrating energy.

A *resistance to interfering emotional forces* should be placed on the same high plane as the emergence of originals, but it, too, is absent from mental testing. It could be generalized to read, "a resistance to all forces that are inimical to straight thinking." For schools in a free society, this is their finest hour; it is not a school's function to prove an irrational point, to sell something, to support dogma, to brainwash, but rather to augment knowledge—to help keep the child's mind open and invested with a desire to take on new learning. In so doing, schools improve the human condition. To get understanding is still the supreme act.

Mental Tests and the Confusing I.Q.

A mental test yields for the teacher a rough approximation of the child's mental age (a normative concept) at the time. It tells something about the probable rate of future progress under predictable environmental conditions. It would be less confusing if teachers would avoid using the term I.Q. or Intelligence Quotient. What the teacher needs to know is the child's ability to undertake scholastic assignments, and the best way to find out is by trial and error. The worst fault of the I.Q. is its innocent air of substance, its masquerading in the minds of many as a thing—maybe a bump on the head! The I.Q. is only a defractionated ratio, and a tricky one at that. The language factor in tests of intelligence is so strong that if teachers will encourage, analyze, and test *reading and writing ability* in every pupil they will reach a close approximation to mental age. A test battery covering aptitude tests in English, science, art, and music, buttressed by reports on physical fitness and personality, will leave practically no territory unexplored as far as the classroom teacher is concerned. The ease of calculating the I.Q. has turned us away from difficult but important considerations in level of expectation, validity of the curriculum, specialized abilities, and the like. Not learning well (for various reasons, genuine mental defect being one), the child receives a low I.Q.; tagged with a low I.Q. he can hardly be expected to learn properly. So the circle closes. It is sobering to discover that children who do well on the limited items in a standard intelligence test do not necessarily go far along creative lines. The older the child gets the more crucial are measures of originality, special ability, and complex structures of thought—all beyond the little games found in tests. Of course, failure at the low level of abstraction demanded by a mental test is hardly indicative of subsequent high-level achievement, though there are exceptions. Whatever the test verdict at age six or twelve, it should be reconsidered at the time of any important decision affecting the child. Perhaps persons who do not choose to think develop a form of mental backwardness; a numerous company, they join the ranks of those with hereditary, congenital, or acquired defects in cerebral structure. In my experience, these corrupted mentalities lack the charm of the truly defective child who, if sheltered against life's problems, rarely indulges in malice, greed, or aggression.

It is clear that intelligent behavior is not the same in man and animal, old and young, primitive and cultured. Perhaps, as suggested, it is not the same in male and female. If we include in the definition the attribute *persistence in a task,* the snapshot, quick answer test may judge persons to be more alike in mental ability than they really are.

It should be said in passing that measuring electrical impulses in the brain (neural efficiency) is outside the domain of educational psychology. It is well known that the ability to perform mental tasks is decreased by the ingestion of alcohol or opium in any form, by emotional upset, and also—perhaps permanently—by a reduction of oxygen supply to the brain. But there is no point in interposing physiological phenomena between, let us say, drinking and learning efficiency, since the causal relationship between these two variables is open to direct study. In a wider consideration, any so-called culture-free test of intelligence has little meaning in the context of psychology and none at all in education. I get less and less interested in what persons do under sanitized conditions of learning and responding. To think straight when the odds are unfavorable, to persevere, to move toward the operational, to face reality, to shun magic and superstition—where are the tests for these intellectual attributes of twentieth-century man?

The Learning Matrix

In a humane society there are limits to the demand for intellectual performance on the part of pupils. A harsh compulsion will not do; differences in ability and interest are substantial, and no child likes to be pushed. Motivation finally is *in* the child—an ineffable force that is nourished through a sense of belonging and adult understanding. In education we are asking the child to take part, to solve problems, to compare, to achieve—to make a few decisions now and to make more later by the same process. We try to guide children expertly and gently, but what we hold out to them is the satisfaction of learning and becoming. Even for the very dull, rewards are not wanting. A fluid level of expectation is ascertained, and each pupil is expected to do his best. He is not permitted to lay claim to mental incompetence simply by omitting the factors of work and concentration.

We learn when we are placed in a learning situation. We learn when it is more rewarding to learn than not to learn. The learning matrix in school can be described in familiar terms. First, there is the teacher, surrounded by visible reenforcing paraphernalia. The teacher faces—or mixes with—an assemblage of like-age children. In essence, we may regard effective teaching as emanating from a person spilling over with knowledge, enthusiasm, and an affectionate regard for children. It is the duty and privilege of the school, as of the home, to keep this field of influence benevolent and child-centered.

In any system of organized instruction, a journey has begun, marked by way stations, a few stopovers, and now and then a retracing of steps. At journey's end, the adolescent emerges as an adult. Beyond the primary survival reflexes, all preschool learning was at root social; now, in school, it is flagrantly so. There is no waiting upon a late-arriving set of tribal rites at puberty; by that time the personal life of the child is entwined with societal demands. Into this configuration the child may enter wholeheartedly, sensing that the school offers a life of interest now as well as the preparatory stages of a mysterious future. On the other hand, he may choose not to play the game; he may cling to the memories of a free-style home, street, or gang. In so doing he can be enormously "successful," that is, resistant to everything the school or the larger society expects of him, but in the long run he loses. A child given to nonlearning in school (in which there is no viable substitute for learning) will endure a long period of frustration. The reasons for refusal to accept and carry through appropriate learning tasks are not to be deduced entirely from a study of the

child himself, important as that is. It is necessary also to analyze the major social impacts upon his life style—parents,
siblings, companions, and heroes. If nonlearning is prevalent,
a correlative study of the school's programs and procedures is
in order.

Assuming that a degree of rapport has been established between teacher and pupil, including group reactions, it is essential that no artificial blocking be allowed to bar the pupil's
progress. Perplexity can be brought out into the open without
censure or surprise, for it is almost never peculiar to a single
pupil. If it turns out that the item or principle is beyond the
mental power of a given pupil—no easy determination—that
line of instruction should be altered. This outcome is the
exact reverse of abandoning the student as a *person*, or indeed
as a learner under different circumstances. Teachers, counselors,
and parents should join forces to find out what Johnnie *can*
learn and will enjoy learning. If it turns out to be nonquanti-
tative items as in language, the arts, or the social studies, the
rest of the journey is clear sailing. As I shall indicate in discussing the Dual Progress Plan, these are the usual means of
communication. If on the other hand the pupil's discovered
aptitudes are in the mechanical or mathematical, the task is
more complex; even at modest levels of expectation the maturing child cannot escape the demands of language and social
competence. An endpoint of sorts is reached when the child's
mind cannot be lured beyond the sheer accumulation of facts
and figures but remains alienated from new awareness, usage,
or generalization. Far better for a child or adult to be firmly
in control of a few principles that unify experience than to be
perpetually bogged down in a mass of confusing "problems."
Not many children are so genetically backward as to be incapable of learning, enjoying, and profiting by *something*, but
what that something is will be discovered neither by the in-
efficient teacher nor by the efficient machine. Verbalization
fails when it takes the place of actions and experiences within
the child's time-bind and place-bind. Visual imagery helps to

sustain esoteric abstractions; the performing arts make sense of words, gestures, and ideas. It is in this complicated framework that we may properly assign intellectual dominance to the language arts. Deeds are the taproot of words.

School Children Are Not Captives

I have no patience with critics who regard the children of America as captives of a school system. The school is neither the child's free choice nor the teacher's. Schooling is *society's* free choice, just as nonschooling, that is, illiteracy, was the choice of nations for most of the world's children only a few decades ago. In what sense are children captives if they are required to comply with laws designed for their own protection and growth? Under a dictatorship they are indeed captive, but no more so than their parents who submit to tyranny. Since we are all the beneficiaries—or victims—of an immense overload of laws and traditions, the need for a free, informed, and compassionate citizenry is obvious. It is no accident that when this goal is set up, the universal education of children immediately comes to the fore. Within this general commitment the child in a free society moves freely.

Language and Thought

To repeat, the frontier in theories of learning is in the field of language and thought. What the teacher knows and what the student learns will at times transcend language—as in art, music, or mechanics—but the means of expression is buttressed by language. Even in chemistry and biology the symbols used are embedded in a complex linguistic structure. Why, then, is there so much psychological research along nonverbal and subhuman lines? Why so much attention to behavior devoid of an interior, word-oriented, mental life? Psychology is no longer vulnerable as a science; it will not return to philosophy and natural history, nor will it be reduced to physiology. Early psychologists in their eagerness to get away from rhetoric turned to psychophysical problems. Brass instruments, mazes, tractable animals, conditioned reflexes, stimulus-response bonds, and the like neatly circumvented the primacy of language in human learning. As a result the psychology of learning as applied to the cognitive process was slow to develop. To a teacher or school counselor objective longitudinal reports on a hundred children from birth to adulthood are worth more than a plethora of studies on the performance of animals.

Few teachers have adequate information on their pupils. There is no time for a halt to discover why Johnnie, who may be one of twenty-five or thirty in the room, no longer listens, responds, or gains ground. At this point, a limited amount of programmed instruction may be helpful in showing not *why* but *whether* Johnnie is making progress. It is then the responsibility of the teacher and school psychologist to undertake the diagnosis. As indicated, a full complement of tests, interviews, and case studies will be necessary. The kindergarten arrives late on the scene, so much so that preschool teachers usually prepare a structured dossier of the child's achievements and behavior patterns. This gives the teacher a base line of mental variability to supplement any I.Q. ratings. This is one reason why university preschool "laboratories" are successful; the teachers get to know the child's behavior, singly and in the group, and they interview the parents. An accumulated record up through the primary grades is thereby made available.

A significant factor in language learning is that children repeatedly make use of what they know. Children do not just "observe" speech; they speak. It is to the discredit of the old-fashioned American school that speech was downgraded, that whispering—as natural to a child as eating or sleeping—became a forbidden activity. Now in the 1970s the practice of discourse and debate, of language as an art form, may again be neglected, this time through the silence of earphones. That constant listening, even to superior speech, will improve the speech of children is simply wishful thinking; it is like trying to play a musical instrument without practice. The test of the usefulness of a model is pragmatic. To watch anything, stripped of its potential as a matrix for learning, is only to develop a taste for more watching.

4

THE ART OF TEACHING

The Teacher's Commitment

A commitment of the teacher to "society itself" as against
"subject matter alone" seems axiomatic, but it borders on the
meaningless. No commitment is ever made to subject matter
alone. Let us not, for all that, downgrade subject matter. Great
ideas as far back as Plato have set fire to the whole fabric of
society; such ideas do not originate afresh in each young mind.
They are *learned*, if only to be revised or replaced. Originality
in any field has its roots in the past. In the United States
organized education is primarily the responsibility of the states
and localities. Is the commitment to them alone? Is "society"
to be identified with governmental authority? The service is
local and thus restricted, but the commitment is to the ideals
of education in a free society. The issue is crucial. We ask what
was, or should have been, the commitment of teachers in
Fascist Italy, in Nazi Germany, in Japan under the warlords.
What is it today for Americans in the context of the recent
slaughter in Southeast Asia? What commitment does the teaching profession have, here and now, with respect to any child
whose chance to learn and mature has been worsened by ex-
traneous events?

Not all items or sequences in the curriculum are of equal
weight. What is lost in information can be made up, provided

we know what is worthwhile. Even for children who never missed a day of school, the amount of forgetting is formidable. The remembered parts are those that help one to gain insights or perhaps to maintain a feeling of adequacy in a peer group. The remembered days are those that carry a feeling tone— through a song, a drawing, a problem solved, an original piece of work done, a cooperative venture, a reward, a reproof, an act of injustice. We assess the school within a double framework. First, what does this lesson, this project, this segment mean to the child; and, second, where does it stand in the continuity of the school's curriculum? It could be an empty exercise. Children, and adults too, may become storehouses of useless information. This is the quiz-kid syndrome; it is not education. It is harmful because it is wasteful.

To observe only the teacher at work is to miss some of the essentials of the teaching process. Very little in the educational milieu was originated by classroom teachers—not the design of the school building; not the textbooks; not standardized tests; not electronic aids; not teacher certification; not the laws concerning age-of-entrance, age-of-leaving, school taxes, transportation, racial integration; not the entrance requirements for college. Nevertheless, these factors enter into the classroom situation.

In like vein, pupil progress cannot be ascertained solely by classroom measurements of skill in subject matter. Of course, teachers and supervisors should be concerned if pupils fail to move toward more complex learning, but we are not faced with mutually exclusive alternatives. Show me children who are letter-perfect in reproducing what they have studied, and I must ask about the teacher's concept of goals. Are the pupils being weighted down with isolated facts and fragments? Can they put ideas together, sensing the inherent problems and coming out with defensible solutions—not the teacher's solutions but their own, even though they may be the same? We need two sets of tests, one to measure mental skills and operations and one to assess maturation, meaningfulness, and originality. The stated aims of education include both criteria, but measurements are so much simpler in the first that the second is neglected. The relevant questions are these:

(1) Is the child developing the habit of straight thinking, constantly drawing new sources of knowledge?
(2) Is the child maturing along physical, emotional, and social lines?
(3) Is the child developing attributes that lead to cooperation and good will?
(4) Is the child able to enrich his personal life through creative work and the enjoyment of the arts?

In any accepted field, it is the business of the school to help the child toward such maturity. Unhappily, for all its good intentions, the school is afflicted with scheduling devices that run counter to achievement. A scattering mental effect is produced by a melange of brief class hours in a variety of subjects. Comprehensive research on the question of interference in learning is lacking. Concentration is a prime attribute for success. To the expert teacher of French, for example, the language is familiar currency—well known, incessantly practiced. When a group of pupils leaves the classroom the teacher gets ready for the next round—of French, conversing, reading, thinking in French, and absorbing French culture. This is a form of learning in depth denied most students. Schools introduced an irrational diversion when they offered students a mosaic of instructional periods with little interaction. Research in learning should tell us what the optimum saturation is— the point of diminishing return, the time to change the subject. Should not some students stay with a single subject for days, weeks, or months in order to achieve a small mastery? Team teaching and curricular coordination were long overdue and have yet to realize their full potential.

Criteria of Teaching Excellence

The most bitter criticism of American educational programs is directed toward methodology. If by content we mean what is actually accepted by the student, the method of reaching, or not reaching, this state is of consequence. Laissez-faire is one method, as are concepts of readiness that lead to a postponement of certain stages of learning. Apart from genetic adequacy, the child "readiness" of John Stuart Mill to absorb Latin and Greek resulted from his father's "readiness" to teach and to insist upon mastery. After all, Roman children learned their Latin at an early age, and Montaigne is frank about the method applied to him: Latin by servants and tutors who knew no French.

All methods, like cults and dogmas, tend to harden in time. They lose their early virtues and are hostile to new discoveries; the burden of proof should always be upon them. In fact, what we now seek is no one method but a diversity of approaches that conform to some general plan. The purpose of educational method is to accomplish what we believe to be timely and desirable. Method does not properly dictate content, but it cannot fail to affect it for better or worse. The slogan, "the medium is the message," contains a kernel of truth, but it is rendered sterile by overstatement. No method, no skill, no bit of information is good in and of itself.

As schools introduce new programs certain criteria of teacher fitness should be met. As I see it, these criteria include the following:

—First, a warmth, respect, and tolerance for pupils that, though short of parental love, is nevertheless an important ingredient in every classroom.

—Second, a knowledge of child development and behavior. This is no simple by-product of a course in general psychology; it calls for the supervised observation of children.

—Third, a knowledge in some depth of a discipline or area of subject matter. The teacher should know the relevant history and what new ideas are being broached. For example, the teacher of English or a second language should understand how language is acquired and be steeped in the appropriate literature. The teacher of mathematics and science should have majored in some branch of science. In the social studies, the teacher should get below the surface of current events, and this means turning to history, economics, sociology, and psychology. If the well-grounded teacher of art is an artist and the teacher of music a musician, so much the better.

—Fourth, a liberal education that is organismic.

In short, teachers should be specialists along three lines: the child, the subject matter, and the methodology of teaching. Superior teachers will know children as even parents do not. Through study and supervised practice they will achieve the distinctive mark of any profession, which is expertise. Classroom teachers of the future are not expected to be paragons of virtue and wisdom, but they should surpass today's prototypes. Incidentally, it is unrealistic for women to be confined largely to classroom teaching and supervising in the elementary grades. They should be found at all levels, from nursery school to college, with no differentiation of salary by reason of sex or level of teaching assignment. There is a catch to the latter stipulation. For example, the teacher of mathmatics in an ungraded elementary school should be technically prepared to teach at least through the high school. Teachers of English are already capable of doing this, for English is their daily diet.

If we agree in principle with the indicated aims of education and with their concomitants in the work of the teacher, we are still left with three questions, How shall we organize instruction? How shall we evaluate pupil progress? How shall we educate teachers? Since I feel the school situation is beyond remedy through patching here and there, I shall shortly describe a plan that attempts to get at the heart of the dilemma that we face in the teaching of young children. It will appear that the villain in the piece is the self-contained classroom.

Where the Self-contained Classroom Falls Short

I hold that the self-contained classroom must carry some of the responsibility for the shortcomings in education. Consider these points:

(1) Grade teachers are unlikely to have gone far in mathematics, science, art, or music. They have trouble keeping up with the

bright students; they are vague about what lies ahead in mathematics, engineering, or other quantitative disciplines.

(2) The supervisor who comes in to share the teaching of specialized subjects finds that the classroom teacher is a poor ally; this is not truly team teaching.

(3) It is hard to convert the ordinary all-purpose classroom into a science room, a social studies room, a studio for art or music.

(4) The situation in English and the social studies is different. Teachers in these fields go far beyond their classroom orbits; they would find it silly to stay on the language level of their pupils in, say, the fourth grade. Teachers also converse with other college graduates on a peer basis with respect to domestic and foreign affairs.

Three-dimensional experience enriches the language arts and rounds out desirable traits in character and personality. The narrow world of the self-contained classroom is a poor place for a child to go "all out" in any direction. Other things equal, the best music teachers are musicians; the best art teachers, artists; the best science teachers, scientists. This statement is axiomatic outside the school; in school we lose sight of it. Of course I am speaking of teachers whose love and understanding of children is unrelated to either "self-contained" or specialized teaching. To be effective with and accepted by children (is there a difference?) is not to try to become one of them or to resemble them. We sense this when an adult uses *baby talk*, yet we indulge a teacher who descends to *baby art* or *baby arithmetic*. The teacher we seek is one who respects children too much to imitate them—one who regards them as precious and altogether the hope of the human race.

Cultural Imperatives and Cultural Electives

I take it there is general agreement on the central importance of English and the social studies; surely they deserve the designation "cultural imperatives." On the other hand, some subjects may be regarded as "cultural electives"—important, but not so universally necessary as the "cultural imperatives." Beyond the elementary stages, science and mathematics stand out as cultural electives. Thus by the age of twelve some pupils will show an aptitude for science; others will shun quantitative manipulations. For reasons still obscure, the girls will heavily populate this latter group; their attention, if they are free to choose, turns to languages, social studies, and the arts. The test of the acceptability of science as a cultural imperative on the American scene will come when the school discovers how to arouse interest with equal intensity across sex differences. A parallel statement holds for the arts.

On the Teaching of Science

In any method and for any content, there is a basic unity to be discerned and put into practice. The question is, What is the teacher trying to accomplish? In mathematics and science the answer is, to familiarize students with powerful tools of thought and with attendant technical solutions. Most students will not go far in science. The blank face toward science is so much a part of our adult culture pattern that it is irrational to punish children for a like indifference. Of course most adults never have had occasion to observe scientific method, much less to make personal use of it. Most all-purpose teachers are out of contact with scientists and are unfamiliar with scientific methods. What teachers and their students respond to is not the esoteric methods or detailed findings but the grand sweep of major breakthroughs that cut across the various disciplines; in short, less of the static and comparative and more of the relation of human beings to the natural world and to each other. If today the total scientific structure is to have a capstone, it will be no Comtian concept of sociology but, more likely, *ecology*.

The future of a small number of intelligent, highly motivated students lies in science as a profession. In the elementary grades it is difficult to identify these future scientists, but it is important to realize they are there. In today's world, the interest is not so much *in* science, as *about* science. How many adults know anything about the substance of the scientific branches or their special methodologies? The affairs of everyday life are indeed affected by the *products* and *applications* of science but only indirectly by scientific research itself, which is nongeographical, nonpolitical, nonreligious. Debates on issues in science can be carried on only by scientists. But when scientific theories impinge upon tradition, dogma, or other cherished belief, as they did in the case of Galileo, Darwin, and Freud, there is a great hullabaloo. The field of combat is not then in science; it is in the humanities.

When science is taught by experts, the interested and gifted receive a boost in morale, and all students deepen their awareness. The term "appreciation" in this context does not imply superficiality, nor does it rule out the attainment of proficiency, provided the latter is considered germane to a liberal (amateur) approach. Thus the study of natural sciences below college can center about problems, demonstrations, and discoveries, about matters that are still intriguing. A spark can be struck for every student. Such teaching is already found in some of our experimental schools, but the frank use of the term "science appreciation" is uncommon. This brings us to the question of what organization plan may promote effective teaching of both the cultural imperatives and the cultural electives.

Origin of the Dual Progress Plan

My discussion at this point will center upon the Dual Progress Plan.[1]

The conceptual framework of the plan dates back to an address I gave at Syracuse University on the occasion of the fiftieth anniversary of its School of Education. It was entitled "New Ways to Reach the Mind of the Child."[2] Following a preliminary refinement of the original scheme, a working party was set up at New York University. With the generous support of the Ford Foundation, a three-year try-out and demonstration was carried on in Grades III–VI of the school systems of Ossining and Long Beach in New York; subsequently the plan was put into operation elsewhere.

Essentially the Dual Progress Plan calls for a graded segment based entirely on English and the social studies (the *cultural imperatives*) and a concurrent ungraded segment consisting of mathematics, science, music, and art (the *cultural electives*) – hence a dual program. Pupils move through the usual grades on the basis of their work in the *cultural imperatives,* but no set amount of work in the *cultural electives* is demanded of them. All classes are taught by fully trained teachers who are expert in a given subject. The ramifications of this deceptively simple plan will now be explored in some detail.

A major reform in the Dual Progress Plan is the abandonment of the self-contained classroom. Pupils spend the day in not less than three classrooms: (1) the core (English and social studies), (2) mathematics-science, (3) music-art. In a comprehensive school, they would have six classrooms, namely, English, social studies, mathematics, science, art, and music, together with a gymnasium and a playground. It is not a case of shuffling children about, although they enjoy that feature of the plan; it is a matter of joining pupil, teacher, and specialized facilities to form a matrix for effective learning. In a large school system a teacher offers either the language arts or the social studies; in smaller schools the teacher is likely to cover both areas. Mathematics and science may be joined as a composite specialization. All teachers are *generalists* along two lines, namely, in the liberal arts and in teacher-preparatory subjects.

Why should we undertake the difficult business of providing *two* pathways for all students? In the Dual Progress Plan, the two paths were not casually chosen. They exemplify the *raison d'être* of the plan. To restate its unique features:

1. A concept of *cultural imperatives* versus *cultural electives.*
2. A grade system based *exclusively* on the language arts and social studies (the cultural imperatives).
3. A vertical, ungraded progression in mathematics, science, music

and art (the cultural electives), the pupils advancing according to aptitude, interest, and achievement.

4. A reform of teacher preparation consistent with the three points above.

The Cultural Imperatives Form the School Grade

Why should the cultural imperatives be the only measure for the grade placement of the pupil from Grade III through Grade VI? The answer lies in another question: Are not language and the social studies the source of most communication in our society? As it happens, the factors common to reading comprehension and mentality are so pervasive that tests of general intelligence rely heavily on vocabulary, the understanding of sentences, and the solving of verbal problems. Mental tests contain little of significance in science and nothing at all in art or music. Since under the plan the whole system of ladderlike grades is based on the *cultural imperatives,* we are entitled to ask for "a reason." To find the reason, we need only look about us. In our culture pattern the English language and the social studies carry almost the full weight of the common learnings. True, adults are expected to master a few arithmetical skills and to have a small store of information *about* science, art, and music. But skills and insights in speaking, reading, and comprehension are called upon all the time, every waking hour.

The Cultural Electives

The situation with respect to art, music, mathematics, or any branch of science is quite different; there, for the most part, adults resort to a happy neglect of science, and to arts *appreciation* only. Beyond simple arithmetic, including fractions and decimals, few adults are called upon to display either skill or understanding in mathematics. Some residual geometry may on occasion be called forth, but no algebra, trigonometry, or analysis. Elementary statistics through central tendency, dispersion, probability, and correlation would prove valuable to some high school graduates, but that is precisely the type of mathematics our schools have neglected. Obviously I am not referring to the preparatory work of scientists and technicians but to the general cultural demands faced by the adult population. Of course, the social climate may change. It may be that one day our society will demand a genuine grasp of science pitched to various levels of comprehension. Presently American adults are a long way from that, as ill at ease in science or engineering as they are in medicine, musical composition, or a foreign tongue. Given a massive cultural shift, we should expect the school imperatives to follow suit.

It is important to note that by placing mathematics, science, and the arts in the vertical or ungraded segment of the Dual Progress Plan, we do not thereby reduce their significance. We simply recognize and incorporate in the school plan some fundamental differences in the *level of expectation*. Pupils in the middle school have both mathematics and science every day—and they take each with a teacher who is thoroughly familiar with the subject. But the students are not expected to progress any faster than their comprehension allows, and they are free from that dread feeling of being unable to escape the assignment of tasks beyond their grasp.

The Place of English and the Social Studies in the Dual Progress Plan

It is held that every child should feel at ease in the understanding and use of the English language. Nobody is going to avoid speaking, listening, reading, and writing, or escape problems and actions that involve English. Moreover, we expect children, as they grow up, to know something about economic, social, and political affairs. Relevant questions in these areas are regularly discussed in newspapers and magazines and on television; they enter into conversation at home

and at school. In fact, the language imperative begins soon
after age one, with the child's first word, and it develops intensively through the preschool years.

If, after a reasonable amount of effort in school and out, the
child does not prosper in the language arts—cannot learn to
read or write—we are properly concerned. We have his eyes
examined for double vision, mirror images, or other defects.
It is well known, too, that a child may be deaf years before the
parents notice it; they think the child is dull or misbehaving.
For children with hearing defects, language is a very trouble-
some matter. Aside from such physiological handicaps there
is the possibility of a general mental defect; only an expert
can determine this, but teachers should be alerted to persistent
backwardness in reading comprehension and to a conspicuous
lack of interest in current happenings. Except for a child's
inability to do simple arithmetic, no such involvement adheres
to slowness or disinterest in the cultural electives. Who would
want to lose I.Q. points because of inability to carry a tune,
to paint, to act, to solve algebraic equations? As adults we
skirt all such tests, but every day of our lives, willy-nilly, we
undergo tests of comprehension and judgment.

Teaching the Language Arts

Nothing is fully learned unless it is learned for a purpose
and utilized in fulfillment of that purpose. The language arts
are no exception to this rule. Reading is a venture into the
unknown. There is a pulling power in the next paragraph, in
the next unturned page, that is a function of mild tensions
already present in the reader. Too much saturation with the
unknown will kill the curiosity of the learner, while too little
will waste his time. Language simplification will fail if it stays
simple; Basic English is neither basic (to the psychologist) nor
English (to the linguist).

Apparently the flash fire that lit up the drawn-out controversy
between the phonic method and the word recognition method

has died down. Teachers blend the two "methods" in a single approach that capitalizes on both hearing and seeing; they never did assume that a child was either deaf or blind. The essence of reading is to follow the writer's train of thought and imagination and inevitably to supply one's own unique counterpoint. A poor reader is handicapped; an indiscriminate reader is overburdened. In these days of "junk mail" the reader must choose what to read, what to believe, what to throw into the wastebasket. Why be literate only to be fooled or insulted? An occupational hazard in a democracy is one's susceptibility to free advice.

Not much time, in school or out, is allotted to speech; for most persons it is a lost art. A standardized test does not allow students to ask *their* questions, nor does a large class. While the up-to-date teacher has turned from a silly abhorrence of whispering to a tolerance for talking, I note that effective speech is still uncommon in the classroom. On television the clear speech of announcers and actors rarely serves as a model for the viewer who sits passively before the screen. The truth is that sustained conversation in depth is a rarity; we lack the time, the place, and the patience for it. Speech is of immense value in communication, but today, like almost everything else, it comes to us at second hand; it is a casualty of the electronic age. Thus far the schools have done little to repair the damage. Students hooked up to mechanical or electronic devices, eyes and ears alert to external stimuli, are in no position to converse with each other. I rate effective speech on a par with reading and writing. Of course I am not referring to declamation, oratory, or dramatics, but simply to the art of talking and listening, of *communicating*. The sophisticated by-product of good speech, debating, should be encouraged from the middle school up as one means of discovering not only what "the other fellow" thinks but also the soundness of one's own views. Learning of this sort is applicable to numerous life situations.

Teaching the Social Studies

The teaching of some branches of the social sciences—history is an example—is often a statutory requirement. There are textbooks galore but no definitive studies of the merits of different teaching plans. History, geography, economics, and government form a natural grouping, as do anthropology, psychology (behavior), and sociology. Regardless of the titles of textbooks and lesson plans, such forbidding terms will be lost upon the young mind—on the whole, a good thing. In the elementary and middle school, "Social Studies A" and "Social Studies B" will suffice. Access to resource materials cutting across all academic disciplines, together with freedom of movement on behalf of projects, is the *sine qua non* for success in teaching the social studies. In fact, the teaching of the social studies has much in common with the teaching of English. It is for this reason that the Dual Progress Plan permits teacher teams to cover both fields, particularly in the smaller systems.

Teaching the Arts

In 1966 a conference on the place of the arts in the schools of New York City was held in Tarrytown. The following highlights of the conference are of interest as a flexible scheme for implementing this segment of the Dual Progress Plan:

1. The group suggested that the arts and humanities be considered in three categories: (a) visual; (b) performing; and (c) literary. The dramatic arts will cut across these headings.
2. Firsthand experience in the arts and humanities was held to be crucial—experience in understanding, appreciation, and participation.
3. The activist role was stressed. Performance is salutary as long as it is consistent with aptitudes and interests, but children should not be made to feel inferior through lack of talent. Since every child has a voice, it was felt that singing offered wide opportunities for individual and group achievement. Similarly, reading and writing could be made to embody creative

elements at all levels of skill. The principal aim should be to get the child *involved* in the various arts, for they are in no sense "frosting" or "additives."

4. Stress was placed on out-of-school experiences by way of museums, concert halls, theaters, libraries, and nature walks.

5. A nongraded approach to art, music, and creative activities was favored. Abilities along these lines do not fall into neat chronological or grade categories. The self-contained classroom is not conducive to excellence in artistic endeavors.

6. A repeated question was that of *evaluation*. What valid measures of progress are available? What new ideas and methods are indicated? To win student acceptance, the arts should be alluring and satisfying—at no time reduced to a mechanical system. Interviews, portfolios, auditions, films, tape recordings, and group productions could enter into the framework of evaluation.

7. The preparation of the curriculum was acknowledged to be a complex matter in which teachers, specialists, and practitioners in the arts have a role to play.

8. It was held that familiarity with the arts in some form, bolstered by participation for each child, would lead to a lifelong commitment.

Some Features of the Dual Progress Plan

In the Dual Progress Plan the pupils have general science in a special room every day—more science than is likely to be found in the self-contained classroom. They also have a daily class hour of mathematics. Every other day they devote an hour to music and an hour to the arts, each subject in a room specially designed for the purpose. It is to be noted that the *cultural* electives are not the equivalent of *school* electives; a certain amount of study in science, mathematics, and the arts is required of all pupils. This requirement may be waived subsequently if it is discovered that a pupil simply cannot meet minimum scholastic assignments.

In the ungraded segment (the cultural electives), the pupils are redistributed; the teachers who teach them now, starting with the third grade, will remain with them for some years to come. In fact it is desirable to organize a team of teachers from the third grade up through senior high school. It will be a team of specialists. So, if somebody asks, "What do you teach?" the reply is, "I teach mathematics," or "I teach science," or "I teach mathematics and science." Similarly for music and art. If somebody asks the same question about the cultural imperatives, the answer may well be, "I teach English and social studies—in Grade IV."

The pupils do not have the same teacher for a full day in a given school year. They have either one teacher or two teachers for one half the day and two or three teachers for the other half. Under the prevailing grade system pupils lose all contact with a given teacher at the end of the school year. Under the Dual Progress Plan there is a cadre of teachers in the cultural electives who are in a position to understand and encourage the same pupils year after year—a vertical continuity, as it were.

A Further Note on the Place of Science in the Curriculum

After *Sputnik* and up to a few years ago, there was a national drive to train more engineers and scientists, but educators were loath to predict that few experts would emerge from the lower half of the school's population. We may as well admit, too, that the recruitment of women engineers will be slim unless we change our ways or young women change theirs. In the United States the requirement that girls should take pre-engineering mathematics in high school is largely unwarranted. In the Soviet Union they compel women to take engineering courses. We do not.

The teaching of science is complicated. How can a "specialist" in science cover physics, chemistry, biology, and geology with sufficient knowledge and enthusiasm to hold the attention of pupils from Grade III to the junior high-school level? It is not easy, but some common elements can be exploited. These branches need not be named at an early stage—perhaps not at all below the junior high school. There need be no distinct separation between any two branches in the early stages; in fact, the pupils' questions will not permit it. The most successful science teacher in the early demonstrations of the Dual Progress Plan was a biologist by training who was happy to escape from the fuzziness of the self-contained classroom. Utilizing biology as a rallying point, she succeeded in bringing in something relevant from all the branches listed above, and the pupils prospered. As every teacher knows, a child's curiosity may spread over a wide range of science. If the concept, *general science,* has lost ground it is because "general" so often came to mean "superficial." Personally I had rather see a teacher thoroughly grounded in *any* scientific branch teach *all* the branches than turn the job over to a "self-contained" teacher without depth in anything scientific.

An example of future trends is found in the science teaching materials developed by Professor Jerrold R. Zacharias and his associates at the Massachusetts Institute of Technology. They have prepared modules for instruction periods of four to six weeks. These can be fitted into various types of curricula, and they are flexible with respect to place of usage—classroom, laboratory, or lecture hall. Teachers are in no way absolved from their teaching duties—variations in local and state requirements, not to mention the differences among pupils, see to that. Combined with a certain amount of student teaching (as a part of the process of learning) and self-teaching, the plan is potentially timesaving and money-saving. Moreover, the incentive of being allowed to assist a student who needs help is not without charm for young people who stress mutual helpfulness.

Mathematics: Cultural Imperative or Cultural Elective?

In mathematics, except for the required work in computation, each pupil is expected to achieve in accordance with his aptitude as observed and measured. The child may with dignity omit the more abstract levels or, on the other hand, advance rapidly to higher levels. Mathematics is an esoteric language; it is "terrific" for those of either sex who like it and want to go far in it. We should discover such pupils early and give them a chance to move up fast.

It is not my intention to follow the maze of developments, charges, and countercharges that beset the teaching of "the new math" but only to point up some issues that bear upon mathematics in the elementary and middle schools. Is mathematics in the United States truly a cultural imperative and therefore, like English, a subject to be required to the full extent of a pupil's ability to master it? Or is it, as in the Dual Progress Plan, a cultural elective that sharply differentiates among pupils and permits those of low aptitude or mental ability to abandon it altogether once they have passed beyond the computational stages of arithmetic? To what extent does the transition from the "old" to the "new" mathematics affect the answer to these questions?

A report provides the answers to some extent.[3] There are differences in emphasis among its seventeen contributors, and a group led by Professor Morris Kline of New York University remains unconvinced of the overall effectiveness of the new approach. Professor R. L. Wilder, of the Committee that produced the *Yearbook*, comes to the brink of the fallacy of mental discipline in the following statement:

> After all, except for those areas in traditional engineering and science in which special mathematical skills are still required, the chief equipment for the mathematically trained individual who goes into the ramified branches of modern industry and government is that he be trained in mathematical *ways of thought*. Probably the major task of the framers of modern curricula is to keep this latter equipment in mind while still heeding the necessity for supplying those technical skills without which the purpose of the new structures cannot be made clear.

How do mathematical *ways of thought* differ from chemical, geological, medical, or legal ways? I should say only in the recourse to mathematics as a means of rigorously defining and solving problems not otherwise solvable. In this sense, mathematics comes alive in the mind of the student as a function of its usefulness; the mathematical sciences predominate. Solving problems in mathematics without ever leaving the field is an enticing activity for the mathematician, but for most students the ideas and processes thereby engendered are only a game already played unless the procedures lead to something else, namely, to applications in physics, engineering, accounting, statistical prediction, and so on. In such manner the student will discover useful and perhaps original approaches.

Mathematics is a tool of thought, not a way of thinking. The way of thinking embedded in all logic and science is the disinterested formulation of procedures as a means of acquiring knowledge and testing hypotheses. A student will not derogate or lay aside tools of thought if he can make use of them, now or in a realizable future. However, if mathematics, physics, or chemistry are only played as a game, the student will feel free to yawn, to forget, to dismiss; poker, chess, or politics might be more fun. In any case, there is a vast amount of "forgetting," that is, rejection, of school-induced mathematics. This is not to say that *understanding* in mathematics or any scientific branch is of small importance; quite the reverse. Rather, we do not seek understanding as an intransitive phenomenon — one that carries no object.

In the future, mathematics may become a highly specialized tool or an intellectual interest for the gifted, while offering nothing beyond arithmetic and a touch of statistics for all others. As for technology, a little mathematics, physics, chemistry, or biology goes a long way. In short, intermediate and higher mathematics as an ingredient of education is a lost cause unless teachers and practitioners are able to demonstrate its usefulness over a wide range of student interest. Otherwise students, far from acquiring an aid to thinking, will persist in learning not to learn.

On the "New Math"

In making flat statements about the teaching of mathematics, I am aware that they are not becoming to a psychologist who never got beyond the calculus and the mathematical theory of statistics. Actually they are a layman's version of what Professor Kline has been asserting for the past fifteen years. He deplores the introduction of any methods that restrict mathematical performance. To quote: [4]

> The modernists would replace material currently taught by such topics as symbolic logic, Boolean algebra, set theory, some topics of abstract algebra such as groups and fields, topology, postulational systems, and statistics. I have no objection to the introduction of statistics, but I should like to examine the value of the other subjects from the standpoint of their central position in the body of mathematics and from the standpoint of application. As for importance in the body of mathematics, I believe it is fair to say that one could not pick more peripheral material.

Kline also feels that the "modernists" slight the application of mathematics to

> mechanics, sound, light, radio, electricity, atomic and nuclear theory, hydrodynamics, geophysics, magnetohydrodynamics, elasticity, plasticity, chemistry, chemical physics, physical biology, and the various branches of engineering. If there are ten people in this world designing switching circuits, there are a hundred thousand scientists in these other fields. And what mathematics is used in these fields I have mentioned? Because I work in a large institute devoted to applied mathematics, I believe I can tell you. The subjects are algebra, geometry, trigonometry, coordinate geometry, the calculus, ordinary and partial differential equations, series, the calculus of variations, differential geometry, integral equations, theory of operators, and many other branches of analysis.

Kline is firm in his belief that the first duty of a teacher of mathematics is to arouse the student's interest. Motivation is the key. He adds:

But what interest can young people find in simplifying fractions, in factoring, in exponents, in the quadratic formula, and in all the other dirty, intrinsically meaningless, boring processes that we teach in first-year algebra? The fact is that we have been guided in our choice of material not by the effort to arouse interest but to teach the mathematics that will be needed in the subsequent study of the subject. Our concern, in other words, has been with preparation for the future. But with such an introduction to mathematics, few students want a future in the subject.

Finally, Kline, like everybody else, favors curriculum reform and better teaching. He would approach *understanding* through intuition and utility.

Mathematics is primarily a series of great intuitions. The way to make the meaning of an idea clear is to present it in the intuitive setting that led to its creation or in terms of some simple modern equivalent. Physical or geometrical illustrations or interpretations will often supply this meaning. Thus $s = 16t^2$ is not just a quadratic function. It is a law of falling bodies, and s and t have definite and clear physical meanings. The fact that $s = 16t^2$ and not $16t$ also has an important physical significance and makes the quadratic feature impressive.

For the general run of technologists and sideline students in our time the great mathematical archetype might be Archimedes; he was equally at home in the theoretical and the practical. It appears that the principal centers of research on the teaching of mathematics are moving in this direction. If it supersedes the vagaries of "the new math," this approach will lead to an interlocking cluster of mathematics *cum* science appropriate to the domain of the cultural imperatives. In spite of my strictures regarding the present status of mathematics in school and society, I should favor this outcome.

The Teaching of Mathematics: A Summation

To sum up, computational skill and elementary statistics excepted, mathematics as taught today is as esoteric and useless to the majority of students as Sanskrit grammar. Having taught statistics for some years, I could be charged with favoring it unduly. Nonetheless, I am convinced that some concrete attention to matters of reliability, validity, and probability would yield a corrective to the claims of advertisers, politicians, and soothsayers in general. Presently students lack statistical *savoir-faire*.

I see no objection to the offering of middle-range mathematics in high school in terms of two criteria: (1) As a response to student aptitude for and interest in mathematics; (2) As a prerequisite for advanced work in some branch of science. In short, if the student enjoys mathematics and prospers in its study, he qualifies. Even if he does not enjoy mathematics but is able and willing to succeed in it as a prelude to, let us say, physics, engineering, or computer technology, again he qualifies. All other reasons for retaining mathematics in high school strike me as unrealistic; they are a concession to lingering fallacies, three in number:

(1) Mental discipline ("mathematics trains the mind").
(2) Mathematics is a part of the American culture pattern ("a knowledge of mathematics is a mark of the educated person").
(3) All children and adolescents can perform reasonably well in mathematics, given the opportunity.

The third fallacy is rarely mentioned, because up to now the esoteric nature of mathematics has been glossed over.

The Foreign Language Option

Some fixed goals are unattainable or perhaps ill-considered. Having lost Latin and Greek, most American students slyly abandoned the learning of any foreign language — and for similar reasons. The claim that one cannot master English unless one is fluent in at least one foreign language has never achieved research backing. Shades of Shakespeare, Shaw, and Churchill! More insidious was the belief that studying an esoteric vocabulary and grammar, if accompanied by halting translations, would "improve the mind"—the ever-arising fallacy of mental discipline. Once, conversing with two boys in a Dutch village, I asked how it was they had learned to speak English so competently. The older boy said, "We studied it for six years in school—reading, writing, and conversation." The father spoke up, saying, "This is a very small country; we can go only a few miles without encountering another language, and moreover no foreigners seem to be willing to learn Dutch." There we witness an immediate, durable incentive that Americans lack.

Most American children who speak a foreign language do so from association with parents, siblings, and companions for whom English is a second language. This is less common than heretofore, a notable exception being the stream of several hundred thousand Spanish-speaking Puerto Ricans who have come to our large cities in the last thirty years. The educational issue relates to children who rarely hear a foreign language spoken and if they do, ignore it, perhaps scornfully. Thus in New York City, vocal fluency in Spanish or Italian is looked down upon. In school and college the elitist concept of a "reading knowledge" of a foreign language is often substituted for the lively if inaccurate speech of the late arrivals. A student may speak halting French and still feel at home in French literature. For any native tongue the natural progression is from speech to reading and writing; for the acquisition of a second language this principle needs revising. By school age the child no longer wants preschool French. Visual and auditory cues and a transfer of common elements are of increasing importance. Individual differences in performance are sharpened, year by year.

A large-scale example of the importance of language in all learning is found in the schools of New York City, which enroll a quarter-million Spanish-speaking Puerto Ricans. Assigned to standard classrooms where all subjects are taught in English, the children are confused and frustrated. They soon fall behind, and the stage is set for truancy and delinquent acts. The decision to allow Puerto Rican students to receive instruction in the standard school subjects through Spanish was a compassionate move, but to my way of thinking unfortunate. To teach in Spanish is to nail down Spanish at the expense of English and to make it harder eventually to think in English. A more realistic approach is, at the beginning, to center formal instruction on the English language, with the exception of activities in shop work (if offered), health and physical education, music, and the visual arts. In short, teach the students English as a second language in process of becoming the first language. For these students, with the rare exception of those pointing toward linguistic scholarship, there is no future in keeping up with Spanish. To implement this proposal will take time and patience, but there are compensating factors, as, for instance, in the assurance that the intensive study of English will call upon resource material in literature, American history, geography, and current events. After three years, or even six years, depending upon the child's age and aptitude, it will be time enough to introduce a sequence of specific courses in mathematics, science, social studies, and the arts following the principles embedded in a dual progress plan. In subsequent years there will be a high correlation between the students' mastery of English and their ability to succeed in a scholastic discipline, or for that matter, in a chosen career.

In demonstrating the Dual Progress Plan, following proposals developed in the movement called Foreign Language in the Elementary School (FLES), a satellite program in French was offered, beginning in Grade IV. Early instruction was chiefly audio-lingual. Of immediate significance was the presence of a fluent, lively teacher. The prime factor in learning a second language is *motivation*; the teacher's first task is to arouse and sustain interest. A few statements on the rationale of foreign language study in American schools that were made at the time the Dual Progress Plan was presented are still applicable.[5]

While it is feasible for a normal child to learn two languages simultaneously, it may not be educationally desirable. He simply will not be as good in either language as he would have been in one of them, given equal time, instruction, and encouragement. In this respect bilingualism is no more desirable than ambidexterity. The experience in France some years ago bears this out. It was discovered that teaching English and French with equal vigor in the first school years was not conducive to rapid advancement in French; it was, in fact, associated with symptoms of insecurity—nervousness, obstinacy, stuttering, and the like. The mind of the young child seems to need a taproot and a solid trunk before branching out; this stability is to be found in one's native tongue. A second language is, and should be in part, a grafting upon the first. If attempted too soon, the process weakens the parent structure; if too late, it meets resistance and may fail altogether.

The inherent value in mastering a single tongue is indisputable. We need language for the social fulfillment of our biological structure. Language makes us human. It is as central as the nervous system itself and, as shown by the remarkable Helen Keller, it can develop with small aid from ordinary sensory cues. It is, however, unrealistic to argue that a second language also satisfies a deep need. It depends. Greek, Latin (as modified by the Romance languages), and Old English are "good" to the extent that they contribute to a command of English. They contain generic terms and grammatical forms that aid generalization. If studied as rigid systems, they may interfere with contemporary style and spontaneity. That the burden of proof for a foreign language as a desirable academic accomplishment of the American student must be established, is seen as soon as practical questions are asked. What language? For what levels of talent? With what degree of proficiency? By what methods? With what opportunity for practice? Toward what ends? There are no complete answers.

A scholar may be pressed to search beyond the limits of available translations. Linguists, anthropologists, and sociologists crave a firsthand contact. There are other examples of need: study abroad, foreign service, the performing arts. Still, it is hard to build up a nonvocational, nonprofessional case for competence in a second language. The language permutations among the one hundred and forty members of the United Nations are a case in point. For the official languages, simultaneous translation is in vogue; it has the effect of requiring minority groups to learn one of the languages that come through the earphones.

Accordingly, children who for any reason are keen to learn a second language should be encouraged to do so; as with middle-school mathematics, all others should be allowed to refrain gracefully. Students who elect to become proficient in Russian, Chinese, Japanese, Hindi, Arabic, or Swahili are likely to be strongly motivated. I feel that federal and state funds should primarily support centers for the training of teachers in languages and culture patterns that have hitherto been neglected. Difficult they may be, but they reflect the ideas and aspirations of much of the world's population. A reading knowledge of Chinese, for example, should be more alluring than a reading knowledge of French, Spanish, Italian, or German, from which everything important is soon translated. But let us not again make the mistake of imposing a study of *any* foreign language upon inert or resistant students; as in grafting foreign tissues upon the human body, compatibility is the key to success.

A Follow-up Study of the Dual Progress Plan

The second major reference is the report by Glen Heathers who assisted in the development of the Dual Progress Plan from the beginning.[6]

To quote from my foreword in Heathers's book:

> Students in the "core" subjects did as well as or better than comparable students in the self-contained classroom, and the standard deviations were higher. Still, the prospective gains for ungraded subjects that even now seem logical did not materialize. The question is, Why? If mathematics, science, art, and music are taught by experts in well-appointed classrooms, studios, and laboratories, with no grade restraints, how can pupils fail to profit thereby? Perhaps the answer has been previously adumbrated. What is sought in DPP is not so much

a greater *average* achievement along orthodox lines, as it is a significant upturn in the *range* of accomplishment—a better chance, for some, to "get off the hook" and a better chance, for others, to achieve insights and performances far beyond any "standardized" test. As for the slow-moving sections, a prior question for all new plans is: What can we reasonably expect of the lowest quarter of the school's population and along what lines? In follow-up studies the preceding considerations should carry weight.

On the other side of the ledger, there is evidence from a dozen school systems that pupils, teachers, and parents are favorably disposed toward the plan. Once the plan is installed, it is retained, though at times with modifications that all but defuse its instructional potentials.

The plan itself was not expected to supply the teacher with subject matter content. At various research centers there will be found massive materials on the substance of English, mathematics, science, foreign languages, and the arts. Also the up-to-date textbook, reinforced by books, journals, films, tapes, and laboratory equipment, provides the alert teacher with resource material. Fortunately, much is left to the teacher's discretion. The dropouts from a particular cultural elective, such as mathematics beyond computation, a foreign language, music or graphic arts expression, should not be subjected to invidious comparisons. My feeling about the place of science in the Dual Progress Plan is indeed ambivalent. As indicated, science may eventually be moved over to the graded segment—an imperative for one and all. But technology is really what most adults have in mind when they clamor for more science in the schools—not seminal discoveries but machines, rockets, and electronic devices.

Dual Progress or All Ungraded?

Is a modified version of the Dual Progress Plan the mark of the future for the middle school? It is too early to tell. Thus far only about fifteen school systems have overtly tried it. While there are favorable signs for above-average pupils, we have run into a difficulty yet to be surmounted, namely, that to nurture talent year after year in an ungraded sequence will call for a new type of longitudinal evaluation. At the same time, to release a captive student demonstrably out of his depth, strikes some teachers as derelict.

There remains the question, Why not go "all out" for a nongraded school? A substantial number of school systems are doing so, usually in combination with team teaching. As a rule they display certain advantages over the traditional grade system.[7] The difference between a completely nongraded plan and a dual progress plan does not lie in their amenability to team teaching or in utilizing new concepts of learning and evaluation. After all, half the day in the Dual Progress Plan is devoted to nongraded teaching. The real difference is in their respective rationales. John Goodlad and his associates would abandon the grade system; as refashioned, I prefer to keep it. The basis for this preference is found in the concept of cultural imperatives—what every student and adult *should* learn up to the level of his competence and energy. In the grade system we retain a series of plateaus or changeover points; we know where Johnnie stands in school without having to decipher a series of profiles. We discern a readiness (or nonreadiness) for the subsequent high school program. Students like to climb steps—not just to climb a steep ramp with no landings. To set up "grade equivalents" in a nongraded school is to reveal its weakness, whether the reference is to tests, transfer to another school, or the nagging questions of parents. In short, the reference to age placement is significant, and this is true in other areas of life. A grade system based on cultural imperatives is an arrangement that permits pupils to reach scholastic stations on the way to more remote goals. It is worth having.

Wherein Is the Specialist Teacher Unique?

Schools have a long tradition of calling in experts to teach music or physical education. A feature of the Dual Progress

Plan is that *every* teacher is a specialist, relatively speaking, though certainly not in the sense of research. Specialists should be equal to generalists in professional competence; presumably they have taken the same methods courses in preparation for teaching. In a methods class and in supervised practice teaching, the neophyte learns to speak and write clearly, to listen to each pupil, to encourage participation, and so on. These are useful virtues. What the expert adds, or rather exemplifies, is a *style*—a manner of teaching that does not derive from such courses but is a direct energy output arising out of saturation with a particular scholastic discipline. Thus the biologist as teacher is subtly and perhaps dramatically a biologist—a person who gives out what is within himself and a part of himself. In the arts the mood is that of the atelier. We cannot reasonably expect to discover the spark of genius in many classroom teachers, but when we find it, the attributes are always the same: a unique approach that wells up from within and stirs up the interest of pupils. The dedicated teacher works in the same league. Perhaps a definitive study of a few outstanding teachers would be more rewarding than a dozen monographs on methodology, taxonomy, or classroom management.

5

SOME THORNY ISSUES

What Is Relevant?

As of now, a striking social phenomenon is the ability of children and adults to put off any form of systematic learning that can be dubbed "irrelevant," "boring," "repetitive"—or just plain hard to come by. The schools are not blameless; at times they seem oblivious to the wave of nonlearning and antilearning. If in advance of overt instruction in subject matter it takes a teacher a month to convince his pupils of the relevance of, let us say, the English language, or arithmetical computation, it is a month well spent. If by high school the relevance of the social studies is still a puzzle to the students, a month spent on that issue alone will be defensible. The time will not be lost. To improve the school as a comprehensive social resource we need thorough studies of the total environmental impact on child health, mental growth, and personality. The persistent question is, *What do we expect a child to know, to do, to be, and to become?* Thus far, as inquisitive followers of Dewey, Binet, Lewin, and Piaget we have done little more than map out the problem. There will always be a place for imagination and adventure—for the art of education that embraces the subjective aspects of life. Contemplating the schools for tomorrow, we discern an incredible potential for extending the range of human endeavor. Within their self-imposed limits, foundations and governmental agencies will play the game once it has been invented, but only the school people themselves can bridge the gap between ideation and fruitful implementation.

Of course, relevance, motivation, and intention have always been the concern of the teacher and the school. In the precipitate drive to categorize school subjects and curricula as "relevant" or "irrelevant" this fact is lost sight of. To illustrate, in a vertically mobile American community, when will the language arts—speech, reading, writing, literature, drama—be considered irrelevant? If we have learned anything at all from the world history of education, the answer is, *never*. The brain is a vast network of cells whose principal function at the cortical level is integration and communication. To be deficient in the understanding and use of one's native language is, as every mental tester knows, to be scaled down in intelligence. Similarly for the social studies: we cannot escape their impact, for they penetrate every major decision in life. Rather than depreciate these imperatives we should seek to discover the roots of their disparagement by indifferent or rebellious students. Incompetence in English is a most effective blight on the promise of youth. Ignorance of the social forces at work in such pervasive matters as government, labor, management, economics, education, and health protection will plague the individual all his life. The academic load seems heavy, but in twelve years of schooling there is time on the calendar, provided the schools capture the learner's interest and interlace the mental process with firsthand sensory experience. Neither in school nor out will a concatenation of impacts and bits of information effectively "add up" by themselves.

The end sought and the steps toward it must be accepted by the student himself. If he assumes the role of a nonlearner or an antilearner, teachers should stop right there; the first stage, no matter how long it takes to reach it, is to induce the desire to take part. The password is *attention*. Let the fielder sit down just once, and he is off the sandlot baseball team.

Let a coach discover any player in any sport to be soldiering, and the heat is on; the player is told to "shape up" or get out. Is this a resultant of the voluntary nature of sport as against the compulsory feature of schooling? Not at all. If competitive sports or extracurricular activities were compulsory, as indeed they almost are in some places, this condition would still obtain; it is a way of life. Competition is always a factor. Strangely, it is the one academic motivating device seized upon by the school's critics as obnoxious. What hypocrisy! Adults cannot be lured into playing or watching any game or contest unless someone keeps score, that is, assigns marks. When, strictly for noncompetitive pleasure, they hike, swim, ski, skate, or climb mountains, they often reveal an inner clocking and comparing propensity. On the cultural side, either as participants or spectators (appreciators) they tend to rate everybody and everything, if only subjectively. But in the academic world it is fashionable to postulate some self-fueled flame of interest and endeavor, such that marks, promotions, honors, and the like are not only superfluous but also undemocratic. Actually, even the highly talented, inner-directed student welcomes personal attention and the outward signs of achievement.

The Bright Student Also Deserves a Hearing

The test of superiority is performance. We read of plans to push bright pupils up through junior and senior high school so that they may escape boredom. Now, to be bored is a sad experience even for the dull, who are as much entitled to a juicy life as anybody else. If the bright ones in a school system burst ahead, does this prove we have a good curriculum? Not necessarily. The bright ones may be just as bored a few grades higher up or in college. Dull children left behind may dislike being placed in an aura of contempt. The task is to reduce boredom without surrendering the pupil's personal responsibility for continuous learning—to take reasonable precautions against failure and to open up new vistas of the mind. One way *not* to accomplish this is to permit pupils to advance by way of test-brightness alone, receiving academic credit for work not done. Such a plan falls into the category of pseudo-progress. If a student is able to complete a four-year high school program in three years, or two, very well, let him do so; let him accomplish in superior fashion all the work of bright students who remain the full four years. More often, enthusiastic principals and eager college recruiting officers conspire to withhold segments of the high school program from the student, not requiring him, if he seeks to enter college ahead of others, to cover the ground and to lift his accomplishments qualitatively beyond those of his classmates. Grade acceleration as a release from boredom at any level from Grade I up may be desirable if these conditions are met:

(1) The pupil is superior in all-round mental ability.
(2) His grade achievement would earn a superior standing in the grade above.
(3) His general maturity is average or better for the grade above.
(4) *All* the grades under consideration are conducive to learning and creativity for the range of pupil talent enrolled.

Achievement along a single line is another matter. The ten-year-old musical prodigy may or may not belong in high school; there is no rational relation between musical talent and grade placement. Extreme talent is best nourished in an ungraded sequence. To advance students in the visual or performing arts on the same basis as students in English, science, and the social studies would be to recognize a new constellation of cultural imperatives. Actually it would be a return to the conservatory system, which flourished for many decades. Such a shift in priorities is not in sight.

Of course superior pupils frequently do well in the company of average and below average classmates. There is a natural division of labor in regard to this, in or out of school. The world of learning and creativeness is without limit, and there is really no such thing as mastering a language, a scientific discipline, or an art form. No child should be expected to cram everything into his head; the brighter he is the sooner he will want to express thoughts of his own and to risk their testing in a common market of ideas. The problem of getting in meaningful touch with the world outside one's experience— of accepting or discovering communicable verities—is so difficult as to defeat many a mind of early promise. Our mental cases that fill hospitals and nursing homes bear witness to the total victory of the private self over disdained external reality. The talented pupil is not immune to this unhappy outcome.

Homework: Its Limitations

Children who attend private schools are a selected group on several counts; the most conspicuous is the ability of the parents to pay the tuition, though to some extent scholarships ameliorate this situation. In either case, an atmosphere conducive to learning is postulated. A high income is positively correlated with living space, learning facilities (books, journals, urban contacts, travel), and a smaller family. The parents show a higher level of expectation for their children along both scholastic and career lines. While some students break away from this "square" attitude, most conform if they are not unreasonably pushed. Homework is usually required; *under favorable conditions* it is a useful adjunct to school work. Ambitious parents do more for Johnnie than provide a pleasant setting or a bit of advice; they become partners in the work to be done. (It is indeed hard for parents to tell where "help" stops and "cheating" begins. Even at the university level I favor supplementing the writing and reporting required as outside work by similar but shorter assignments to be met during the class period—a procedure that leads to some fascinating disparities.) But the child from a poor home in a poor neighborhood, if given the same home assignments as other students, is loaded with a double handicap: his store of learning is often deficient, and he can expect little help in any subject.

One way to help the underprivileged child is for the school to furnish each child with a kit of reading matter and audio-visual materials as a self-sufficient backstop to the assignments. Also, *every* child should be given a desk or locked space at school, together with a briefcase that can be taken home. The question remains: Why send pupils home day after day to attempt further work under poor conditions? Without research attention to this question, the case for homework as a global classroom assignment is suspect. Prior to definitive findings, I should be inclined to restrict homework to supportive assignments in the language arts and social studies.

The Open Classroom?

A great deal is heard these days about the virtues of the "open classroom" and very little about its possible defects. As imported from England it seems familiar to anyone who observed "progressive" education in its waning days. The child's experience apart from school is so unstructured that hundreds of visual and auditory impressions may leave him uninformed and indifferent. Trees, ponds, parks, woods, animals, vehicles, roads, streets, reading matter, people, and small events jostle in his field of sensory perception; these contacts, lacking form, may be only accretionary. For random-stimulated children, the very first day in school is a mind-opener. The school draws upon the stored items of sensory experience, but it also adds new ones. It brings them all into focus by encouraging each child to ask questions, to make comparisons, to reach out toward meaning. "Activities" the child has had since the rattle in the crib, along with a budding curiosity, but reasoning and a latching on to society's peculiar ways is not so easily come by. Sophisticated testing in English, science, and the social studies will reveal whether the open classroom helps the child along cognitive lines. The large room, with "workshop" centers scattered about is familiar, as is the designation of "play" as "work." Much learning goes on in a play situation, and certainly in a playful or joyous mood. In open education, English style, there is a return to the downgrading of time in human affairs. After all, a sense of time is as characteristic of man's rise above the other animals as is the acquisition of language; it is a way of distinguishing among the concepts *past, present, and future.* For the young child a gentle approach to time-binding situations is desirable, and it works.

Then there is the durable question of marking, testing, promoting. A teacher's devotion to minute record-keeping on every child soon evaporates; besides, hardly anybody will wade through such remarks to find out where the child really stands. More important than such jottings is a case history of the child's progress year after year, together with the results of occasional tests and photographic copies of his original works. On the credit side of the open-type school we find teacher attention to each child and encouragement for social interplay among the children; the atmosphere is "loose" and friendly. Yet these favoring factors do not necessarily culminate in productive activities. No magic resides in cardboard, wood, or other raw materials, as such. At a demonstration in St. Louis of an open classroom imported "live" from the East Coast, I noted that the children banged around aimlessly, while the teacher might as well have stayed at home. In the course of an hour, by sawing and discarding various sticks of wood, three of the boys managed to nail a fifth leg to the center of a card table. I asked them why, but there was no answer. Does not *some* reliance on modern textbooks and teaching plans aid both teacher and child? Could not the children themselves profitably engage in the design and production of such materials? To both questions the answer is *yes.* Motor experience as a bridge to thinking in spoken and written language provides a good start. For the underprivileged child, motor skills may be a ramp toward the cultural imperatives; it is the teacher's responsibility to conceive them as such.

As indicated, we do many things together, but we mature

alone. How they learned, what they learned, and why, constitute the students' chief personal gain as the school door
closes behind them. Are we thus pointing the child to the life
of a bookworm or pedant? The French system has perhaps
erred in this direction, although it has rewards for the few who
push through to the top. For the American student excessive
bookishness can be dismissed as a rare cultural mutation.

The Year-round School—A Sign of the Future

In my opinion the schools of tomorrow will adopt a year-
round plan that includes a merger of outdoor recreation and
education. The underlying principles are well established. We
have long known that learning can be exciting and enjoyable,
that play as a form of learning is as old as man.

Some years ago I outlined a practical plan whereby a large
school system (or smaller ones, cooperatively) could move into
the year-round school. There would be some extra costs in personnel, but an annual salary for teachers is overdue in any case.
It is certainly feasible to make use of buildings and facilities
that now stand idle during the summer months. Since I do not
believe local real estate taxes can provide the basis for this
reform—or for any other of large scope—wide acceptance of
the plan depends upon a substantial upturn in state and
federal aid to public education.

The plan, in brief, is this:

A. A regular school year of 175 days of attendance (5 days per
   week for 35 weeks), to extend from September 15 to June 1,
   two weeks to be given to the holiday seasons. This holds for all
   students, Grade I to Grade XII.

B. For students in junior and senior high school (all students in
   Grade VII to Grade XII), add one calendar month, to be
   taken during the period June 1 to September 15, with state
   and federal aid. Each teacher, on an annual salary basis, would
   teach two summer months. This plan would allow the students involved two and one-half free months and teachers a
   vacation of one and one-half months. The students would be
   offered two options for this summer session:

> 1. A month at camp devoted to outdoor recreation and education under expert supervision, or
> 2. A special summer program in the community consisting of indoor-outdoor education. It would be based on a systematic selection from the following: motor skills, games, demonstrations (including films, filmstrips, and educational TV); short hikes, arts and crafts, nature study; music, dramatics, and the dance; visits to zoos, parks, museums, galleries, historic sites, and nearby natural scenes.

C. For Grade III to Grade VI, the elementary and middle grades, only option 2, above, would ordinarily be offered.

D. For Grade I and Grade II, the regular school year of 175 days would be offered, supplemented by 5 (or more) days in spring or summer to meet the standards of the respective states for length of the school year. These extra sessions would resemble option 2, with the parents free to join their children or to observe.

Since there are not enough camps to meet the probable demand for option 1, there would need to be granted the legal power to rent camps from agencies, to establish temporary facilities, and to acquire permanent camps. Such permanent camps would be less expensive than agency or private camps; for one thing, schoolchildren are already organized in groups, and there would be no problem of selection among applicants. School buses could be made available, together with some types of equipment, as in science and physical education.

With this plan fully in effect there would be

(1) New elasticity and richness in the curriculum.
(2) A flexible deployment of the teaching staff.
(3) A greater demand for specialists.
(4) A fuller use of school and community resources.
(5) A new educational aid to parents.

The experience of schools that have moved in this direction is reassuring. This merging pattern of outdoor recreation and education provides a more exciting life for pupil and teacher alike. It is consistent with the burgeoning projects backed by federal funds for the conservation of natural resources; it transforms "ecology" from a slogan to some real sensory experiences.

As far as I know, the year-round school, as outlined above, has not been tried. It is a more radical departure than most existing plans for student work during the summer. It is not based on economy or the occupation of empty schoolhouses. It rests upon the observed needs, interests, and drives of children and youth. It calls for a setting different from that of the prior standard school year. Although the expected gains are in the sensory-motor aspects of behavior, there will be side effects in the mastery of abstract subject matter. English (conversation, imaginative writing), science (botany, zoology, geology), music, and the visual arts thrive under informal outdoor conditions. Teachers who find it hard to change their ways should be excused from summer assignments. Doubtless the main load of teaching, counseling, and sharing under outdoor conditions will fall upon the younger staff members. In carrying out these suggestions is there any way to overcome the inertia of school boards and school executives? The hesitancy and anxiety of the teaching staff? The United States Office of Education could help by supporting a few major pilot projects. Good starts could be made in Michigan, California, and New York; these states have much to offer by way of expertise in combining outdoor education and recreation. I predict that when the year-round school is accepted in principle by school authorities and community leaders, its implementation will produce a commendable feedback into the "regular" classroom work.

Performance Contracts

Under a performance contract, a privately owned contracting firm, in business for the profit it can make, takes over the instruction of children and is paid in accordance with the measured learning of the children involved. Such a scheme is likely to be geared to evaluation by national achievement tests, which are notoriously rigid as applied to any particular group of students. If the contracting company is allowed to choose or construct the tests, we have a closed circuit of judgment that lends itself to abuse. Doubtless the pupils involved will improve their relative standing for the duration of the contract, in part because novelty is a spur, but the use of performance contracts is a hazardous business.

Beleaguered school executives are apt to reach out for a particular line of student achievement they can hold up to public view as evidence of good administration. A commercial agency can easily promise "quick tricks" if it is not held responsible, as the school is, for the totality of the student's learning, experiencing, and behavior. The scheme is an updated version of the carrot-and-stick stimulus, defective in principle and a mixed blessing in practice. The truth is there is not a single device or reward an outside firm can offer that could not be duplicated at less cost by the school itself. The prizes offered for acquiring bits or sequences cannot be separated from the linked process of stimulus-response-reward. Premium stamps, candy, radios, TV sets, athletic equipment, time off from the school day, and assorted "privileges" of this type get embedded in the child's mind as a part of the game. In high school or college athletics we frown on that type of reward, for it comes close to straight cash payments. Should a basketball player be paid for each basket made in scholastic competition? A baseball player for each hit, a football team for each first down? Such a scheme would disgust anyone with a liking for sports.

The issue should not be ducked: the rewards offered by some contractors are the same as cash. If learning under these circumstances becomes the order of the day, the rewards will have to be ever-present and escalated. The sense of achievement, the desire to learn and to strengthen one's fitness for a career, or as Lincoln put it, "to study and get ready," will be minimized. What moral justification is there for substituting an artificial gimmick designed for animals in captivity? Consider, too, the power suddenly placed in the hands of reluctant learners, who are the particular target of external contractors. Resentful of school assignments, of teachers, of the whole Establishment, students can get even by the simple act of refusing to learn. This is no new stance on the part of some students, but hitherto, apart from the teachers' obvious distress, it was hard to discern any effect. Now the contractor loses money, the school loses "face," and the school board loses confidence in the competence of its executive officers!

The School and the Bus

In rural districts busing to a consolidated school is a well-established and desirable practice. For the crowded inner city the grade school belongs in the neighborhood, but its housing should not usually be *like* the neighborhood's. In a depressed area the school should be a beautiful, shining departure from its surroundings, just as churches have so often been, and for the same reason. Parents, teachers, and pupils will come to take pride in such a school if they believe it to be truly *their* school. To what we cherish, we give our best. In the case of the school, not flamboyance, but a handsome, well-designed school surrounded, if possible, by free space and playgrounds that tie in with an all-year plan. Every facility should fit in with the purpose of the school. Given equality in equipment, curriculum, teaching excellence, and financial support, the observable differences between two schools will be in the race or national origin of the student bodies, *not* in the potential intelligence of the two populations. If a significant difference develops it will spring largely from differentials in home life, that is, in motivation, example, and cultural resources. These differences an excellent school will help smooth out, especially if the whole neighborhood is on the upswing.

Accordingly, we should take a close look at the effects of busing that is undertaken for the sole purpose of achieving a racial balance. There are four fallacies in large-scale busing that its advocates tend to ignore, namely:

1. That being nonwhite or Puerto Rican or Mexican is a sign of mental backwardness.
2. That it is better to bus some city children long distances to other schools than to send *all* the children out on visits, field trips, sports, camping, and the like.
3. That a city's neighborhood elementary school is in itself regressive if not obsolete.
4. That the chief block to racial integration is the composition of the school's population (actually it is the adult residential pattern).

Nevertheless scholastic gains will accrue to a busing system if the pupils are sent to a specialized or superior school. Such a plan should serve as a prototype for doing in the community what was hitherto feasible only through the transportation of students.

Of course, busing students to and from school is common practice the country over. It is estimated that busing accommodates 40 percent of the total school population of 46 million. Busing to achieve racial desegregation is a small enterprise (3 percent of the total), although in some cities it is substantial. Regardless of the cost or effect of busing "to achieve racial balance," it is out of character—and a dangerous precedent— for Congress to enact any legislation whatever by way of prohibition. All school people and concerned citizens should unite to prevent such legislative action. The public schools need to be on guard against the political opportunism that has recently characterized the legislative and executive branches of the federal government. Neither busing nor any other educational issue affords justification for moratoriums from "on high."

The bus is needed for transportation within the city, as private schools discovered long ago. Distance in a city is more than a matter of miles; the factors of safety and time weigh heavily. Still, a giant crisscrossing of routes from home to school is wasteful unless all the children involved gain thereby. The test of the value of the neighborhood school—or of its successor—lies in its ability to provide a fine educational experience for all children and encouragement for their parents. Neither busing nor any other school service will result in equality of performance on the part of the pupils. And that is a very good thing, unless we prefer the life of an ant or a robot. The aim is to achieve an equality of opportunity. We are entering a period of progressive desegregation in the school's racial composition, but reform in financing should not wait on this outcome; it is needed *now*, and only the states and the federal government can give it a strong impetus.

Surely black children are not being bused to a white school because of its whiteness, but only because of the superiority of its program. Should not the same criterion be applied to the busing of white children to a black school—namely, to improve the children's educational opportunity? To require that children be bused to an inferior school or neighborhood is wrong in principle and self-defeating in practice. After all, no shuffling of children, no exchange of unequal opportunities, will improve the lot of the total school population. The only rational, long-range plan is to improve *all* school systems, without restricting variability, that is, without homogenization. In the meantime, since there is a certain amount of busing whereby some students are sent long distances to schools inferior to those close by, it is essential to move fast toward educational improvement *everywhere*. The bused students themselves cannot be expected to accomplish this difficult feat. As a kind of first aid, a platoon of highly qualified teachers— black, white, or some of each—should be moved into the impoverished districts that receive students, together with the books, equipment, and movable teaching devices that characterize a superior school. This arrangement would "hold the fort" while plans were completed to effect permanent improvements. In short, the aim is eventually to replace the goal of "busing to achieve racial balance" by "busing to achieve excellent schooling for every child." In some areas, racial desegregation would follow as a desirable by-product. It is to be noted that the successful plan of busing rural students to consolidated schools was established on the principle that *every child* should be given an enriched educational experience. This plan led to the demise over the country of tens of thousands of hopelessly inadequate one-room and two-room schools. I believe the parents of today will accept that principle as a basis for city and intercity busing. It calls for a massive replacement of crowded, run-down schools by fine schools in attractive parks; it calls for a teaching staff that would be rated excellent in any community.

Racial Desegregation

Who does not have a mental image of the blindfolded figure of Justice holding balancing scales? No differences of color, sex, social status, or nationality are allowed to penetrate the great barrier of impartiality. Since her eyes represent all sensory impacts, only the abstract principles of justice are to be placed on the scales, and the verdict is to be rendered accordingly. The courts have come a long way from this idealistic stance. In some of the most pressing decisions of the middle decades of the twentieth century, directly affecting tens of millions of American citizens, they look sharply to distinguish black from white. They separate persons by color in order to intermingle them in education and to guarantee freedom to work, to vote, and to hold office. The only wall left to be fully breached is that of miscegenation—an irrational and doubtless unconstitutional carry-over from the past. It is reasonable to hold that if the Negroes had come to this country as free men, on equal terms with immigrants from Europe, they would have intermingled and intermarried on a peer basis. The Latin American countries furnish examples. Having directed a major educational project in East Africa, I can testify at first hand that the blacks there are emerging as quite the equal of any other race. They are developing the leadership in business, industry, and education that we have traditionally denied their black counterparts in the United States.

The Supreme Court properly recognizes a huge backlog

of debt to our nonwhite citizens and seeks to redress all major grievances. I do not regard any of its decisions in the field of education as regressive, but I am left with a certain unease. Matters will not be set aright *on a grand scale* until the biological factor of skin color makes absolutely no difference in any determination of rights, duties, or opportunities—until color is as evenly regarded as the genetic accident of being tall or short, blond or brunet, blue-eyed or brown-eyed. The Supreme Court has moved further in this direction than the lesser courts or the general run of corporations and governmental agencies, but it has not gone the whole distance. Still, the Court has taken steps that prepare the way for the final stages of racial blending. Actually, if the last steps are to be taken they must be taken by the people themselves. What we have now in the North as well as the South is a quietly sustained social apartheid, with occasional token breakthroughs but with no great haste on either side to alter the social *status quo*. Pride of race works both ways.

Accordingly, I believe the tensions aroused by *forced* integration in housing, education, and employment will taper off when racial polarization is a matter of free choice unaccompanied by economic or educational penalties. All of us have heard persons, perhaps liberal persons, make pronouncements that hold the blacks, *ipso facto*, to be inferior. For such persons, a black neighborhood is a sign of backwardness. The correlation is indeed high, but it is often misinterpreted. For example, sociologists in a series of studies extending over several decades have shown that the same impoverished areas in Chicago have spawned mental deficiency and lawlessness no matter what groups took over—Polish, Italian, Irish, or Negro. The relation is circular; underprivileged families drift toward the slums, and the slums push hard against every parent and child.

The way to restore the neighborhood school and the school park close by is to replace all slums by attractive modern housing in a setting of trees, playgrounds, recreation centers, and cultural attractions. For a long time to come, domestic projects of this type, together with massive efforts along ecological lines, will supply William James's "moral equivalent of war." Of course, new buildings and facilities alone are not enough to rehabilitate persons who have suffered indignities and chronic neglect in a blighted neighborhood. It takes care and thought and patience, bolstered by group planning, to prepare persons, young or old, to make the most of their new surroundings. In all this the schools can render invaluable assistance.

Since we have all-white or nearly all-white schools, both public and private, that are widely held to be superior, it is time to encourage the development of their all-black or nearly all-black counterparts. The question is, How is this to be done? Thus far, local affluence that generates a high tax return or the payment of high tuition has furnished the financial wherewithal. Since it is not feasible today to reproduce this suburban-type wealth in black communities, we must look elsewhere for financial support. The immediate targets are the state and the federal government; they can supplement the local property tax and provide an equitable distribution of funds. As a start, state, federal, and philanthropic funds should be poured into a network of small-city and big-city projects to demonstrate what happens when a neighborhood, a local school system, and a community college combine their educational resources. The demonstrations will demand careful planning and research. They must be flexible, long-range, and community oriented at every stage. My faith in the ultimate success of such ventures rests upon studies of the genetic potential of children and youth—an inheritance that responds differentially to environmental impacts. There will remain a high degree of variability in the population—the genes determine that—but what is genetically *possible* will more often come to pass. No utopia is envisaged—do we have it in Westchester County, the Main Line, the North Shore?—but we shall more closely approach the promise of America. In the meantime we cannot afford simply to stand and wait.

Is a virtually all-white school *ipso facto* segregated? Yes, if it became white through gerrymandering or any other prejudicial device. If, however, it is all-white because it conforms to the principle of the neighborhood, regional, or consolidated school, "segregated" is not an accurate term. The same can be said for an all-black school under similar conditions. We would be clear-minded on this issue if an all-black school were rated *superior* on the basis of valid criteria, while a nearby all-white school were rated *inferior*. I am dubious about the assumption that a school population should differ in color from the population of its locality. As indicated, the truth is that the *populations* of children in the United States — white, black, red, yellow, or mixed — are equally endowed at birth; subsequent departures, plus or minus, from a curve of average growth are environmentally induced. When districts are honestly laid out, the *de facto* racial segregation of school children is a replica of the same condition in housing; that is where the problem resides, and it can be met by reducing segregation at the "home base." Controversy on busing does not arise in thoroughly mixed communities; there, integration in schools, churches, parks, and private enterprises is taken for granted. Every school executive should visit Hawaii!

National Assessment: For and Against

Comparisons of the effectiveness of whole systems of education call for research projects beyond the capability of the systems concerned. Apart from the natural tendency to "put the best foot forward," most school systems do not have the resources in time, money, or personnel to develop and validate a comprehensive research plan. It will be necessary to turn to either a university research group or a special research institute. However, the personnel of a school system will play a dominant role in field-testing and demonstration. It was originally intended that the United States Office of Education should not only make annual statistical reports on the status of education but also provide some means of making comparisons.

Our pluralistic society has developed under a Constitution that did not mention education for the reason, sound at the time, that the control of education was left entirely to the states and localities.

Federal aid to education has now extended far beyond the confines of agriculture, mechanic arts, home economics, job preparation, manpower, the Indians, and the military. It is a bit early to appraise its impact on education across the gamut from nursery schools to universities and research centers. Nevertheless I shall venture two predictions:

(1) The nursery school experience that would be helpful to most children in our business-industrial-urbanized style of life will be denied to the majority of children at ages three and four unless substantial federal funds are added to state funds on a straight basis of the number of children whose admission to the program is requested by parents. Local funding, based primarily on real estate taxes, cannot be stretched to render this service. A carefully planned program beginning at age three or four would give children a sound platform from which to launch their entry into the elementary grades. Since the physical, mental, and emotional needs (with allowance for individual differences) are the same for all *populations* of these young children, there should be an absolute disregard of the factors of race, national origin, and socioeconomic status.

(2) As the states and the national government take up more of the burden of taxation in order to equalize educational opportunity, no public agency will be allowed to deny the right of citizens to raise private funds or to tax themselves additionally in support of educational variations, however defined. Private schooling at any pupil-age level from the nursery to the university years may be supported by groups of like-minded persons as long as it meets state requirements as to curriculum, safety precautions, and health protection.

In this frame of reference, the prospect of a national assessment of educational achievement, not as a basis for federal control but rather as an extension of the business of reporting and comparing, may prove enlightening.

The specific project entitled National Assessment of Educational Progress has been in the making for nearly ten years.

Tests have been constructed in the fields of reading, writing, mathematics, science, social studies, fine arts, and citizenship. They are designed for four age groups: nine, thirteen, seventeen, and young adults. The results can be tabulated and compared by age, sex, geographic location (regional), socioeconomic status, and the like, entirely on the basis of a sampling of scores rather than on a sampling of persons. Each person submits to only an hour of testing on a battery that would take perhaps fourteen hours to complete. This plan shields individuals and school systems from comparisons, invidious or otherwise. Unlike the Iowa Every Pupil Tests, or test batteries emanating from "College Boards," the Educational Testing Service, or the American College Testing Service, these NAEP examinations cannot be used to measure pupil or school progress.

The verbal approach predominates, but there is also some attempt to arrive at attitudes and imaginative responses. However, I doubt whether the final reports of this program will yield results that could not be predicted on other grounds or from less elaborate testing programs. The young adults will be adept at forgetting what they learned in school or college; the students from homes that rate high educationally and socially will outpoint other students; the southern region (with some exceptions) will fall below the average; speech, if measured, will get a low rating by any standards; facility in a foreign language will be hardly worth measuring; the attitudes of seventeen-year-olds and young adults will be so overlaid by new mores regarding sex, schooling, parents, jobs, clothes, music, profits, ecology and the Establishment as to defy any brand of testing short of case studies in depth.

For all that, school people will be given some insight into the results of instruction in subject matter long considered to be basic. Much of what has been observed locally or grasped by intuition (that is, extrapolated from noneducational data) will be confirmed or modified. Most parents will pay no attention; only what happens to Mary or Johnnie can hold parental interest. The *less* attention legislators pay to the findings, the better; each one will denounce every putative inferiority in his constituency and praise unduly every favorable showing. The school people themselves will do nothing at all about the conclusions, for no single school or school system can be singled out for praise or blame; all wholes have been reduced to parts and reassembled anonymously. It is as if, without identifying a single household, a sociologist were to report in separate tables on furniture and fixtures, finances, literary interests, and recreation. Such disembodied data are for the dealer in abstractions. Doubtless some cause for cheer will emanate from the findings, even though the paranoid fringe of the school's critics will find occasion to justify their hatred.

The tests themselves strike me as an improvement over previous tests in the fields represented. For example, I am impressed with the Assessment's measurement of art appreciation. It would be good to see the expertise displayed in the various tests applied to a systematic appraisal of programs and instructional outcomes in *named* schools and student samplings. The test results could then be used confidentially in aid to both student and teacher. As matters stand, the Assessment findings will be brushed aside. Among the professionals, surveys of this massive type scarcely match the excitement stirred up by a report that something different is to be found in a particular school located, let us say, in New York, Pennsylvania, Massachusetts, Michigan, California, or Oregon. As the Assessment teams break up, I expect to find their members colonizing research institutes, or perhaps local school districts newly awakened to the place of tests and measurements in a well-ordered plan of educational inquiry.

How Finance the Public Schools?

For decades to come the issues that boil up in education respecting curriculum, technology, teacher training, teacher unions, racial imbalance, and parochial aid will be matched by crises in school finance. It is an issue that has been slow to take form. A nation that had enormous funds for foreign aid and Asian wars should have guaranteed a first-class opportunity for every American child. It did not. Despite continued exhibitions of affluence and power, the nation as a whole was not winning any blue ribbons for its support of education. After all, *federal aid to the public school should have followed upon the adoption of the federal income tax, and progressively with every increase in that particular tax.* Why public authorities failed to predict the intolerable effect of the draining away of financial resources, leaving the support of education tied to real estate and sales taxes—even to lotteries —I leave to the political scientist. Apparently the concept of local control through local taxes was a watchword that fitted in comfortably with the modest aims of school boards.

Of late, the repeated failure of communities and states to approve badly needed capital expenditures has brought matters to a head. Amidst deficiencies in housing, employment, health, and welfare why should the schools be singled out for "favoritism"? That a sound education was the best-known means of combating social ills was indeed emphasized by educational leaders, but their ideas were regarded as visionary. Now, caught in a financial squeeze play, the taxpayers are taking action—that is, inaction, by failing to approve school budgets and bond issues—as a prelude to reform. I for one do not interpret the widespread "rebellion" as a sign of indifference to the maintenance of good schools; I see it rather as a determined stand against the inequities of an outmoded system of taxation. The movement carries the seeds of a genuine reform whose initial steps have already been taken in legal and political circles.

California: The Serrano Case

California is out in front. The decision of its supreme court [1] in the Serrano case in August of 1971 raised the question of *equal protection,* as contained in the fourteenth amendment of the United States Constitution. The court noted the tremendous range in the ability to pay, from the poorest school districts to the richest, resulting in differentials that could not be overcome by local effort and that thus far had not been sufficiently reduced by state aid. (Unlike New York, California allotted state aid on a straight per-pupil basis.) Some districts had ten times the property value of others on the basis of dollar support for each schoolchild. The California court abandoned the uncertain principle of *need* in order to rest the case on the matter of discrimination in rendering a public service (education). Regardless of a locality's financial status, public school children were to benefit by equal payments for their education. In so holding, the court reiterated its previous stand on the crucial importance of public education, not only to the students and parents concerned but also to the strength and progress of the nation. Courts in other states are certain to pick up this general argument; in fact, Minnesota, Texas, and New Jersey have already followed the lead of California, thus eventually bringing the matter before the United States Supreme Court.

In October 1971, the California Supreme Court clarified its August decision. It pointed out that existing statutes and procedures were not automatically invalidated thereby. Schools could not be expected to meet their immediate obligations in a kind of financial limbo. New decisions will be forthcoming, and all actions should be based on a thorough study of this momentous problem. Furthermore, the court indicated that it will take time to devise and put into operation a new financial plan consistent with legal and educational principles.

In short, the courts have no intention of taking over the administration of our public schools. They simply are alerting all authorities to the constitutional implications of the *Serrano* decision.

Adjusting the Flow of Money

If verdicts similar to that given by the California court are affirmed and put into practice, presumably the first steps will be taken by the respective states. Each state would deliver to school districts an annual payment designed, by itself alone, to ensure a satisfactory educational experience for every child of school age. However, this amount would not equal the highest cost per student presently in effect over the state. Differentials in costs require higher appropriations in large cities than in rural areas to pay for equal services. Though there is a correlation between expenditures per child and the quality of the educational experience, it is not a one-to-one relationship. The all-round educational superiority of suburban children, when found, rests in part on the excellence of the home and the community. In the future, a single factor, the extent of the family's addiction to commercial TV, will modify financial differentials.

The well-documented maldistribution of wealth among the states, as it applies to education, can be corrected only by federal acts. Northern states and cities—New York is a prime example—have long wrestled with the effects of low standards in Puerto Rico. In both education and welfare "upward mobility" is a geographical phenomenon. What happens to the children of cane-cutters in Puerto Rico is of direct concern to every city in the United States. However, I feel it would be a mistake for the Supreme Court to merge the two questions of in-state equalization and interstate equalization. On the average, the states already assume nearly half the cost of public education, and there is no legal block to their increasing this proportion. How they can do so without reaching into localities for a share of the revenue from real estate taxes is a serious question. Some states teeter on the verge of financial insolvency; they, too, are victims of the enormous flow of tax income to the federal treasury. What the federal government needs, in the view of competent critics, is not more tax income but a shift of priorities from sterile military adventures to domestic enterprises, of which education is the most pressing and the most rewarding.

On balance, it seems unwise to eliminate the real estate tax.

When real estate taxes are fairly assessed, efficiently collected, and their proceeds wisely apportioned, they yield substantial support for the educational budget. They are not easy to evade. To relinquish a well-established system of taxation in favor of a national plan would reduce the power of the local community and the state in the management of school affairs. Having examined at first hand the effect of Japan's prewar monolithic education structure, in which all money and power trickled down from the ministry of education in Tokyo, I am not enthusiastic about adopting a highly centralized educational plan in the United States. The schools need both federal aid and state aid, and it is possible to provide such aid while allowing a measure of control to the state and a still greater measure to the local authorities. Only general accounting should remain a prerogative of the federal budget.

That is indeed the dilemma: how to have a large measure of state and federal financing while guaranteeing local control over all key decisions affecting education. My contacts with the chief state school executives lead me to believe they could set up a special committee fully capable of resolving this issue.

6

SECONDARY EDUCATION
AND TERTIARY EDUCATION

The Comprehensive High School

A comprehensive high school whose curricula include career options and the arts is sufficiently flexible to meet the needs of most students. Until offerings are strengthened in science, business, and the arts, a few specialized high schools may continue to flourish in a large city systems. The nongraded high school is not likely to take hold; it lacks focus in terms of the choices a student must make in his immediate future. Ability grouping as an explicit track procedure is not called for, although remedial work is still in order for slow learners. As a matter of fact, students at every level of ability still need work in speech, reading, and writing. No restrictions should be put on the performance of superior students. Some students could meet all the requirements for the diploma in less than four years and be eligible for college entrance; if they elect to remain for the full high school term, advanced placement in college is to be expected.

For all high school students the language arts (conversation, reading, writing, and the appreciation of literature) should be given the highest rank. There are several reasons for this view:

(1) Most students are still deficient in this essential area of learning. The elementary school, unless strongly backed up by a

113

superior home, has proved to be unequal to the task of ensuring pupil competence.

(2) Language is deeply embedded in all the other academic disciplines and is a source of their fruitful integration.

(3) The recrudescence of latter-day progressive education under
the guise of openness and free choice has reduced some classrooms to a hodgepodge of offerings and a forum for shrill
verbal activity.

(4) Instruction by computers, devices, and television has reduced
the student's opportunity to exercise the language arts; it has
downgraded language as a tool of thought and a medium of
intellectual exchange.

On Grade Organization

Unless it connotes substantial changes in the school's
program and the quality of teaching, the organizational plan
of a school system will have little effect upon student learning.
A perennial question is, What should be the nature of the
program in Grades VII and VIII, or at the corresponding
starting ages of twelve and thirteen? An answer that has proved
reasonably effective is to combine these two grades with the
former first year of high school to form a junior high school,
leaving the last three grades for the senior high school. This
is the familiar 6–3–3 plan. Its chief values are threefold:

(1) It relieves a mounting boredom of students who at age
thirteen still have a year of "elementary" education ahead of
them.

(2) It puts a stop to the self-contained classroom.

(3) It requires subject matter expertise on the part of the teacher.
However, the claimed advantages are based on empirical
grounds; there is little research that would lead to an extensive changeover on the part of school systems that are
accustomed to an 8–4 plan.

This is a propitious time to carry out comparative tests of
plans that cover the range from nursery school to community
college, inclusive. (Instruction in the latter may be designated

tertiary education.) As a model with which other plans could be objectively compared in terms of student interest and achievement, I propose the following schema (JP = Junior Primary):

Grade	Age at Start	Grouping
. . .	3 4	Nursery School
JP I II III	5 6 7 8	Elementary School
IV V VI	9 10 11	Middle School
VII VIII IX	12 13 14	Junior High School
X XI XII	15 16 17	Senior High School
XIII XIV	18 19	Community College

The above arrangement could be called the seventeen-year plan. If the school system maintains a four-year high school, the seventeen-year schema would be modified, becoming 2–4–5–4–2. The middle school would then cover five grades, preferably through the Dual Progress Plan or some derivative of it.

With an ungraded nursery school for children at ages three and four in operation, the term "kindergarten" for five-year-olds is misleading; everything good about the kindergarten concept will have been applied to the younger children. It is well to include the three- and four-year-olds in any educational plan, even by way of blank spaces for school systems that have overlooked this group of educable children. Day nurseries for aid to the children of working mothers (now numbered in the millions) represent only a transitional phase far below the quality of the university-sponsored "preschools" maintained since the 1920s. By joining the junior primary to the next three grades we get a unified elementary segment in which the self-contained classroom eventually gives way to teacher specialization.

Given a junior and senior high school of three years each, the middle school comprises Grades IV, V, and VI. The middle school may be graded, ungraded, or mixed as in a dual progress plan. Under any scheme it will call for teacher specialization. A tying-in with the junior high school would be helpful. The junior high school should take special account of the adolescent need for action, for "belonging," for grasping the essentials of the social structure. Its curriculum should allow a certain amount of free choice on the part of the student. As a variation, a school system might offer in Grade IX the seven-way choice of fields I am proposing later in this chapter for the senior year of high school. This would come prior to the legal school-leaving age and might help to arouse interest in further schooling.

What Counts in Secondary Education

My remarks on elementary education obviously bear upon secondary education and the course of its future development. Accordingly, without fitting any proposition to a specific year of high school, I submit the following by way of supplement:

(1) The crucial element in all learning under the auspices of the school is the teacher—at once a generalist and a specialist.

(2) A major determiner of student success or failure, or something in between, is the curriculum—its content, fitness to promote the stated aims of education, and student appeal.

(3) A varied action component of instruction involving student choices and community resources is an aid to motivation, especially for the lower ranges of talent.

(4) All-round teaching success calls for special attention to students who have high I.Q.'s or who are gifted along some line such as music, art, or creative writing.

(5) A team of teachers should offer a continuous strand of articulated subject matter throughout high school, polarized in relation to *great issues*, such as personal health, employment and recreation, the national economy, race relations, politics, ecology, foreign relations, war and peace.

(6) A high school year devoted to an intensive exploration of a single subject or cluster (the student to choose one of several options) will invigorate the student body.

(7) In addition to traditional subjects the high school should offer a strong program in the arts.

(8) More persons and personal contacts—fewer machines and electronic devices that isolate the student—will serve to strengthen morale.

(9) A year-round program with a merger of outdoor education and recreation appropriate to the adolescent years is indicated, but time should be reserved for summer work for pay.

(10) Near the start of the program in a comprehensive high school, an introduction to career choices, with the option of transfer to a job-oriented curriculum, will reduce the percentage of school leaving.

Of course, it is not feasible for a junior or senior high school to offer job preparation for the hundreds of occupations in business, industry, and technology. A clustering will serve the purpose of discovering aptitudes and making useful starts; at the same time it will enlarge the scope of the student's choice of a career. (I find the term *career* a bit pretentious as applied to an ex-student's first exposure to the world of work-for-pay. *Job* is perhaps a better designation, for it emphasizes the temporary nature of early occupational choices.) In school districts that have access to an area vocational school, busing is indicated as a means of supplementing a high school program.

Student Choices

For high school students the most popular choice in science is biology. Under skillful direction biology can become an exciting experience that brings into play statistics, chemistry, and physics as supporting studies. In this way biology approaches the amplitude of "general science," with some likelihood of achieving depth for the average student. In view of its bearing upon ecology and the study of human development, biology is well placed to meet the student's constant search for "relevance." It lends itself to the utilization of films, field trips, and laboratory demonstrations, and to the recruitment of community talent as a means of enlivening discussion. While the number of students who will enter physics, chemistry, or biology as a profession is small, their important role in technology (nutrition, engineering, manufacturing and the like) leads to numerous career choices. Hence two parallel lines of curricular development can be discerned: (1) *the appreciation of science*, perhaps centering in biology, as a broad elective, and (2) technical preparatory work in a discipline as an elective for the talented student. For such plans, a comprehensive high school is indicated.

In the social studies, as in the physical sciences, the high school student should be able to choose among the various branches or to be content with a single broad confederation. For talented students who are pointed toward professional careers, specialized work that can be joined to college programs is a good solution, but again it calls for a comprehensive high school. The usual disciplines are history, political science, economics, sociology, and psychology. A skimming over the ground is to be avoided. The various subjects may be clustered to form a unified curriculum in the social studies; in small high schools this is a necessary outcome. The major interest of the teachers in charge will determine which academic field is likely to become the academic centerpiece—on the whole, a defensible practice.

At the high school level of instruction in a foreign language, all that I have said about FLES (Foreign Language in the Elementary School) applies. A reading knowledge and a phrase-book vocabulary are scarcely worthy of inclusion in the curriculum. Rather, for those students who have already gone some distance, the high school should provide intensive experience in speaking, reading, and area studies—as an elective. For the beginner, it is again a matter of free choice. Of course the high school student looking toward college will be expected to meet standard admission requirements. In my opinion, foreign language study should not be required except to meet a clear preparatory need in terms of the probable choice of a career or a college major.

Back to the Fundamentals in High School Mathematics

The replies of sixty-five distinguished mathematicians to a memorandum entitled "On the Mathematics Curriculum in the High School." [1] indicate the source of the contemporary debate. In summary:

> The mathematics curriculum of the high school should provide for the needs of the students; it should contribute to the cultural background of the general student and offer professional preparation to the future users of mathematics, that is, engineers and scientists, taking into account both the physical sciences, which are the basis of our technological civilization, and the social sciences, which may need progressively more mathematics in the future. [P. 189]

The question is, What "cultural background" is meaningful to the high school student? Literature and the arts provide immediate enjoyment and the prospect of a lifelong interest. By the time of high school, the social studies commingle with events and decisions close at hand. Throughout the memorandum the authors rightly insist that if mathematics is really to be comprehended it must be in the context of "concrete applications which would challenge the student." For the majority of students, the "old" mathematics beyond the elementary stages produced little that was either useful or enjoyable; it remains to be seen if the "new math," which, as I have noted, Kline regards as tedious and irrelevant, will fare much better. A second quotation from the above memorandum:

> Elementary algebra, plane and solid geometry, trigonometry, analytic geometry and the calculus are still fundamental, as they were fifty or a hundred years ago: future users of mathematics must learn all these subjects whether they are preparing to become mathematicians, physical scientists, social scientists or engineers, and all these subjects can offer cultural values to the general students. The traditional high school curriculum comprises all these subjects, except calculus, to some extent; to drop any one of them would be disastrous. [P. 191]

Here the key word is "users," but the total number implied in the professions listed above is comparatively small. The truth is, cultural value, devoid of either enjoyment or application, is a will-o'-the-wisp.

The Most Neglected Area in Secondary Education: The Arts Program

In the fall of 1970, as director of a project, I submitted a report[2] to the three sponsors of the project, namely, the National Endowment for the Arts, the United States Office of Education, and the JDR 3rd Fund. The yearlong study was conducted within the framework of Educational Systems for the Seventies (ES '70), a voluntary consortium of sixteen school systems, that was formed to initiate new plans for high school instruction. An advisory committee for the project consisted of professional artists, educators, and philosophers; a curriculum team was formed of artists, art teachers, and curriculum specialists. Both groups were drawn from across the country. Altogether the working parties, which met in New York City, comprised forty persons. All the ES '70 school systems and several others were visited by the director; in this way a large amount of firsthand material on the teaching of the arts was assembled and analyzed. The objectives of the study were stated in capsular form as follows:

> The aim of the Arts Curriculum Development Project is to organize, apply, and evaluate relevant experience in the arts for students enrolled in the innovative high schools comprising Educational Systems for the '70's (ES '70). The plan will involve students at every level of aptitude or interest, on the ground that creative art experience is as appropriate as the study of science or literature. This approach will not preclude the encouragement of students for whom an intensive pursuit of the arts is indicated. However, the main thrust will be toward active participation for all. It is held that a thorough demonstration in ES '70 of the significance of the arts for students will lead to: (a) A wider acceptance of the value of the arts curriculum, (b) More careful attention to the arts requirements in teaching, demonstration, and school facilities, (c) An understanding of the reciprocal relation between the arts and

other curricular offerings, and of the place of art in personal
and social maturation. Art as a basic factor in life. [Pp. 18–19]

At the beginning of the report the director distinguished
between the two "domains" of art in this way:

> *Art appreciation* embraces the graphic and plastic arts, the
> performing arts (music, theater, film, dance), and the literary
> arts (imaginative writing). The aim is to enhance one's under-
> standing and enjoyment of the arts. The emphasis is upon per-
> ception, insight, relevance, and response, all to be woven into a
> pattern of liberal education. *Art expression* is not an activity
> commonly engaged in by adult Americans. They are rarely
> called upon to draw, design, paint, carve, sing, dance (sym-
> bolically), play an instrument, compose music, write imag-
> inatively, or take a dramatic role. This restraint is not a universal
> attribute of human nature. In Italy, music is saturating; in
> Japan, graphic art. The question is, "What, other than jazz,
> rock, pop art and the like, do we foresee for the emerging adult
> society in the U. S.?" And further, "What is expected of the
> schools by way of *arts education?*" [P. 25]

In the course of the year the group projected a few caveats
that are relevant not only to teaching the arts but to all
teaching. In the words of the director:

> In arts education it is unwise to separate the attributes of
> cognition and emotion. There is no membrane between them.
> They are not in compartments. They interpenetrate; they modify
> each other. The senses on which both reason and feeling are
> based involve the whole brain. We need not resuscitate the
> psychology of instincts to observe that the human body is de-
> signed physically and physiologically to respond to some stimuli
> and not to others. The term *experience* applies to the used
> part of the environment. From birth up, every person selects
> from a multitude of potential impressions those that appeal to
> him at a given time. We should not make the mistake of re-
> garding the learner as someone who simply responds to external
> stimuli. Of more interest to the teacher is the way in which
> psychological patterns are formed that, through habituation,
> limit the actual choices even when numerous choice-points are
> available. . . . In discussions of art teaching there is so much
> emphasis on *process*, on what goes on in the mind of the child,
> that we need to ask how we might measure or assess this in-

terior, arcane phenomenon. Not knowing what tests to apply, we refer to process in vague terms as much or little, conscious or subconscious, fruitful or sterile. The way of art, like the way of thought, is sometimes fragile; it may be wholly or partly concealed from the person involved. We can discover process only by its observable outcomes—by the object, the writing, the musical composition, the performance. Binet's unique contribution to the understanding and measurement of intelligence sprang from his abandonment of attempts to get at reactions inside the nervous system. He turned to items of external behavior. Process was inferred. So it will be with any predictable success in the measurement of arts outcomes. [P. 35]

The Arts Are for Everyone

As might be expected, the study deplored the relatively low place of the arts in the curriculum (the text is the director's, but the sentiment was widely shared):

> In high school are the arts ever to any degree vocationally or professionally oriented? The obvious answer is yes, but only for the small number that elect to follow a career in arts or crafts or in teaching. Perhaps students and teachers sense a vocational "dead end" for the arts curriculum. At least, this hypothesis may partially account for the massive indifference of administrators and school boards to the absence of arts programs in secondary education. The irony is that mathematics and science are not similarly held to be devoid of vocational application. Not questioned on this score, they are blithely assumed to be crucial and are therefore required subjects. Nevertheless, between science and the arts in the framework of either vocational or liberal education, the laurels belong to the arts. The memory of technical subjects taken in school fades away fast, often with residual distaste. Not so with the arts. By deepening his understanding and extending his vision, the arts lift up the worker and add meaning to the work. To put it plainly, the arts for one and all celebrate the joy of living. [P. 39]

The Artist as Teacher

It is sound in principle to enlist artists as teachers; however, it may be well to add a cautionary note. Certainly not all artists would be good as teachers, and that is no reflection on their standing in the world of art. An artist, having exercised his freedom to produce anything out of any materials, may still be circumscribed by defects in technical skill or deficiencies in imaginative talent. He may not know what to teach if his own work imposes no standards and sets no aims beyond the exposure of his inner self—or one of his selves. If, like a mathematical series, his work approaches zero (the Whitney Museum in New York has exhibited "white-on-white" and "gray-on-gray"), the nothingness is not in the art form but in the artist. There is a literary analogue: according to the late A. E. Housman, it is possible for a poem to have nothing to say while saying it beautifully.

Sights and sounds stimulate automatic responses that arise from a person's accumulation of impressed events. In this sense the artist plays upon us and upon the experiences, frustrations, and hopes of mankind in general. For example, the members of an audience by definition have something in common. For the artist-in-residence or the artist-teacher, the audience is replaced by a group of students who are expected to go beyond immediate, unstructured responses. Students are there to change, to accept, to reject, to learn, to try out—all polarized toward what each one in his own way can make of the contact. To his feeling for art, to his originality as an artist, the artist-teacher is expected to add the ability to establish rapport with a group of students. As an artist he need make few concessions to individual differences, but as a teacher he cannot ignore them.

Accessibility Counts

I feel that high schools and cultural centers are both missing an opportunity for effective interaction. To paraphrase a well-known principle, a school's utilization of metropolitan resources is inversely proportional to the square of the distance—distance being measured in time and cost. Hence a system-wide, city-wide plan should be developed for bringing museums, galleries, and performances directly into the schools. For the performing arts, Lincoln Center of New York City is already doing this, but not many institutions have followed suit. Just as a museum exhibits numerous works of art that are "on loan" and confines others to hidden recesses and basements, so a school could acquire on loan from a museum many a work it would be unlikely to purchase—and nothing would be tucked away out of sight. Similarly, if dance and theatrical companies held their rehearsals in school auditoriums the student body—and perhaps the artists as well—would profit.

A New Plan for the Senior Year of High School

Later on, in discussing higher education, I shall outline in some detail a plan for revamping the four-year college program. One feature of the plan could be initiated in the senior year of a three- or four-year high school. It is designed to counteract the frequency of academic starts—"introduction to," "survey of," and the like. The plan requires every student to choose a field of interest and to carry work in it *exclusively* for one year. It may or may not indicate his subsequent choice of a career or a college major. By the end of the year, each graduating student will have attained some indication of where his interests lie. Suggested choices, to be covered only by teachers at once expert and enthusiastic, are these:

(1) Natural science—an integrated program in mathematics, physics, chemistry, biology, and ecology: the great constructs, problems, and issues.

(2) Social studies—social anthropology, psychology, sociology, history, and government.

(3) English—speech, composition, imaginative writing, literature.

(4) Foreign language, with correlated area studies. French may be the most popular choice, but a large high school system might also offer other European languages, along with Russian and Chinese.

(5) The visual and performing arts. Collaboration with a college or with a city's cultural agencies is indicated.

(6) Child development and behavior. While this choice may appeal to students who plan to become nurses, teachers, counselors, or social workers, it should be centered in education for family life.

(7) War and peace.

The construction of appropriate courses in this plan calls for a new approach to subject matter. Having freely chosen a last-year program of study, the student can be expected to give his best to it. (If some students display no interest in any one of the seven options, the choice—now the school's choice—is easy: put them in the third option, English.) To avoid premature claims as to the desirability of such a plan, I suggest that a consortium consisting of a university, a state or federal research agency, and a school system carry through a three-year demonstration and evaluation. The undertaking might be entitled "A New Plan for the Senior Year of High School."

The Community College Movement

It is unrealistic to omit the two-year community college or institute from the plans of a local school board. As we look back, it was indeed a strange academic world that required the high school graduate to embark upon a four-year college course or to abstain completely. By combining "terminal" sequences in technology and liberal arts, the community college does more than reduce the number of college dropouts; it offers programs that bring to a reasonable completion what was begun, or perhaps only hinted at, in high school. (Of course, "terminal" is not a good designation; these colleges expect the student to move toward a baccalaureate degree if his ability and drive warrant this decision.)

In a lecture at Harvard University, I once made an estimate on empirical grounds of the growth of the junior college;[3] it astonished most of my colleagues and frightened a few:

The limits of growth in junior colleges, institutes and junior
divisions are not easily foreseen. If tertiary education were to be
established with a full utilization of resources along mental,
recreational, artistic and vocational lines, I should expect eighty
percent of the secondary graduates to begin, and a very substantial portion to complete, a two-year program. For many, work
in school and work on the job would involve a tapering process.
To many persons these estimates appear outrageously high.
They look about, seeing no such reservoir of talent, even as the
czars of old observed that the masses were doomed to poverty,
illiteracy, and degradation. [P. 18]

Although at that time the scholastic base-line, high school
graduation, was more selective than it is today, the estimate
is still viable. The Census Bureau reports that enrollment in
the two-year colleges quadrupled between 1960 and 1970.
The enrollment is now 2.5 million and it may reach 5 million
in ten years. The designation *Junior College* is giving way
to the more accurate term, *Community College*. This movement toward some form of postsecondary education is one of
the most striking phenomena in contemporary American education. Other great issues, such as racial equality, a fair basis
for school taxation, and the growth of the four-year colleges,
are deeply affected by it.

The fact is that the experience of studying in a community
college conveniently at hand is infectious; it leads to a career
and opens new avenues of intellectual and social inquiry. For
the adult whose work week has been drastically shortened, it
fills a gap in a manner not given to casual reading and commercial television. The serious student whose progress toward
a baccalaureate degree has been halted for one reason or
another is encouraged to get on with it. The plan of mixing
adults in a "student body" of widely varied interests is not
new; a remarkable example is the Collège de France in Paris,
which has prospered for over four hundred years. The American
community college movement, already over one thousand colleges strong, is healthy because it fills a need—a vacuum in

the lives of men and women—especially of young persons who did not get on, or stay on, the road to college.

The community college has certain attractive virtues; it is accessible, inexpensive, and versatile, and it adds seasoning to any part-time occupation. These are the familiar attributes of motivation, but taken together, they do not carry the restless eighteen-year-old, the bored housewife, or the tired worker much beyond what can be squeezed out of television, cinema, games, sports, travel, and party-going. The hard-core lasting appeal will rest on the same basis as any other educational experience, namely, career advancement for some, and for all the promise of life enrichment through learning. If the community college edges away from these two basic supports, all the gadgets, programming, and games-playing in the world will not save it as an educational institution. To be culturally additive, to be meaningful, to justify the billions in public funds required to support its huge body of students, the community college must find its place, not in the overpopulated world of escapism but in the grand continuum of education that begins with the child's first day in school and need not end short of senility.

Another way of putting it is to say that the community college should in its own right offer substantial nourishment to the seeking mind. For example, the persons I have labeled "intermittent students" should be given special consideration. In a large "free-wheeling" enterprise such students could form an academic enclave whose program would be accepted en bloc as a ticket to third-year standing in a four-year college. But the community college, out of some irrational desire for prestige, should not make the mistake of imitating the standard baccalaureate curriculum; with only a short history to look back upon, it can afford to be venturesome. It has a wide-open opportunity to prepare for dozens of subprofessional careers.

Presently there is a scarcity of well-financed research teams to undertake the validation of new plans. The truth is, this Topsy-like growth of tertiary education has fallen between the high school and the college, insofar as research support is concerned. A graduate student in search of a thesis, a foundation sifting applications for project support, a governmental agency bent on standing "where the action is," should look to the community college movement—the most spectacular development in American education since the rise of the land-grant universities.

The English View

Having conferred extensively with advanced students from the United Kingdom while I was a summer Fulbright Lecturer at Cambridge, I have concluded that one of the most stimulating observers of the English educational scene was Lord Crowther. Crowther was of course widely known as the chairman of the committee that produced the comprehensive report *15 to 18.*[4] While this report gives American educators something to ponder, the pluralism of our educational system—its close financial and political ties at the local and state levels— renders all comparisons difficult. Of special interest is a compilation of Crowther's views as conveyed to an American audience of high school principals and supervisors and reprinted in the *Atlantic.* Speaking of the abandonment of the "famous or infamous eleven-plus examination," Crowther states:[5]

> I have several times seen this movement quoted in America as evidence that English education is turning away from selection. I think this is a grave misunderstanding. The public objection to selection at eleven is social and political, not educational. It is an objection on the part of parents to having their children sent to different schools, not to their having different educations. And the remedies that are being applied are wholly in terms of institutions, not in terms of the education they provide. [P. 39]

The situation described has its parallels in continental Europe but not in the United States. Now Crowther points to a major difference in academic upward mobility:

Nonselection—if that is the opposite of selection—as it is practiced in America is totally unknown in England. By non-selection I mean the principle of treating all children alike, allowing them to sort themselves out by their choice of courses, by what they find easy and difficult, or by their varying ambitions—with counseling assistance, no doubt, but without any compulsory segregations. I am sure your system seems as odd to us as ours does to you. There is no retreat from selection in England. [P. 40]

Actually our system is not quite as laissez-faire as Crowther would have it. There are hidden—and not so hidden—hurdles in economic status, family level of expectation, and state or institutional examination systems. True, some public universities accept all high school graduates, but there attrition works massively and fast.

Crowther's concluding remarks are perhaps the most disturbing to American educators:

The sharpest difference of all between our two systems [is] our system of specialization. A student will take the examination for the Ordinary Level of the General Certificate of Education at the age of fifteen or sixteen in a wide range of subjects drawn both from the humanities and from the natural sciences. But once he has passed that examination, he will specialize. That is to say, he will devote two thirds, or perhaps even more, of his time in school to a narrow range of subjects. . . . and he will take the advanced level examination at eighteen in his special subjects only. When he gets to the university, the specialization is even more intense. [P. 41]

In short, "the English boy or girl is a specialist from the age of fifteen or sixteen." Under Crowther's leadership this plan was reviewed at length. The recommendation to the minister of education was that it be continued. Crowther and his colleagues could see no point in having students after age sixteen go over the same subjects they had had in school for ten or eleven years; now was the time for knowledge in depth, and for reaching out.

We in England argue the case for specialization not primarily on the score of the information it provides but because it awakens interest, teaches clear thinking, and induces self-discipline in study. This sort of intensive study takes a great deal of time, and that is why it can only be applied, for any one student, to a restricted range of subjects. No doubt you will say that the boy must be very narrow as a result. That may be. Are you sure that being narrow is worse than being shallow?

I find that English education has a high reputation among Americans. I am often asked, for example, whether it is not true that the eighteen-year-old boy in England is a year or two ahead of his American contemporary. I always answer that question, or assertion, by asking some others. What boy? If an English boy is still at school at eighteen, he is necessarily in the upper quartile in intelligence. Are you comparing him with the average American high school graduate, who is of average intelligence? And ahead in what? In the subjects to which he has been giving nearly all his time and attention for two years? It would be strange if he were not a long way ahead in those. Or over the whole range of a broad curriculum? He has been taught different things, by different methods, with a different purpose in view, in a different sort of school. There is no fair basis for a comparative judgment. [P. 42]

Not sitting in judgment, but curious as to what English practices we Americans might adopt for high schools and colleges, I feel the answer lies in increased specialization at the level of tertiary and higher education. That an American student may be awarded a bachelor's degree with a "major," say in economics, of only forty credit hours out of perhaps one hundred and twenty that comprise his total collegiate program is a contradiction in terms. The important issue is this: after college few persons, apart from the demands of a job, study *anything* in depth. Those who have done so in college can rely upon associative mental activity to fill in some of the gaps. To learn something thoroughly is to call out all one's reserves in mental capacity, interest, and perseverance. Such learning is of a different order from casual conversation in a broad range of disciplines, and it is infectious—one can hook on to it, as it were. In sum, we should consider moving in the English direction for students at the age of sixteen, perhaps joining the heavier specialization to career sequences. This plan would fit in well with the seven-option senior year in high school I have briefly outlined.

7

INSIDE THE AMERICAN UNIVERSITY

Alma Mater

In higher education, there is a fallacy that has not yet been extirpated from the main body of our thinking. It may be called the *lump of learning fallacy*. It holds that there is not enough higher education to go around; what there is should be reserved for the highly talented or the socioeconomic elite. Having entered the ivied halls, the student is told there is a fixed amount to be learned, and the faster he learns it and gets out, the better for everybody. We are asked to believe that college should be a short-term experience, especially for the bright student. The duller you are, the more college you need. Since professors are expensive, machines will attend to your wants. There is said to be an impatience in the best minds; if you keep them full term to their books and discussions and laboratories, they will run out of ideas. This fallacy is a by-product of the boredom that afflicts many students as they move up from high school to college. Some college advisers, determined to rescue the bright students, push them out of the classrooms. They contrive the all-purpose examination. If a student can pass it, though failing to show up as a warm body and a glowing mind, that is considered a very good thing. It saves the wear and tear of instructors; it reduces costs. Between intellectual splurges, the student can go carefree.

A lesser fallacy that has plagued some college students will continue to cause confusion. This is the *semantic fallacy*, the identification of the word with the thing or the experience. We talk about and about, using words to describe other words. Having called a set of performances *intelligence*, we vainly proceed to look for it as a structural entity. What, says the geneticist, are its microscopic determiners? What, says the physicist, are the operations? What, says the psychologist, are the internal sources of drives? Of course the key concept is found not in a reduction to discrete elements but in cooperative and integrative action.

The conditions of learning strongly influence its effectiveness. Learning is not something poured over a person like a rich sauce. It penetrates the nervous system; it shows up in what a student knows and what he does. It goes far to determine what he *is*. A college graduate is not only different from what he was when he entered; he is usually different from what he would have been without college. The hope is that the difference is in a favorable direction. To the inspired teacher in close touch with the individual student (a somewhat rare situation) standardized testing provides a confirmation of intellectual progress already discerned by both parties.

Since the learning process is not one of accretion but is organic and organismic, a college does well to resist both shortcut and packhorse procedures. The lockstep, which is a considered risk of the credit system, is an unconsidered risk of "open" systems. Credits, marks, courses, prizes, honors—all are flexible. No two persons take the same course or make the same progress, for what they do is intertwined with what they bring and how they react; statistical dispersion is the rule.

We learn to do neither by thinking nor by doing, but by thinking about what we are doing. If a student working *in absentia* is better prepared for a college degree than one taught by expert instructors with the aid of books, periodicals, laboratories, and the give-and-take of critical discussion, there is something wrong with the college. All experience is life experience; it is the business of the college to make the brief life experience of a student uniquely rewarding. Incitement to learning is enhanced by both private thought and public exchange. Time is nothing but the theoretical framework in which these events take place. The college experience implies a good use of time at a most significant season in life.

The University and Its Surroundings

The outer boundary of a university, like the skin of the human body, is no inert wrapping; it is a part of the whole and can expedite or restrain. A university is neither subservient to its surroundings nor immune to their impact; it neither conforms nor condones. Like a church or an art center, it will raise beautiful structures in the midst of a slum. It will develop magnificent campuses in a cornfield. If its facilities prove inimical to learning, sooner or later they will be replaced. If new plans are developed, eventually they will be adopted. That such a renewal process may require ten or twenty student generations is easily documented.

There are indeed values that students can derive from the resources of a great city; the question is, Do they take advantage of libraries, museums, theaters, concert halls? If literature and the arts are to emerge as meaningful attributes of the student's personality, he must get involved. That a student may write, compose, perform, criticise, compare, appreciate— see things through on his own terms—these are the priceless opportunities in art. So it is for other collegiate experiences. For the student to abstain from all this is a case of not learning by not doing.

History is written as much through cities as through states and empires, and the city needs a group of scholars and students detached from the give-and-take of everyday life to give it light and a sense of direction. Leaders in art and thought who live in small towns transcend their environment without transforming it, but the college may take on a "local coloration." In the Southwest, Indian settlements and Spanish culture patterns favor social anthropology. In metropolitan areas like New York, Philadelphia, Chicago, and Los Angeles, there is an emphasis on the arts and professions, along with business and finance. However, let us abandon the idea that a city-located university should be extremely city-centered, that is to say, provincial. A university can be weakened by an excessive sharing of functions. A university should not get so deeply involved with matters of town-and-gown that the gown is practically dispensed with. No university can supply the primary needs of a metropolitan area. Precious freedoms derive from not being beholden to any governmental agency, business corporation, labor union, or religious body. In a time of public dissent and distress, the tradition of academic distance takes on fresh meaning.

Citizens crave economic security, good homes and schools, safe streets, access to parks and cultural centers. They need, but often fail to get, political leaders who are at once informed, energetic, and incorruptible. But what is the source of these important virtues? The answer, to my way of thinking, is education, in the widest sense of the term. A university is a living example of what can be thought and done and proclaimed when minds are set free to search for truth. The university sets up a tolerant milieu in which students are expected to transmute learning into attitudes and insights that will serve them well throughout life. Schools, colleges, and universities are not the only guides to ethical conduct, but the least among them will proclaim straight thinking, moral courage, and the right to differ. They will send their graduates out to translate ideas into action, ideas they formed when their sense of being mentally alert was at its peak.

The academic world cannot be hemmed in. The university embraces all past knowledge; it looks to the future. It reaches into the origin of life and the springs of human behavior. It explores the universe. The university encourages the scholar to break away from campus pursuits and local activities. Thus, a Johns Hopkins anthropologist traced the Indian migration from Mongolia to Tierra del Fuego. Fermi did his famous atom-splitting work beneath the stands of a defunct football stadium at the University of Chicago. A team from land-grant Cornell University pioneered in the science of cryogenics, which is about as far as one can get from agriculture. The great magnetic belt surrounding the earth was discovered by and named after a professor at the University of Iowa. Two scientists trained at the School of Medicine of New York University developed both the live and dead vaccines against polio, while a member of the faculty of the school—as he says, between glances up and down the East River—won a Nobel Prize for his work on RNA and DNA. Various diseases, including cancer, may yield to the work of a team of research workers at Rockefeller University in New York. To track down one of the world's most spectacular designers, one need not go to Europe or South America, only to a college town in "Little Egypt," which is in southern Illinois. To millions of students and anxious parents across the country Berkeley was the eye of the storm of student protest, but to some of us it remains the home base of a dozen Nobel Prize winners and the discovery site of man-made chemical elements.

The Liberal Arts

To express culture, the choicest words in the college world are *the liberal arts and humanities,* science in this context being relegated to a lower if not antithetical status, and the professions (education in particular) most likely excluded. It is no secret in academic affairs that what comes after affects what comes before: the college influences the high school. It is appropriate, therefore, to ask what is meant by the term *liberal.* Shall we go as far as Whitehead? He holds that "there can be no adequate technical education which is not liberal, and no liberal education which is not technical." For me, the expression *liberal arts* carries these connotations:

(1) *The subject matter is enduring.* It must not be ephemeral, trivial or simply descriptive. "How-to-do-it" courses do not meet this test. There must be a search for abstract principles and for achievements that enhance the meaning of life.

(2) *The subject matter is whole.* It is not an isolated segment. The course will start with questions; it may end with more questions and perhaps with a few answers, but it will require the student to think for himself. Such courses are essentially "task-force" operations; they are not particular steps in a series of advances by which a scholar achieves his status.

(3) *The method of teaching is adjusted to the nonspecialized interests of the students.* The biologist teaching his subject as liberal arts may be unable to bring his students to a high level of proficiency in laboratory procedure or research, but he will help them to weave facts and theories into a consistent pattern that will ready their minds for the great sweep of biology in our time.

(4) *The student approaches the subject matter without reference to practical application.* He may like the subject, nevertheless, and work hard at it. It should not take him long to discover that he is learning a common language—achieving a new literacy, as it were—that will enrich his life on many occasions and in all cultures. Later he will discern, faintly at first and then with appreciation, a relationship between what he learned at the periphery and what he most needs at the heart-center of the career he has selected.

(5) *The university plan embraces the liberal arts.* In liberal education we acquire a language that all persons may employ apart from "shop talk." Many subjects contribute to this pool of knowledge and communication. However, at advanced levels a subject is rarely liberal. As the scholar moves up in his chosen field, his subject becomes less and less liberal, more and more esoteric. There may even be a loss of communication among members of the guild. On the other hand liberal studies, while based upon the most advanced thinking and creating, are expected to reach students at all levels of talent. In the past, some disciplines were held to be more suitable for the liberal approach than others—language, literature, and history, for example. Provided they are not given a dry, pseudo-scientific, true-false treatment, they will continue to be a great source of liberal education; taught by persons without vision, they comprise an elaborate mechanism for sterilizing thought. Aware of this hazard, American colleges are vigorously exploring both subject matter and the art of teaching. They are discovering, on the way, that a grasp of science gives a new dimension to the arts and humanities.

General or liberal education must get below the surface at first contact. Subject matter pursued with intensity will link up to other material similarly offered; that is the way the mind works. As a rule, general education is confined to the appreciation of the works of persons who were not generalists. The generalist derives satisfaction from a brush with specialized achievement and draws intellectual nourishment from writers, actors, musicians, artists, explorers, surgeons, and scientists. But as long as we confine general education to bits and pieces, we shall miss the key factor in the liberal arts. What really frightens the tender-minded is expertise in any field, at any level, under any circumstances.

There is of course an essential role to be played by the scholar who is at home in several scientific or cultural branches. The historian in science, medicine, or art comes to mind. Such versatile scholars are also specialists, but of a different order. Joint advances in physics, biochemistry, and genetics depend upon a convergence of insights that must first be reached by specialists. The work on DNA and RNA is a remarkable example. The symbols man uses to disentangle these genetic intricacies make sense to us because they fit into a system of our own making; we do not retrace nature's steps, for they are not given to us.

Public enlightenment is the task of the few who are expert through liberal and technical study and of the many whose education prepares them to weigh the options. Schools and colleges have no monopoly on learning, but they are bound to review the lessons of history, science, and social policy. They are joined on occasion by journals, churches, and political agencies, but above all other institutions the schools remain free to get the data, to test hypotheses, and to examine values. Education spreads its services over the vast range of human curiosity and without stint to each person. Education is the solid rock on which the professions build their structures. Illiterate peoples, lacking this base, cannot develop the professions, nor can they, in today's world, cooperate effectively. Always the first move is toward literacy, in the faith that from literacy the great enfranchising arts and sciences will arise.

The Decline of the Cultural Tradition

Since the decline of the classics as a basic ingredient of secondary and higher education was contemporaneous with an upsurge in scientific interests, observers have complained that science destroyed the older learnings. Actually a weakness had developed within the humanities. In a memorable address to the Sixth Congress of the Universities of the British Commonwealth at Oxford in 1948 Professor John MacMurray laid the blame squarely upon tradition. The liberal subjects, he said, were infected, for "logic is but a technology of knowledge." Culture came to deal with the certain past, science with an uncertain, exciting future. Thus science captured the imagination of men, pushing the scholastics to the wall and itself unlocking new doors to humane and creative enterprise. In MacMurray's words, "A successful science, aided by technology, has fragmented culture, and cultural tradition is fundamentally to blame."

To turn the question about, Why was the cultural tradition vulnerable? Only the naïve expected science to reveal the basic values of life. Still, it was a mistake to assume that the search for values would be unaffected by scientific progress. Laws, customs, and religious beliefs bend before the findings of science in its ever-widening field of competence. The physical sciences have answered not only scientific questions but also questions long held to be peculiar to philosophy or theology— questions on the origin of sun, earth, and life. The answers found are more closely related to man's ultimate destiny than any based on blind faith or speculation.

To engage the mind of modern youth, we must include in history courses more than accounts of kings, wars, and tribal journeys—more than the rise and fall of nations. There is a place for the history of the natural and social sciences. To put it bluntly, Why did questions on the structure of the universe, the origin of species, the transmutation of the chemical elements, or the nature of intelligence lose their appeal as case materials *for the liberal arts?* The answer is that scholars in the humanities looked away at a time when scientists were first able to give valid answers to what had previously baffled all mankind. The fragmentation of the liberal arts coincided with previously unheard-of opportunities to enrich the life of the mind. Many teachers in the humanities, having deplored the "vulgarization" that science was supposed to produce, were unable to warm themselves at the new fire. Other teachers of the liberal arts, observing the success story, attempted to be "scientific." This is shown in part by their readiness to employ teaching and testing methods not suitable to the appreciation of literature, to the lessons of history, to the growing understanding of man in society. Having lost their birthright, which was to inspire through creative works, these teachers did not thereby discover any humane virtues in science. A pettiness of spirit developed in areas that should have been reserved for sorrow and joy, for love and beauty and courage, for the intact works of the masters.

We can all name great teachers who were exceptions to the rule, but "orthodox" teachers indulged in these practices:

(1) They reduced subject matter to discrete courses, emphasizing drill, dates, fragments, and stereotypes—the bric-a-brac of "culture."

(2) They fallaciously ascribed the general excellence of students in the classical curricula to *mental discipline* or *transfer of training.* Greek, Latin, and ancient history would "sharpen the mind." (The error was in the sampling. Students did not get brighter through such studies; they were already a selected socioeconomic group with a correlated rating in intelligence.

Superior conversation and reading habits at home buttressed the work at school.)

(3) They failed to note the increasing divergence between life in America and traditional subject matter. Gettysburg, the equal of Marathon or Waterloo, was outranked. The grand sweep westward of American enterprise, with its colorful overtones and its emerging significance in world affairs, was too close, too rough and contentious, to make its way in the curriculum of advanced studies.

(4) They rarely aroused students to a defense of political and religious freedom. With the coming of millions of impoverished people to our shores, a new conservatism developed. Political faintheartedness reduced the American Revolution from a violent upheaval to an alarming episode. This mood is strongly upon us today. It is a deep-lying force that acts against the revival of the rebellious, free spirit exemplified in great writers and leaders, ancient or modern. Now in the 1970s, sobered by bloody misadventures that strike home, the American people appear ready to return to some first principles in the pursuit of justice and peace. Now for the first time humanists and atomic scientists have joined in a common cause.

Conant on Teacher Education

Ten years ago James B. Conant, former president of Harvard University, published a book destined to be a blockbuster in education.[1] Since the reviews and commentaries number several hundred items and range from enthusiasm to outrage, I shall simply recapitulate some of the highlights and a few of the more reasoned criticisms. Conant sets the stage by referring to the persistent quarrel between the "academicians" and the "educationists":

> Why are the academic professors angry? What are they angry about? Many academic professors believe that the courses given by professors of education are worthless, and that the degrees granted students who have devoted much of their time to these courses are of little value.

Since my observations do not constitute a review of Conant's book, I shall stop along the way to set the record straight.

Having worked on both sides of the fence, I believe the liberal arts faculty is not so much angry as contemptuous, while the education faculty is angered by attacks its members regard as misinformed and insulting. In any event, the amount of student time devoted to professional courses to meet state teacher certification requirements is less than is the case for engineering, nursing, law, medicine, pharmacy, dentistry, accounting, or their satellite semiprofessions. Since no one holds that teaching the young is less socially significant than these other occupations, the argument shifts to the *quality* and *relevance* of the program in education. Here again teachers point out that all professions and many disciplines — chemistry and psychology, for example — jealously safeguard the territory they regard as their own.

Conant's criticism is more valid with respect to those courses in the liberal arts and science offered *within* schools or colleges of education; there the academic gulf is wide and deep. At a time when teachers presided over self-contained classrooms and taught across the whole spectrum from art to arithmetic, such terms as *subject matter, content, structure of knowledge* carried little weight. The theory was that anybody could teach anything. That there is more than a remnant of that attitude today is borne out by the alacrity with which thousands of teachers relinquish instruction to a machine, a computer, or a programmed book. Students in academic departments learn more than they are likely to learn in a course entitled "On the Teaching of" science, mathematics, English, French, and the like, but the persistent question is whether they have also learned how to inspire, instruct, and guide students.

I recall the case of a brilliant teacher of Romance languages at New York University. Since she held a doctorate from the University of Paris and had "published," her credentials as a scholar were impeccable. At the university she had the rare assignment of teaching students in both the School of Education and the College of Arts and Science. She stated that she preferred teaching the future teachers to teaching the liberal arts majors, for a reason that had not occurred to me, namely, that the students in education knew why they were studying French or Spanish and had a keen perception of what they would face after graduation. As a result they were not only willing to study a language in depth, including literature and history, but also to pursue it as a living, speaking language. The other students rarely took fire; for them the common goal was "a reading knowledge."

It follows that college teachers should be aware of the differentials in motivation among their students. There is, first of all, the student—the serious student who aspires to become a scholar, writer, critic, college teacher, and will therefore study a foreign language as Americans study advanced English. For such a student tutoring, seminars, and supervised self-directed study are indicated. There is also the future teacher of a foreign language in the elementary grades, high school, or junior college; here, I feel, is a good opportunity for collaboration between two colleges. For example, let the Arts College teach French to these students and simultaneously call upon the College of Education to offer a correlative course entitled, say, "Teaching French in High School," or "Teaching Beginning French."

It is well known that the chronological or historical approach to subject matter may be inferior to a psychological approach. The young child learns a language fast—he has a built-in cerebral mechanism for this task—but the older student has ingrained habits tied to English. More subtly the older student will ask, "Why should I put myself through this tedious business?" The child's mind is no blank, but neither is it overcrowded with "furniture." As for the graduate requirement of a reading knowledge of a foreign language, I suggest we abandon altogether the hope and the insistence.

The issues that have taken form since 1963 revolve about such terms as *relevance, meaningfulness, freedom, society,* and *environment*—all capable of endowing subject matter with tremendous appeal. As never before, it is the task of the teacher to help students see the connection. However, I am with Conant in holding that whatever is placed in a curriculum should be studied in some depth; the rubric of "general education" is not to be accepted as an excuse for skimming over the surface.

Conant favors a state certification for teachers at the elementary and secondary levels based on three requirements: a baccalaureate degree, successful practice teaching, and an official statement by the college or university that the graduate is prepared to teach "in a designated field and grade level." In view of my endorsement of specialized and ungraded sequences, as in the Dual Progress Plan, I am distrustful of certification at a "grade level." All teachers in the elementary grades should be capable of teaching their chosen subject matter up through high school. Since teachers in small high schools will be asked to teach a cluster of subjects, their preparation should take that into account. Conant recognizes the special nature of art, music, and physical education by advocating a teaching diploma in these subjects without grade designation. Conant's plea for reciprocity among all the states is unrealistic; New York, for example, cannot be expected to honor a Mississippi teaching certificate.

Teachers have been pleased to note Conant's liberal views toward financial aid and released time for scholarly work. Teachers would also like to receive credit for courses taken on campus while they are teaching full time. I think such credit should be allowed. Also a school of education should resist the temptation to pry into the noncampus occupations of its students. There are other, more effective, benchmarks, the surest one being the quality of the student's work as a student.

One emphatic pronouncement of Conant's is just as emphatically rejected by schools and colleges of education over the country. It reads:

As far as adequate preparation for teaching on the elementary or secondary school level is concerned, I am certain that four years [of college] are enough, provided first, that an adequate high school preparation is assured, and second, that the subjects studied are adequately distributed among general education, an area of concentration, and professional education.

The provisos themselves are enough to "kill the bill!" Limiting preparation to four years would strip teaching of any claim to professional rank.

How One University Faculty Reacted to Conant's Plan

All the comments above are "mine own"; if in the aggregate they seem weighted toward the negative, it is a matter of space-saving on my part. The majority of Conant's recommendations on teacher education I endorse, subject to the modifications Conant himself might make if he were writing today. I had at first thought to summarize the reactions of teachers, school executives, and school board members toward Conant's comprehensive report, but that would take us far afield. Instead I shall cite a few of the responses to Conant's recommendations recorded at the time by the late Dean Walter A. Anderson of the School of Education at New York University:

(1) Of Conant's recommendations, seventeen are given "unqualified approval by the faculty," six are approved in part, and four receive negative votes.

(2) The deans have negative reactions to these items:
  (a) Allowing each college and university to determine that a person is adequately prepared to teach. (Taking this power away from the state would lower standards and produce chaos.)
  (b) Calling for reciprocity among the states.
  (c) Proposing that colleges and universities should "go it alone" in teacher education. (Although New York University exceeds the standards set by the state and the National Council for the Accreditation of Teacher Education [NCATE], it does not object to their activities and recognizes their usefulness in setting minimal standards over the country.)

Conant's "batting average" at New York University was very high; in fact, the major portion of his set of proposals was already in effect there. As the immediate predecessor of Dean Anderson, I may reveal that the action approving seventeen of Conant's major items was a rare phenomenon; both faculty and administrative staff at New York University are seasoned protagonists of the "right to differ." Incidentally, many of the professors of education at the university are themselves products of graduate colleges of arts and science—a transfusion that makes for academic health.

The Education of Women

The new age for women, as for men, contains the threat of total war—a war waged right at home. This is the dark curtain against which we must project our vision of "women's liberation." For this type of war women really need no education at all; they cannot prepare for it, they cannot wage it, and, like the men, they cannot recover from it. Tomorrow's war calls for no personal weapons, no battlefields, no marching troops— only thermonuclear rockets and possibly the nursing of those who unluckily manage to survive.

We are most human when we live in societies, and for unnumbered centuries the family has been the basic unit for man's life as a humane and social being. World emergencies overshadow but do not replace personal affairs. Children are born and grow up, multiplying their insistent wants for food, shelter, and care. Somehow the young must be fitted into a pattern of social control far removed from the anarchy of "mother nature." Old virtues, like physical strength or hunting prowess, recede, to be replaced by others that are less conspicuous. Social consciousness and love, as a counterforce to violence, take on new dimensions. Nothing in biology or the social structure has changed the need of children for steady, affectionate care especially on the part of a *woman*—a mother or mother-substitute. To be wanted is the unconscious goal of every child. Where this is denied, the quality of family life is diminished.

It will not suffice for the liberated woman simply to copy men's collegiate education, serving it up as fit for a new world. Higher education was not designed to be men's education as opposed to women's education; it was offered to all who were traditionally sent to college, namely, men. To this day it ranges from a tight engineering curriculum to an assortment of fragments available under the banner of "free electives." The system operates smoothly up to a point, but it does not lead to genuine involvement in any branch of the liberal arts.

It is possible to design women's education independently of what is found in men's colleges or coeducational institutions. The main structure would consist of three elements: (1) liberal education, with a field of concentration; (2) home education; and (3) career education.

Liberal education consists of a sequence in science, the arts, and the humanities. It need not be a patchwork of courses loosely put together. Conceived as a direct response to the demands of a culture pattern, liberal education is the same for both sexes. It varies a little in response to regional interests, but it requires no subscript; a course in English literature may be the same for students of chemistry, psychology, or home economics. Students will bring their differences to the course, and they will learn, or fail to learn, selectively. In the vast range of abstraction and application that characterizes modern culture, the aim is to achieve insight and awareness. Since girls excel in acquiring a spoken language, a phenomenon noticeable from the preschool and kindergarten years, a choice among the world's languages should be nominated for an important place in the future education of women. In view of the need for international exchange, a newly developed zeal for the principal foreign tongues, including Russian, Chinese, Japanese, Hindi, Arabic, and Swahili, would place women's education out in front in a hitherto neglected field. Similarly in the arts we should search for and develop talent in performance as well as appreciation; in the beginning stages, they interlock. It is not that all talent resides in performance; it is rather that, stripped of all action components, a wordy familiarity with art will reduce pupils to tame little tape recorders. It is time to abandon the scholastic fallacy. We do not live in two separate worlds: to be educated is to know, to do, to be, beyond any ability to chip off fragments from the works of others. Memory is useful but limited; in demanding so much of it, higher education has rendered a disservice to superior minds.

The second element in women's education I have designated *home education*, in simple recognition of the fact that a large proportion of American women are, or expect to be, home-makers. Actually this segment could be called general education for women. Let us admit at once, before temperatures mount, that much of the college work proposed for this part of the curriculum is suitable, if not indispensable, for men. Thus far, however, men have paid little attention to it, and I doubt whether they will unless women lead the way. Home education consists of two major units: *child development* and *consumer education*. The mother or mother-substitute carries the chief burden of understanding and educating the child from birth to the age of five or six years. It is a major undertaking. The fathers are helpful, but not reliably so; in any case, for these ages they do not dictate the course of instruction. The mother, loving her children, also needs to know them, perhaps in the way a doctor knows his patients. For the college graduate this knowledge is not confined to how-to-do-it recipes. It takes on the full stature of science, technology, and art. As I remarked some years ago: [2]

> To the alerted mind, the fleeting reflexes of the newborn infant will carry as much weight in understanding life and human relationships as philosophic questions brought to us through cultural channels. When you watch an infant what do you see? Is it nothing but the wiggle of a pink toe? Or is it also a sign of nervous maturation building slowly upon inherited structures and pointing toward further development in an endless con-

tinuum from child to youth to adult? The gorgeous phenomenon of growth, equal to anything in the heavens, is there before our eyes. It should be a part of everyone's college experience to open the mind to such revelations. Seen against a background of biological knowledge, they are the basic elements in human understanding. They are to society what the electron, the proton, and other basic particles are to the physical structure of the universe. If these sense-data are lacking, words about them and words about words will lose their significance, leaving us as empty as a room from which loved ones have departed. The liberal arts, to be liberalizing, need to be re-enforced constantly in these humble ways.

Domestic servants and baby-sitters cannot be trusted to guide children in accordance with modern psychology; they are untrained. The homemaker is indeed entitled to assistance, but she cannot in good conscience abdicate. For parents who are college graduates, day-care centers are a poor substitute for home life. The same high standards such parents exemplify in their work should be attained in child rearing; not "day-care" but nursery education. In this segment of the curriculum entitled *home education*, chemistry and physiology will be applied to the nutrition of children. I have heard women deplore this practice as interfering with an artistic and affectionate approach to family life. Perhaps, like the dirt farmer upset by his son freshly returned from an agricultural college, they have encountered eager young graduates who wrap their conversation about these technical matters. Actually, the more parents know about nutrition, education, and child psychology, the more they will seek the deeper meanings of life. The first use of scientific information is to free energy and thought for what lies beyond. Women may justly claim that men need all this, even though a father's contact with the child is less exacting. There is certainly a division of labor, but it is not equal for men who are expected to concentrate on making a living and "getting ahead." What a man learns along the lines of child care is often learned at second hand; the woman who guides the young child can teach the young man.

Consumer Education

It is strange that the field of consumer education has been
so long neglected. A strong case can be made for inserting a
sequence on consumer education in the home education unit.
Through the unbeatable combination of the wife's longevity
and the husband's estate, women finally inherit much of all
personal wealth. They are potentially in control of vast corporations. Governments are different; women legislators are still
rare, and they seldom exercise much budgetary influence. This
is a pity, for women would be more intelligent than men in
striking a balance between, let us say, the need for high-speed
throughways and the need for education and environmental
improvement. Women would be more likely to bring state
and federal appropriations to bear on community problems.
In terms of daily living we need protection against the claims
of advertisers who exploit every medium of mass communication. If a new consumer awareness on the part of women should
culminate in a League of Women Consumers, so much the
better. The advertisers of superior products should lend a
helping hand, for they, too, suffer from the antics of the
uninhibited. It is encouraging to note that local, state, and
federal authorities are now calling upon women to plan and
administer agencies devoted to consumer interests. One of the
requirements of straight thinking is to formulate the right
questions and then to insist that answers be given to those
questions. To cite an example: the big issue in the sale and
consumption of cigarettes is not found in any detail of size,
filter, or flavor, but in the question: Is there a causative relation
between cigarette smoking and lung cancer? Thus far a dozen
major studies indicate there is such a relation, and the surgeon
general has helped to publicize the danger. While men lead
in the conduct of the basic medical research, on the whole
they are reluctant to support programs of public information;
they habitually align themselves with production, distribution,
and finance.

Career Education

The third element in a design for women's education, *career education*, is distinctive only in terms of the careers chosen. Women's major collegiate choices have been in home economics, teaching, social service, library and secretarial services, and nursing, with a scattering in almost all other occupations. Lately business, public service, editing, publishing, and mass communications have greatly widened the field of choice. The whole spectrum of the arts is as open to women as to men, but may not be equally appealing. Musical composition, like quantitative science and engineering, seems to represent a true sex difference in both aptitude and interest. This part of the curriculum can be bracketed with the sequences available to men. We may expect the career choices increasingly to involve a five-year university program, with a tendency, as in teaching and some aspects of nursing, to go beyond the master's degree. There should be no bar to the entrance of women in any profession, provided we keep in mind that it is unrealistic on the part of married women with children to disregard homemaking. At least it seems unlikely that a wife, having given birth to a baby, will be able from that moment onward to enlist the husband for an equal share of time. With the abandonment of breast-feeding, women took a long step in that direction, and it may be that some women will settle for nothing less than equal time on child care. Still, my observation is that when man and wife share and share alike in domestic duties, the sum is less than two for achievement and less than one for individuality.

Liberation for Everybody

Any "victories" gained by one sex over the other afford no basis for a sound future in education. What we all seek, beyond the famous *reverence for life* of an Albert Schweitzer, is a *zest for life*. Schweitzer himself showed his reverence for life not in idle contemplation but through serving in a sea of activity that would have drowned lesser men. We may as well abandon the illusion that we are storing up little items for some vague use in a more perfect world. There is not going to be a more perfect world, or any world at all, unless we act fast to get governments to abide by the deep longing of their peoples. It should strike home to us that women, more than men, are *people*. Women are the intuitive, sheltering ones, more likely than men to cut through to the essentials of life. More often than men, women think as persons and not as robots; they do not crave a purely rational analysis. If they distrust a man, they also distrust his ideas, his work, and his politics. At times, this habit betrays them, for they can be misled by eloquence or personal charm. On the other hand, men are misled by rhetoric and false promises; more often than women, they accept others at their word value.

Obviously the education of men and the education of women have much in common. The long future belongs to coeducation. Anything said about either sex as a whole can be said of the other in exceptional cases. Nature itself maintains no perfect dichotomy, physically or psychologically. The genetic determiners of both sexes are found in either one. What we have now in our social structure is a division of function, based in part upon tradition. I predict that sooner or later the education of men will parallel patterns newly set for the education of women. The massive educational breakthrough for American women came in 1862 with the establishment of the coeducational land-grant college system, signed into law by Abraham Lincoln, who is truly the patron saint of higher education for women. The emerging design of education for women is a response to social forces that have been boiling up these long years, far in advance of the stimulating movement we call "women's liberation." The majority of males, too, would like to break loose from the school's infatuation with quantitative memoriter items. The educational outcome will doubtless be liberation for everybody.

8

STUDENT AND FACULTY UNREST

A Decade of Trouble

Since the outbreak of student violence on the Berkeley campus of the University of California in 1964, deeply laid troubles have continued to surface well into the 1970s. Although not as shocking as the Berkeley, Kent State, Jackson State, and Cornell uprisings, the incidents reported by over four hundred institutions of higher education during the 1970–71 season have indicated that the era of massive protest was not over.

Of course, university turbulence is not new; over the centuries there have been hundreds of incidents involving students, faculties, trustees, townspeople, the police, the military, the clergy. Student power was decisive in chasing back to England Harvard's first, and rarely mentioned, president—a scoundrel in any age. Boredom, a lack of emotional stimulation, a sense of neglect or unfairness—from the beginning these have provided fuel for student and faculty demonstrations and occasional acts of violence. (I confess to having taken part in several street demonstrations of a quasi-academic and political nature as a graduate student at the Sorbonne, though I had only a foggy notion of what the grievances were.)

As we look back on the American scene with a degree of detachment we see that the fire was fanned at times by rigid, unfeeling attitudes on the part of administrators and trustees.

155

All that was then needed to start a "confrontation," if not a riot, was a provocative incident, with a radical student leader or committee to capitalize on it. By *radical* I do not mean students with real grievances who were using sit-ins and demonstrations to bring about some redress and reform; I reserve the term for those paranoid "walking delegates" who strove to beat down the university as a social institution. Agitators of this type are no different from anarchists elsewhere.

I doubt whether the extremists could have enlisted much support from students or faculty had there not been a strong undercurrent of revulsion at the deeds of American troops and bomber squadrons in Vietnam. Everything students had been taught to think of their beloved country was being washed away in a blood bath of intolerable dimensions. The United Nations was virtually abandoned by the United States government. Racial issues had produced a flood of hypocrisy, North and South. Among young people in or out of college there was a widespread feeling that the president of the United States was not a man to be trusted.

Students and members of minority groups, like all other persons, have no instinct, no inherited drive, to exhibit aggressive behavior. Human beings are endowed with the genetic potentiality of either violence or peacefulness; what emerges depends upon environmental conditions *as perceived by the individual or the definable group.* The common precursor of aggressive action is frustration, but once indulged in, violence may be self-generating. Moreover, contemporary society sanctions and sometimes rewards acts of violence as a means of achieving its ends, and student leaders are quick to exploit this Janus-like posture.

To the extent that such national troubles prevail, we may expect further campus disturbances. Eventually the idealism of youth in college will find other, more effective ways of registering protest. Their complaints about the standard curriculum are well founded, but reforms do not come about instantly, and certainly not through the pressure of "non-negotiable" demands. University administrators and faculty representatives are wisely asking students to participate in matters of academic program, management, and governance. The vote at age eighteen will permit almost the total college population to carry ideas and ideals into political action. If collegiate voters respond sensitively to the great issues of our times, old-line politicians will take heed, and the wavering ones in the middle will be won over. This tendency is already discernible. When a campus disturbance can be traced to an issue directly affecting the lives and hopes of students, it is actually a mark of awareness that adults should welcome as a counter-force to their own passivity.

It is, of course, the right of students to complain and, in a renewed dialogue with the teacher, to change the pace, the methods, the assignments. The curriculum is not sacrosanct either, but there should be sound evidence to justify radical departures. Reforms instituted by ballot or in an atmosphere of emotional outbursts tend to peter out. A watering down, a submissive tolerance of insults and disruptive behavior, a "selling short" of the students' preparation for the future, will go far to convince the malingerer that he was right in the first place; to such a student the school will remain a throwback, an enemy of free choice.

Somewhere between the two extremes of recent violence and former placidity there should be a decent, amiable place for all students, a place from which patronage and personal antagonism are excluded. There is progress toward this goal. It was in defense of human rights, freedom of speech, and freedom of assembly that students and faculty were united; these rights and freedoms are now regarded as equally applicable to the classroom, campus, and lecture hall.

We have witnessed the avoidance-of-pain syndrome that has long been the province of S-R (stimulus-and-response) psychologists. Through every student excess there is revealed a desire to seek orthodox approval. The destroyers are as strong for subsequent amnesty as they were at the start for non-negotiable demands, a stance that is truly childlike. As for the pronouncements and actions of some college trustees and presidents, the less said the better. For all their faults, young people see through hypocrisy, bluster, the false front. Now that students are penetrating the inner circle of policy and executive action, a sobering feedback to the respective student bodies may be detected. End war, eliminate poverty, subdue racial prejudice, pay attention to the needs of students *as persons*— these are the basic demands that underlie the wave-surface of campus frustration. Stripped of this idealistic override, the standard college curriculum seems stale and unappetizing.

The Free College Student

The hope is that student bodies will not return to that midstation between adolescence and adulthood that year after year characterized the American college population. The road from apathy to action eventually leads to the examined life. Any American youth is free by the age of eighteen to attend primarily to his intellectual, artistic, and emotional drives. Most students soon realize that the putative restrictions of college life are fictitious; never again will they feel so free, so responsive to their inner selves. There is indeed competition; in student patois, it may be "for real." When competition is overdone, students are on the right track in softening it and orienting it to constructive acts. William James, who flourished in a time of business greed and the debasement of labor, took a dim view of what was then regarded as "success." But James did not give up; he became a renowned scholar and one of the half dozen most original thinkers of his generation. He, too, was a "success," but in a different way. And there, I think, we glimpse the light that will not grow dim for the rebel walled in, or walled out as the case may be.

The test of student readiness for social change is twofold: (1) What is the quality of the substitutive plan, and (2) How and by whom will it be administered. Are we about to witness the emergence of an elite corps of students steeped in mechanical instruction, addicted to "rapping," taping, and TV, and subsequently graduating from a nomadic-sporadic university? In these early euphoric days of the movement everything seems possible; there are no flaws in the plan, no rocks just below the surface. The prospect of a spell of free-wheeling toward a college degree is palatable, indeed delightful. On this easy journey students will doubtless find soul mates and a certain amount of practical assistance from the like-minded. If they become sufficiently enamored of nonwork, they may close the door to science, technology, and the professions, but the losses there could be balanced by a newly found readiness for humane service. It took physicists a long time to discover the existence of antimatter, which has a place in the universe. It will not take nearly so long to discover the reality of anti-education, which I surmise also has a place.

In the meantime, the college headquarters—or campus, to use the old-fashioned term—will continue to be the hub about which satellite manifestations revolve. The student exodus does not break the bond; many will return to the campus after a season of independence and wanderlust. The college, for its part, should take stock of itself, not to appease its wayward sons and daughters but to discover where the seeds of alienation lie. It need not go overboard, though some of the insistent demands of disenchanted youth touch the nerves of honest men who are proud of their work. Our basic social institutions have in some ways betrayed the young, but many older people refuse to believe it. Adults—poor, middle-income, or rich—are being assaulted by new forces that stir up guilt in their hearts for failing, for succeeding, for trying to succeed in a perfidious world. The American, unable to explain or justify the war in Indochina, is a stranger to his friends abroad, while the circle of nations that trust and follow the United States has decreased year by year, as witness the voting in the United Nations. As for religion, its downward course is common knowledge; the signs of its decay appear in the weapon that youth keeps always near at hand: *indifference*.

Sick of hypocrisy in a world "they never made," young leaders are trying to fashion a better one. They are handicapped by their own paranoid fringe groups and by the resistance of the older generations who fear, not without reason, that things could get worse and that young people, however idealistic, will do no better than their elders. That is certainly the risk, but it is a risk we must take. To my way of thinking a revitalized university is still the best hope of young and old. It is an easy target for the vengeful; up to recent years it has not had to fight back. Whenever a university does have to fight back, its most effective ally will be the young people themselves. They have the most at stake, and they learn fast.

We cannot aspire to a pulling in of the extremes of poverty and wealth without expert help from sociologists, economists, and psychologists. These experts, as such, will not take over the job; their function is to provide a critical, long-range analysis of causes and of proposed legislation. Now, as never before, student insight and student power carry an impact at every level of government. By voting, organizing, and demonstrating, young people can take the lead in revising attitudes toward the "good life," whether we speak of a person or a nation. I think they have already done so in the impending conflict between industrialization and human welfare. Over the years this great issue emerged only in the minds of "eccentric" reformers or in the fictional works of a Tolstoy, Hugo, Dickens, or Steinbeck. Progress in this area is sure to be difficult and painful; without careful planning it will conflict with the aspirations of an army of workers in jobs to be phased out. Advances in the conservation of natural resources are easier to come by; we may expect to see some remarkable reforms in this sphere, provided the activists are willing to undergo a season of learning and preparing. In the meantime a healthy camaraderie is springing up between student leaders on the one hand and "philosopher-statesmen" on the other. The whole movement would be immeasurably strengthened if religious leaders would put their creeds to work as a third force. They are in a position to offer what the students lack, namely, some time-tested moral convictions that should precede action.

It is improper for the university faculty to be found on the barricades, even to safeguard the president's office. Its classic responsibility is of a different order, namely, to discover more about barricades—when, where, by whom, and for what purpose should they be erected, and if erected, how manned. All options are to be coolly examined, as they rarely are by extremists in the line of fire. A paramount university function is to provide an informed, objective, and fearless criticism of what has happened and may in future happen to the body politic. A university is a path leading to maturity in its student body, compassion in its faculty, and common sense in its administration. Since individual students or professors are not *the* university, they can do what they please, up to a point, and that point is usually well beyond what is condoned in any other social setting. (In forty years of administration in higher education I had cause to "transfer" only three professors to a more congenial climate: one for willful plagiarism, one for habitual drunkenness—i.e., dereliction of duty— and a third for stealing United States mail.)

So, let the student join any cause, *provided* he does his work as a student and does not interfere with the rights or safety of others. Faculty members do not quite share this blue-sky freedom; they are required to perform certain duties. If, like Socrates, they get into situations that are repellent to the ruling powers, unlike Socrates they do not stand alone; inevitably there is a measure of identification with the university or research unit. However, I regard it as a function of the president and board of trustees to free the university from this entanglement, for it involves a false premise. "Academic freedom" is not designed to condone criminal acts. Whether or not an action is illegal is best left to the law, but the university authorities have a duty to work against a miscarriage of justice. What is against the tradition or aims of a particular university should be left to the judgment of the faculty as a whole; there is usually a stated procedure for such cases. The president then may act as a court of appeal, and he should accept the role without turning to a board of trustees. If things go wrong at this level of authority, there are formal agencies to step in to appraise the total situation, to censure or to acclaim. The whole sequence of events may disturb the usual course of university affairs, although of late presidents and board members have been more fearful of the student body than of the faculty. Stirrings are good, whatever the source; stoppages are bad, since the university is not a destination but a mode of progress.

A Return to Normality?

Having passed through a season of sit-ins, nonnegotiable demands, strikes, lockouts, and acts of violence on the part of dissident student bodies, university administrators are certainly wiser than before. Perhaps newly appointed counselors, deans, presidents, and trustees may look forward to a return to "normal" conditions. But a better understanding is still a factor if tranquility is to prevail. After all, the total university experience of a student body is brief, and much as the students may reject the term, it is preparatory. Students in science and the professions have sensed this all along; they are eager to work and study under conditions whose chief excitement is in learning, experimenting, getting ready. The faculty, having listened to the students' pleas for "fairness" and "relevance," are expected to bring themselves and their students to a reasoned concurrence on the aims of higher education. In so doing, the faculty cannot in good conscience relinquish its final role in curriculum construction. For the student body the key force is *influence through consultation*; for the faculty it is *responsibility after consultation.* The ends are the same: the intellectual and personal maturation of the students.

If the structure and growth of knowledge are proper concerns of a faculty, what can be said of the student body? There is no single answer in terms of curriculum, but one factor is conspicuous. Some students—the restless ones—are not oriented toward departmentalized subject matter. Their antennae are keen to detect social defects, evils, and dangers. Academic preparation for an attack upon such defects is viewed with distrust. "Let's *do* something" is the battlecry, and it should not be ignored. Instead, students should be shown that by expanding their knowledge and their *savoir-faire* they are not marking time but are in fact deploying their energy and ability to the best advantage. "Let's *do* something," indeed; the question is, Do *what, by what means, toward what ends?*

Student activists do not consult college catalogues to discover what they choose to study. They get the issues of the day out of newspapers, journals, and TV, as filtered through their own publications and "rap sessions." Their choice of burning issues appeals to serious reformers at any age level: war, poverty, racial discrimination, unemployment, the plunder of natural resources. Toward delinquency and crime, the student lens is less sharply focused. Illegal acts of students and sympathetic faculty members are condoned, but the reaction to police brutality tends to divert attention from the daily blotter of sordid crimes in the United States. As everybody knows, crime is rampant. Court calendars are crowded, and convicted criminals are kept in limbo for years on end. Police authorities are jumpy; they find it hard to distinguish between proper law enforcement and the invasion of civil rights.

For all the headlines on student violence, the college campus is the safest place in America. It is supposed to be the sanest as well; perhaps on balance it is. But neither safety nor serenity is a sufficient condition for the nourishment of the mind and the maturing of the personality; knowledge is essential, and truth is still the watchword. The university will endure. It has a special place in our thoughts and aspirations. Jefferson underscored this feeling in the obituary he composed for himself. While neglecting to mention that he had been president of the United States, he proudly listed his founding of the University of Virginia.

The State as a Superpower

More insidiously disruptive than student demonstrations is the drive to reduce the authority of a university's chief executive officer and board of trustees by a state controlled superpower that is callous to the institution's record of education, research, and public service and contemptuous of its thrust toward excellence. The public universities of Illinois are presently suffering from that malaise. A recent report of the executive director of the Illinois Board of Higher Education flatly ignores the appeal for funds of the president of the University of Illinois, backed by its board of trustees, and freezes new appropriations at a level insufficient even to maintain the *status quo*. Furthermore, this overall state board has arrogated to itself powers long reserved to the university's board of trustees. I predict that these happenings in Illinois, if they indicate a trend, will reduce a great university to the level of run-of-mine. The president of the university has expressed his view in forthright fashion:

> The Holderman report uses a criterion of "population fraction" in weighing programs, concluding that the state is underproducing bachelor's degrees by 15 percent and overproducing doctorates by 30 percent. This discussion defies description. Based upon this reasoning, Illinois has too many corn growers, too many farms, too many urban dwellers, too few ski resorts, and too few mountains. Where is the evidence that there is an oversupply of doctoral manpower with doctorates from the University of Illinois? Where is the evidence that in so-called "austere times" graduate education loses its importance? There is no such evidence and, as a matter of fact, convincing arguments can be made on exactly opposite sides of these claims. (*Illinois Alumni News*, February 1972, p. 1)

Illinois is not alone. Universities across the nation are accused of *contributing* to the nation's troubles. The paranoid power-hungry fringe of those hostile to education cannot be placated; it can only be bested by standing firm.

Unionization

In the next decade university faculties will have to face up to an important decision: to unionize or not to unionize. As in all shifts of power, the walking delegates of the unions paint a rosy picture of the benefits to be derived from collective bargaining. Experienced labor personnel will man the negotiations, which will be directed to the top of the university's governance. Under unionization, increases in faculty salaries will be by formula according to rank and seniority. In the case of a dire financial emergency, which is just around the corner for hundreds of colleges and universities, the newest members of the faculty will be let out first. Such academic virtues as productivity, originality, and potential value to society (as in medical research) are not in the vocabulary of labor organizers, although the university faculty may be able to write such factors into new contracts. Whatever the faculty hopes to retain of independence, open-market opportunity, and individual zeal should be safeguarded through binding agreements in advance of joining the union. Since only a small group of faculty members is at present working under contracts, there is time for assessing the experience.

Analogies to the origins of the labor union movement in the United States are misleading. The salary scales and working conditions in our most humble colleges do not compare to the virtual enslavement of unorganized workers that existed only a few generations ago. In the anthracite region of Pennsylvania, I have heard old men recount tales of long hours and pittance wages, of cave-ins and explosions, of company-owned stores to which the mine laborers were perpetually in debt. Unionization then was a godsend to the worker and his family, as it was in factories and a dozen major service organizations.

Ultimately it gave a lift to the whole economy. But of late the labor movement has developed the defects that go with power.

This is not to say that the big American corporation is above all criticism. Although few corporation executives today assume the attitude of "the public be damned," even under the attacks of political and ecological critics, some industrialists have taken a different line of defense. For example the pharmaceutical manufacturers, on being forced to reveal outrageous profits, claimed, with a show of reasonableness, (1) that the medicinal benefits were extraordinary, (2) that taxes would catch up with both corporate and personal profits, and (3) that vast accumulations of money eventually would be the source of new philanthropic foundations. All true after a fashion, but the person who needs and should have a pill ungraciously prefers not to pay for it ten times over.

As for the most powerful unions, they do not hesitate to interfere with essential public services in order to win their case, and the schools are not exempt. However, there is such a variety of controls among our twenty-five hundred colleges and universities that I question the ability of any union or consortium of unions to dominate higher education. What concerns me, rather, is the beguiling offer of union organizers to free faculty members from such arduous duties as organizing and manning negotiating committees and holding elections — in short, confronting the administration and the trustees with a constant stream of demands. The "grievances" that a labor leader will find or invent in the ramifications of a large university system defy enumeration! It will come about that on occasion a single labor boss, demanding absolute loyalty to the union, will not hesitate to defy both law and academic tradition. For a faculty member subsequently to raise his voice in protest will be a new form of lese majesty; for the "other side" to renege will immediately call for a strike vote. New York City's one-hundred-day strike of schoolteachers was a sad outcome for the pupils and not entirely a happy one for the teachers, whose union leader was sent to jail, but it did not bankrupt the system. The private college or university is more vulnerable; were some of these institutions to close down, they might stay closed. Faculties will lose the esteem of the public and of private philanthropists if they follow the case-hardened example of the longshoremen, railroaders, teamsters, and construction workers.

It is essential that value judgments be made in terms of the aims, the progress, the sense of commitment, that characterize a particular college or university. A leveling off in the manner of trade unions is not conducive to individual excellence or to improved public service. Homogenization is not, and never will be, a decent answer to the problems faced by our institutions of higher education.

THE WINDS OF CHANGE

The Independent Colleges and Universities Are Endangered

The financial plight of the private colleges and universities is too well documented to warrant further discussion. Publicly supported universities have their troubles, too, but they can see a light at the end of the tunnel. The dilemma is described by Alan Pifer, president of the Carnegie Corporation, in his annual report for 1970:

> Private schools, colleges, and universities, while retaining a leavening of low-income scholarship students, will do best financially by turning their backs on the hard-pressed middle class and concentrating their admissions on the children of affluent families which can best afford ever-rising tuition charges. In so doing, they will pay the price of becoming estranged from the mainstream of the populace, which will only serve to increase their growing insecurity. As for the major private research universities, even substantial tuition increases will help only marginally, so small a part does tuition play in their overall financing. Any real solution to the plight of private institutions must begin with a clear appreciation by the nation's top political leaders of what the *collective* presence and vitality of these institutions mean to the nation.

Political leaders can help by seeing to it that funds from philanthropic sources are not dried up by legislation that would reduce the tax deductibility of cultural benefactions. Donors can channel funds to independent colleges and universities, beyond research "override"—which is an unstable base—and beyond scholarships for students whose full tuition rate will not pay the cost of their education.

The independent universities as a group would do well to divorce themselves from the church-controlled institutions of higher education. Some church-related colleges, sensing the drift of the times, are already shedding their religious affiliation. If, however, a church-controlled college feels it cannot survive without public aid, there will be sufficient room for its student body in other colleges, private and public. At this writing, at least, some high-tuition private universities are in search of students.

Enrollment Trends in Higher Education

Up to now, the principal factors that have contributed to the remarkable upsurge in the American college and university population are the following:

(1) Increase in the population of college-age persons.
(2) Increase in the number of high school graduates.
(3) Increase in the expectation of higher education for women.
(4) Increase in the number of graduates of two-year community colleges.
(5) Increase in the real income of families.
(6) Increase in the number of foreign students.
(7) Decrease in the demand for unskilled and semiskilled labor.
(8) National legislation, e.g., the land-grant acts and veterans' aid.
(9) A blurring of class distinctions based on race or occupation.

The contribution of each of these factors to a multiple correlation is hard to compute, but their respective weights will change in the coming decade; some of them are approaching predictable limits. There is in addition the volatile factor of the future attitudes of young people toward the concept of a college education as a preparation for a career or anything else. Still, we should not lose sleep over variations in the size of an enterprise that presently is the main concern of some 8 million students and of 1 million workers that staff and supply it. After eight hundred troubled years the university idea, as we know it, seems disaster-proof.

A few predictions more central to the purpose of education may be of interest:

(1) The majority of high school graduates will seek some form of education beyond the high school; state and national agencies will assume most of the cost. For these high school graduates, four options are envisioned:

    (a) An intermittent student plan, full-time or part-time.

    (b) A community college or technical institute.

    (c) A revamped four-year college involving greater flexibility in content and teaching methods.

    (d) A college-university plan leading to a graduate or professional degree.

(2) For most students, the opportunity to break home ties and move away will be greater than ever.

(3) The search will intensify for students who excel in general intelligence or special aptitude.

(4) There will be a sharpening of the focus on careers for students who are not degree-bound.

Since so many vocations are becoming monotonous and easily mastered, it should not take much initiative on the part of college administrators to lure students to a campus, at least on a part-time basis. Having recruited them, the college should exert a lasting influence on students—something that will stay with them regardless of age, place, or circumstance. This is the stage setting for the arts and humanities.

The extraordinary growth of postsecondary education has engendered a fear among economists and public officials that college graduates may be headed toward a saturated market. At times, because of restrictions on the exchange of persons across state or national lines, there have been pockets of unemployment for the well educated. The symptoms may also accompany sudden shifts in military priorities or a period of overproduction along certain lines. Generally the slack is taken up by a substantial shift to other occupations. If the depression is national in scope, the unemployment that characterizes the whole population cannot be laid to any oversupply of college graduates. In contemplation of a fresh alliance between general and specialized higher education we may predict greater resiliency on the part of each graduate. To this I would add the likelihood that the new crop of B.A.'s, M.A.'s, and Ph.D.'s will in the future be less contemptuous of the "lower" blue-collar or no-collar occupations. We went through all this in reaching the goal of high school graduation for the majority of American youth. We shall do it again for the college graduate. While income differentials have broken down, that is not the basis of my complacence toward this trend. It so happens that the social level of the job itself is coming to mean less and less.

For centuries the elite of Europe could point their sons (daughters did not count) toward four major occupational groups: the clergy, the military, the government, the lord of the manor. A measure of respectability was also accorded scholars, scientists, explorers, and the like. Trade, the crafts, teaching, and agricultural or industrial work were "below the salt." In the United States up to the Civil War, conditions were much the same, except that farming and the crafts, essential to survival, achieved a distinction of their own. There were few colleges. The professions required little advanced learning; law could be "read" in an attic. With the advent of the public high school and the parallel development of the land-grant colleges the wave of the future in American education was discernible. Both movements conformed to egalitarian principles embedded in the Constitution. The high school prepared youth better for the complex vocational demands of the cities. The state college of agricultural and mechanic arts, while catering to a population still largely rural, grew into a tremendous cultural resource for city, state, and nation; it did so by transforming itself over the years into a learning center of wide scope. Thus in the rich Mississippi Valley, the "breadbasket" of the nation, the land-grant network of colleges not only advanced farming as a way of life; it also trained the men and women who would organize heavy industries and build great cities.

That such achievements lacked certain amenities and failed to protect basic human needs—especially for women, children, and unskilled laborers—was no indigenous defect; rather it was a straight transfer of living standards from the industrialized East. Since I hold to the view that education is both cause and effect in the transformation of the social order, I can understand why both East and Middle West at first failed to develop an educational plan that went much beyond an obsession with "making a living." The colleges of the East were small. Students arrived in their early teens and left a few years later, sprinkled with classical "learning" from which the juices of literature and the arts had been neatly extracted. The graduates moved directly toward business, industry, politics, teaching, preaching, law, and medicine. There was little science, let alone social science. The factory profile dominated the city. The churches, one and all, practiced what they preached, namely, a prime concern for better conditions in the next world. It sounds like a tidy social structure, but, as we know, national and world movements were about to give it a hard shake.

Continuing Education and the Intermittent Student

It is against this backdrop that we should interpret today's surge for increased education over a wide range of talent. If by the year 2000 80 percent of the high school graduates have undertaken further academic work, what is alarming about that? For me, nothing whatever. After all, today's figure of 60 percent would have seemed preposterous to prognosticators fifty years ago. Now that everyone becomes a voting citizen at age eighteen this right to vote quite reasonably carries with it the desirability of getting into tertiary education. We should face it: the high school or academy is not a school for adults; it is at best the happy hunting ground of youth. It is a finishing school, and what it finishes is *childhood*. And with what dramatic impact! Now the time to leave home, to work, to vote, to marry, to fight in war (if male), is right at hand. In the light of these new responsibilities, for those able to carry a single postsecondary course, something is added, something gained. For those who continue as students for two or four years, there is the chance to enrich life immeasurably. Even if the chance is faulted in some way, the student will have deepened his awareness of a life "out there" of which he has had a taste. To drop out is no all-encompassing defeat; actually, all its signifies is that a few esoteric professions are shut off, leaving others—the visual and performing arts, business, industry, agriculture, and public service, to name a few—still wide open for the exercise of one's talents. Incidentally, we should abandon the term *college dropout*; it is derogatory and inaccurate. It is better to keep alive the hope of returning—an option accepted today on a large scale. The term *intermittent student* is preferable.

If my concept of the intermittent student is realistic, there will be no permanent dropouts; persons may study and work concomitantly or in blocks of time. Adult or continuing education remains a great boon to young and old. Presently a function of the university, adult education would do well to attach itself to high schools and community colleges, to the total range of the cultural offerings of the city. In short, if a program of education beyond the high school adds to one's career effectiveness and at the same time contributes to one's appreciation of literature and the arts, it will prove to be a fine investment. No college can guarantee this outcome, it is true, but no critic of higher education can deny its desirability.

Reforming the College Curriculum

In the future, every college student should undertake a program in four interlocking segments, as follows:

(1) A specialization, with preparation for a career.
(2) A strengthening of English as a cultural asset.
(3) An interdisciplinary sequence devoted to current issues.
(4) A curricular sequence in liberal education.

Thus if the specialization is in the Romance languages it will include segments basic to such career outlets as teaching, translating, foreign service, international trade, or the performing arts. The strengthening of English will involve speaking, writing, and literary appreciation. It will serve to remove some widespread deficiencies. The sequence of courses in current issues will concentrate on war and peace, the United Nations, human rights, racial equality, full employment, urban renewal, family life, ecology, civil law, and the like. This segment will be taught by experts in the various fields, utilizing case studies of existing conditions and proposals. As we add liberal education, which I have already discussed, the sum of the parts looks greater than the whole. Each segment will expand unreasonably unless there is overall direction and focus.

What makes any subject come alive is its impact on the student's intellectual and personal development—on the level of expectation. This was the aim of liberal education from classical times. During the Dark Ages it was lost by renouncing the realities of this world, and it has not been fully recovered. Today's college students still suffer from common prejudices and superstitions—to some extent an outcome of the fragmentary nature of the curriculum. If we hold to the false belief that all knowledge is of equal worth, we will permit students to take almost anything, setting up only two conditions for study: an avoidance of depth, and a reliance on test-passing.

However, change is in the air. The "major" should demand a true curricular specialization and a solid commitment on the part of the student. The "electives" should apply to integrated sequences in liberal studies, not to a scheme whereby instructors spread out their offerings like so many items in a cafeteria. For each student there should be a core demanded by society itself working through the university, which is its instrument. At the same time, each student should be free to choose an area outside his specialty that he likes and will pursue. This academic duality is abhorrent to pedestrian teachers; for them, the curriculum is not where the fun is. As this message gets across to the student, he becomes resigned to boredom in the classroom. To overcome this lassitude, it is not sufficient to lighten academic requirements, to ask teachers to be more alert, or to rely on electronic devices that "make learning easy." Something more is needed, and it is to be found in the basic structure of the collegiate program. Many proposals are in the air; the plan whose description follows is simply illustrative.

Several years ago, as a consultant to a southern university concerned with the quality and direction of its baccalaureate programs, I proposed a plan of organization designed to improve scholarship by taking into account differentials in student interest and aptitude. A skeletal outline of the proposal, on which this account is based, was published in 1965.[1] The features of the plan are as follows:

(1) The beginning student selects one of three options with respect to the starting year of his major subject:

> *Option* A: The major to be started in Year III (junior year)
>
> *Option* B: The major to be started in Year II (sophomore year)
>
> *Option* C: The major to be started in Year I (freshman year)

(2) A common freshman year.

(3) As part of the liberal component, a *series elective* in the sophomore year to which at least 80 percent of the curriculum will be devoted.

(4) A strong major (specialized) sequence.

The tabulation below indicates the distribution of credit hours under each option, in a four-year baccalaureate program of 128 hours.

Option	Year	Liberal Studies	Major (single or dual)	Free Electives
A	I	32	0	0
	II	32	0	0
	III	4	24	4
	IV	4	24	4
Total		72	48	8
B	I	32	0	0
	II	24	8	0
	III	8	20	4
	IV	8	20	4
Total		72	48	8
C	I	24	8	0
	II	24	8	0
	III	12	16	4
	IV	12	16	4
Total		72	48	8

It will be seen that the plan calls for a common freshman year—32 credit hours of liberal studies in Options A and B; 24 hours of liberal studies and eight hours of specialized work in Option C; a *series elective*—32 or 24 hours in Year II; a major, single or dual, of 48 hours; free electives of eight hours (liberal, major, or unrelated). Hence, for liberal studies the minimum is 72 hours, the maximum, 80 hours; for the major or specialized sequence the minimum is 48 hours, the maximum, 56 hours.

With reference to the liberal studies in Year II (the sophomore year), each student is offered a *series choice* of one or two of five series. This is the radical feature of the plan. Each series is a composite group, consisting of four interrelated courses centered around one of these five areas of knowledge: Choice 1, Science; Choice 2, Social Science, including Child Development; Choice 3, English Language and Literature; Choice 4, Foreign Language and Area Studies; Choice 5, Visual and Performing Arts. Thus in Option A, the sophomore student may spend his entire year in a single group of interrelated courses, or he may choose two groups. He is not allowed to spread over more than two groups. Students are not required to select the major from their series choice; the major may be a completely different field of knowledge, though the two will often coincide. A series choice might be composed of four such courses as (in Science) mathematics, physics, chemistry, and biology, or (in Social Science) psychology, social institutions, anthropology, and child development. The free electives of eight hours consist of any courses in the college for which a student meets the prerequisites. In the aggregate, these four elements of the plan—an optional starting year for the major, a common freshman year, a series elective in Year II, and a strong major or specialized sequence—comprise a new approach for a college of arts and science.

What is the *raison d'être* for this novel design? Surely no faculty or administration will give it serious consideration unless it meets two basic criteria: it must follow the main line of evolution for the American college, and it must fit well into the pattern of a particular college. Accordingly, the points to be stressed and evaluated are these:

(1) The common freshman year will reveal the differences in quality and motivation that stem from different preparatory backgrounds; it serves to enhance the readiness of each student for subsequent studies. In a comprehensive university the common freshman year would be organized and administered by a coordinating college or division having no teaching faculty of its own but drawing upon the resources of all the undergraduate units.

(2) The liberal studies segment ensures that more than half the total program will be devoted to a systematic core without reference to the specialized interests of the student. It gives the "college stamp."

(3) The series choice in the sophomore year is designed to sustain interest. The student chooses a field congenial to him and explores it in some depth; if he so desires, he may add eight additional hours in the last two years.

(4) The major, single (e.g., mathematics) or dual (e.g., mathematics-physics), with a minimum of 48 hours and a maximum

of 56 hours, commits the student to intensive work. It should prepare for a career following graduation or provide a sound base on which to build graduate and professional studies.

(5) A student may start his major in the freshman year (Option C) or the sophomore year (Option B); these options are for students who know what they want, or have started in high school a subject, e.g., music or mathematics, that should not be interrupted.

(6) An imaginatively constructed program is called for in Year I and five such programs in Year II. The student does not pick and choose from a list of courses; in Year II he chooses an *option* whose parts have been knit together. In designing these units, the faculty is expected to call upon seniors and graduate students for aid.

Throughout the plan the keynote in liberal education is *allurement* and the keynote in specialization is *commitment and career preparation*.

Is it reasonable to suppose that a typical faculty in arts and science will consider such a plan? Since the plan goes beyond a patching up of existing programs, it might at least stir up a faculty. One way to test interest in it would be to prepare a "mock-up" of the plan, together with a questionnaire, to be sent to a representative group of undergraduates, graduate students, student counselors, faculty members, and deans. Analyses of the questionnaire results would be distributed on a limited basis to college executives amenable to innovation, with the thought that with aid from a foundation one or more institutions might try out the plan.

Open Admissions and College Standards

As young people elect not only to finish high school but also to go beyond, if not to college perhaps to a business or technical institute, the question remains, Is this good or bad? I should say it is good if most students in the upper ranges of intellectual talent choose to enter college. Today a substantial number of students in the upper quartile of ability as measured by tests or high school standing do not enter college. Whose choice is it when a boy or girl decides not to go to college, or not to succeed there, or not to go beyond the bachelor's degree? Actually the choice, which looks so easy, is for some persons a crazy-quilt pattern with these nine items woven into the design:

(1) Underlying mental ability or special aptitude, however measured or guessed at.
(2) Quality of the secondary school experience.
(3) Cultural attitudes of the family and community.
(4) Financial status.
(5) Circumstance of race or national origin.
(6) Proximity of a public low-cost college.
(7) Changing manpower demands.
(8) War-related factors, such as the draft and scholarships for veterans.
(9) Shifts of values and goals in the youth population.

However we may combine these factors, it is clear that we are changing from a nation of high school graduates to a nation of community college graduates. New problems arise, for example: At various choice points, how shall the group be selected to move upward educationally? Through what curricula and teaching methods? With what incentives and rewards? How shall we take account of sex differences in aptitudes and career interests? How, in short, can we salvage and bring to maturity the enormous intellectual potential of youth in the United States in a social setting of individual choice? The founders of the land-grant system hit upon a precedent-breaking solution, namely, the idea of open admission.

The practice of open admissions is a century old among the land-grant universities of the Middle West. Without fanfare the early leaders of the movement announced that high school graduation, at the time rather a luxury item, would qualify any student desirous of advanced study in the "agricultural and mechanic arts." There was no great rush to enroll in the new institutions. Some of them were late getting started,

for the transformation of a federal grant of land into a viable
and appealing college was not a simple matter. Also, the Civil
War and its aftermath constituted a deterrent, especially in
the South. The elitist university plan of the East had a two-
century start; it was in any case far removed from any thought
of agriculture and mechanics. Closer to the seedbed of the
budding colleges were the University of Michigan (founded
in 1817) and the University of Iowa (1847), but like their
eastern counterparts they showed small interest in applied
science; engineering was eventually added to their offerings
in liberal arts and the professions. An expansion of the land-
grant concept to include higher education in every academic
and professional field produced such outstanding universities
as Illinois, Minnesota, Wisconsin, and California. To this
day, most of the comprehensive state universities and the
separated "technical" universities (Michigan State, Iowa State,
Purdue, and Pennsylvania State, for example) retain a modified
plan of open admissions. Of course these universities are no
longer confined to pure and applied science but are often
distinguished as well for their work in social science, the arts,
and the humanities. Differences in emphasis and achievement
among the land-grant institutions are explored in a book by
Herman Allen [2] that marked the first century of the land-
grant system, 1862–1962. From early days the universities that
accepted land grants promoted home economics for women
and military training for men. Apart from teacher education
and veterinary medicine, the separated institutions have as a
rule left professional education to the comprehensive universities, the non-land-grant state universities, or the private sector
of higher education.

We now find some of our largest eastern universities em-
broiled in a controversy over the desirability of open admissions.
In 1970 the mammoth City University of New York broke
through academic and legal entanglements by announcing that
it would accept graduates from the upper half of the class
in New York City high schools. The issue there, as in other

cities and states, concerns the character of the collegiate program. Will it be weakened? Questions of mental ability, race, and economic status enter into the discussion. Some believe that both bright and average students suffer if intermingled in the same college, but in terms of *learning* this fear is not well grounded. The high school graduate is already an academic achiever to a mild extent. Knowing something about the senior-year offerings in New York high schools and about the distribution of excellence among the state's numerous colleges, I should have difficulty in finding any great intellectual leap from one to the other. The programs offered in the colleges are more sophisticated, but the teaching methods are likely to be inferior. There is a distribution of student talent even at the graduate and professional level; individual differences in general ability, special aptitudes, and motivation are as conspicuous there as anywhere else. This observation applies later on in life. Does anybody hold that doctors, lawyers, engineers, scientists, teachers, writers, businessmen, politicians—college graduates for the most part—are lumped together in some tight circle of ability and professional expertise?

A segregation of students is not the answer, though the observed differences will call for flexibility in student placement and teaching methods. Only bad teaching will prevent the bright student from approaching his potential; only bad counseling will confront the mediocre student with goals and assignments beyond his depth. In the large state universities selection has been left to the process of attrition—an acceptable device provided it is based on a sound knowledge of the student's ability vis-à-vis the demands of a particular career or profession. For example, the record shows that some generals, like MacArthur and Bradley, were at the top of their West Point classes; others, like Patton and Eisenhower, were far down the list. The Military Academy has reported a reliable correlation between class standing and subsequent military success but no point-to-point prediction. So it is throughout higher education. Except in highly technical fields such as mathematics, physics, or genetics—or research in general—the shortage in I.Q. is no greater than the shortage in character and perseverance. The test that faces higher education is somehow to combine personal traits and intellectual abilities into an organismic whole.

The Open University

In higher education there is always the question of comparability. What is considered desirable for the nations of western Europe may or may not be appropriate for Americans. The concept of an "open university," of a university without walls, is a case in point. I do not regard all learning to be confined within the walls of a classroom or school building. As indicated, I look upon playing fields, recreation centers, parks, museums, libraries, theaters, concert halls, camps, and natural scenes as conducive to the well-rounded educational experience—so much so that I am committed to the year-round school as a means of promoting these liberating factors. For the college student all the facilities mentioned above remain desirable, with perhaps some additional emphasis on tennis, golf, bowling, hiking, camping, or winter sports. Either as a necessity or an adjunct, the "walls"—that is, loci—are still there, but they are movable and designed to contribute to the activity itself. On the whole, contemporary college architecture would seem to foster learning, and it is certainly a delight to the eye. To regard these "walls" as meaningless and a waste of money is to depreciate the aims and functions of higher education.

Of course, students working at home are not unwalled; "independent" study is nothing new. Since everything passes through the individual mind, we ask, Independent of what? Of libraries, laboratories, and study halls, of vigorous classroom and seminar discussions? Of direct stimulation by a probing scholar who performs at once the services of mentor, co-worker, and examiner? Free to perform experiments with the aid of crude equipment, or none at all? To speak with no one listening, to challenge without opposition, to proceed without measures of progress?

What hidden springs of self-propulsion and self-direction are to be tapped? Every college was set up to encourage students to learn, to perform, to originate, and this aim has been reached with a modest degree of success. To underwrite that success, it was postulated that the milieu, the teacher, and the presence of other students would be helpful. That most students need external reinforcement of their internal drive for learning and achievement is a sound observation. Exceptions can always be made for the creative artist or the compulsive genius; today's better colleges allow for this. The "open" university as now promulgated in the United States can only be made to look good by comparing a truly stultifying college program—there are some examples—with a pink-cloud vision of what students will do if they are left to themselves except for academic dosages via television and correspondence. (These strictures do not apply to Britain's valiant effort to give an educational lift to a million adults who were short-changed under its former plan of rigid exclusion from higher education.)

To try to hold a student body together by a wholesale loosening of standards or by making irrational concessions will be self-defeating in the long run; it may, in fact, lead to the early demise of any struggling college that chooses that option. A college stripped of distinguishing characteristics, hostile to the so-called restrictive activities of assignments, face-to-face discussions, and examinations—to academic performance of any kind—runs the risk of becoming a diploma mill.

The pass-fail system of marking is, of course, a misnomer; it would be more honest to call it the *pass* system. The point is illustrated in a report by Mathew R. Sgan entitled "The First Year of Pass-Fail at Brandeis University." [3] Of 794 student registrations in 239 courses, only 13 received the mark "fail" —less than two percent. Most of the courses for which students chose the pass-fail option were in the School of Creative Arts.

As I have indicated elsewhere, this is a defensible plan for students in arts *appreciation*, provided they show up. On meeting reasonable conditions that can be judged at the conclusion of a term or semester, students could be given the mark "passed" with the understanding that such courses do not enter into the determination of a grade-point average; that is, "pass" courses are excluded from consideration for competitive scholarships, "honors," Phi Beta Kappa eligibility, and the like. To place most courses on a pass-fail basis is to deprive the student, the college, and the future employer of useful data on the quality of the student's performance; it is, moreover, an invitation to return to the outworn example of the "gentleman's C."

We should be aware that the external examination system implies a curriculum that is externally determined. Individual teachers attempting to avoid this determinism will be alienated if their students fail to earn their share of university honors and scholarships. Moreover, the principle of separating aims, methods, content, and examination is at fault. They belong together. We may allow some division of labor, but not a divorce. Every teacher and every student should feel free to discuss and try to change the aims of education, realizing that generations of philosophers and scientists have done the same. In the prevailing European system, the "out-there-ness" of the examination system debilitates the teacher and frightens the student. Long-deferred examinations tend to make a storage bin of the student's mind.

Graduate Education

It is generally conceded that American graduate and professional education is unsurpassed throughout the world. In sheer coverage of the whole spectrum of advanced education, in accessibility to students, in massiveness, it has no equal. We have perhaps twenty or thirty graduate schools whose general excellence equals the best to be found in all of Europe—the number of Nobel awards attests to this. In spite of the expense, European students apply for admission to our graduate and professional schools by the tens of thousands. This status could not have been reached if our undergraduate colleges and divisions were devoid of merit, for very few Americans carry on baccalaureate studies abroad. There is another factor whose significance has not been appraised. At the graduate or professional level many American students have been intellectually aroused *for the first time*; they now concentrate on mastering a few subjects that are invested with career objectives. In a sense, the majority of students in American universities are "late bloomers."

A significant factor in the American success story is the phenomenon of *pluralism*. The public universities of fifty states, backed by enormous funds, undertake basic research. They may join with a dozen national research institutes on projects of wide scope. Private universities, like Harvard, Yale, Princeton, Columbia, Rockefeller, Johns Hopkins, Duke, Washington, Chicago, and Stanford, together with the Massachusetts Institute of Technology, the California Institute of Technology, and the Institute for Advanced Study in Princeton, constitute an interlocking society of research workers that has no counterpart abroad. Nevertheless, for seminal advances in pure science, we still look to the small, intensive laboratories of Western Europe. The American scholar is more concerned with the linkage of theory and application than with the lonely art of extending the boundaries of abstract knowledge. Our forte is in discovering polio vaccines, developing atom smashers, creating new chemical elements, getting to the moon, searching for a cancer cure, and the like. In spite of our fondness for Greek-letter societies, we are on the whole more Roman than Greek. In an atmosphere of free choice, I predict the serious college student will more frequently than heretofore elect the social sciences (cultural anthropology, psychology, sociology, economics, history, politics) and the arts. Biology, oriented toward nutrition, ecology, and population control, should gain in popularity.

American and English Approaches to Higher Education

In a recent paper, Alexander W. Astin [4] has adroitly labeled three types of goals for higher education *elitist, egalitarian,* and *remedial.* Under the elitist plan, "only the ablest and brightest should receive higher education." Advocates of the egalitarian plan believe "that everyone should have an opportunity to go to college, and that the investment of resources should be about equal across the spectrum of ability." Under the remedial or social welfare plan "special attention should be devoted to the lowest-performing and most disadvantaged members of society." Like many other observers I should prefer to mark my ballot "none of these." They appear to be discrete, but in practice they are not. From its opening days in the early 1600s Harvard College has been considered the prototype of the elitist group, owing to the fact that most of its students were the children of elitist *parents*—clergymen, professors, doctors, lawyers, industrialists, business executives. An *intellectually* elitist student group would show a positive correlation with these families, but there would be many deviations; the percentage of bright children in middle-class families is lower than that of the groups listed above, but the total number that qualify is much larger. As for genius, it is only necessary to look up the ratings of the parents and grandparents of our best minds in any field of creative endeavor— if indeed any records can be found. Talent, like gold, is where you find it.

I find myself partial to the egalitarian camp, provided it remains distinct from a homogenizing concept of education. This means that I want the "ablest and brightest" to get an education that will develop their talents to the full. Too often, the term "ablest" has failed to include persons gifted in the literary, visual, and performing arts, in special aptitudes, in humane attributes that foreshadow great accomplishment. There is no need to play off one extreme of the distribution of ability against the other; an affluent society should try to bring each student up to a high achievement quotient. Astin holds that a double standard of admissions would not solve any problems, and I agree. If held to the same marking and passing standards, ill-prepared students would be at a disadvantage; if not, a schism would appear between the regular students and the favored ones. Holding, as I do, that nonwhites and whites have the same distribution of intelligence *under equal home and school conditions*, the long-range solution is to provide superior teachers and learning facilities for colleges presently rated as substandard.

In Britain higher education has taken a different turn. The proportion of Americans of college age in college is about eight times that of the British. Of those who enter a degree-granting institution in Britain about 90 percent graduate. Students enrolled at Oxford or Cambridge will have studied a single subject for three years. The classes are small; the teachers keep in close contact with their students. General education is uncommon. This is truly an elitist education in depth, but scholars like Lord Crowther and Sir Eric Ashby regard it as well worth the cost. Shortly after World War II, I debated on the BBC the relative merits of the American and British approaches to higher education with Sir Ifor Evans (now Lord Evans). I had to admit that the average British student was academically ahead of the American. On the somewhat vague issue of comparative all-round maturity, we reached no conclusion. There the matter might have rested but for two questions that came to mind: since there were proportionately eight times as many students of college age in American colleges, why not compare only the upper eighth of the American college population with the entire range of British collegians, and second, why not compare the remaining seven eighths of the Americans with Britons of the same age who did not go beyond high school or its equivalent? On this note, the debate ended.

If suitable criteria of fitness could be agreed upon, it would be of interest to compare American students with students from Britain, France, and the Soviet Union and to carry the studies perhaps five years beyond graduation for each sample. In view of the wide variety of universities on the American side it would be necessary to compare not only the orthodox liberal arts college but also graduates from these variants: a "cluster" college of the University of California, a large land-grant university, a comprehensive independent university, a church-related university, a small independent college, a city university on the "open admissions" plan. A by-product of the study would be the availability of a set of benchmarks through which to judge radical departures here and abroad.

For numerous American children the decision to go to college or not to go to college has already been made by the age of twelve or thirteen. Educators who were quick to point out the deterrent nature of the former "eleven-plus" examinations in Britain rarely looked far enough down the educational ladder to discover a substantial blocking in our underprivileged families. For blacks and Puerto Ricans the critical age of negative decision may be as early as age twelve. On the other hand, most students who attend private schools and academies or expensive public schools are tagged as college recruits; that is the expectation, and the children sense it. In segregated nonwhite districts the boy or girl of native talent and creditable ambition has to fight an uphill battle.

Having entered college, most American students are still allowed to postpone study in depth. They mistakenly identify specialization with narrowness. The study of science, sociology, history, literature, or a foreign language is not forwarded by picking up isolated fragments and wearing them down to dullness. Having read hundreds of theses and dissertations as a professor and graduate dean, I have ceased to marvel at a well-documented academic phenomenon—the likelihood that the Ph.D. candidate will publish nothing at all beyond the dissertation. For the doctoral student who goes into business or government service this is understandable; the research aspect of the long journey was never uppermost in his mind. For college teachers the failure to publish is significant, not because of the publish-or-perish fallacy but because of the evidence that they were pressured into producing the dissertation in the first place.

Most professors regard themselves as specialists in a particular academic field, although the field itself may be divided into numerous territories. They speak of themselves first as physicists, psychologists, economists, and the like, with a deprecatory nod to their service as teachers. Professors absorbed in research clamor for smaller classes and a lighter teaching load; when the latter approaches zero the scientist has truly arrived. I have observed, too, that the nonresearcher often jumps on the bandwagon; he likewise aspires to a lighter teaching load, but only to accomplish less of anything. There will be a tightening up here as a concession to financial stringency, but I trust it will not be by formula. The test of a professor's need for extra time for research is not in the realm of promise; it is quite simply in his prior research productivity. Without reliable measures of the potential significance of research in a field—of the qualitative as against the quantitative—the university administrator is at sea. He may straddle the issue by tolerating a decline in both teaching load and research production with advancing professional rank. A more defensible procedure is to encourage and reward superior teaching, with or without accompanying research activity, and at the same time free the truly productive scholar to carry on his work. It is clear that I place the university research scholar on the same basis as the performing artist: he should not perform at all unless he performs well. For deans and presidents who are still content to evaluate research by its bulk or frequency, I suggest a comparable attitude toward teaching: other things equal, pay and promote the professor proportionately to the size of his teaching load. As the late Beardsley Ruml once remarked, this plan would save money and, up to a point, need not affect the quality of teaching.

Having implied that orthodox departments continue to stick to their respective lasts, I should add that many are engaged in elaborate cross-functioning, both in research and teaching. No department flourishes nowadays as an academic island. Medicine rests on biology, biology on a branch of chemistry that dissolves into physics and statistics. Various academic disciplines are brought together in order to attack practical problems in housing, health, transportation, communication, agriculture, conservation and industrial process. Since the unprepared mind can do nothing by way of objective research and not much by way of technical application, concerned students may as well study and get ready. The prime educational issue revolves about the best means of ensuring a rapprochement between a faculty-oriented curriculum and a teaching plan that excites the student body.

10

SCIENCE, PHILOSOPHY, AND RELIGION

The Views of Two Scientists

This chapter contains clues as to the meaning of humanism, but I am indebted to Sir Julian Huxley for a definitive statement. The Huxley of today, like his illustrious grandfather, looks upon man as an evolutionary product of an archaic past. To get the flavor of Huxley's views it is helpful to quote several statements from his article on humanism: [1]

> The Christian system of beliefs is quite unacceptable in the world of today. It is contradicted, as a whole and in detail, by our extended knowledge of the cosmos, of the solar system, of our own planet, of our own species, and of our individual selves. Christianity is dogmatic, dualistic, and essentially geocentric. It is based on a vision of reality which sees the universe as static, short-lived, small, and ruled by a supernatural being. The vision we now possess, thanks to the patient and imaginative labours of thousands of physicists, chemists, biologists, psychologists, anthropologists, archeologists, historians, and humanists, is incommensurable with it.

Once the scientific mind confronts a series of related facts and events, it feels at home. No one gets lost in tracing the history of science from its crude beginnings to a concern with galaxies, nuclear particles, or the phenomena of life. But, *all this from what starting point? To what end point?* There the mind boggles. Of course some ancient beliefs are quite unacceptable to the clergy as well, but there is a reluctance to abandon those regarded as central to Christian theology, no matter what the scientific view may be. In contrast to traditional articles of faith, Huxley envisages a humanist religion that will

> have the task of redefining the categories of good and evil in terms of fulfilment and of desirable or undesirable realizations of potentiality, and setting up new targets for its morality to aim at. . . . [It] differs from all supernaturalist religions in centering its long-term aims not on the next world but on this. One of its fundamental tenets is that this world and the life in it can be improved, and that it is our duty to try to improve it, socially, culturally, and politically.[2]

In short, Huxley's grand aim is to work toward a Fulfillment Society. (I have long defined the aim of education as *life fulfillment through learning and the creative process.*) Can our dominant religious leaders, by and large, accept this goal? I am convinced they can, since so many of them already have done so. As major social reforms are chalked up, an implicit dependence on the Golden Rule, with or without supporting dogma, is apparent. Through societal "natural selection" what is obstructive or nonfunctional is likely to be sloughed off, but the level of confidence in this outcome has been reduced by the prospect of a nuclear war. Huxley believes there is a cosmic trend toward mind, and toward greater minds than we have known. To be designated Homo sapiens after eons of evolutionary change is no small thing!

In Pierre Teilhard de Chardin we find that rare combination, a distinguished scientist (paleontologist) and a Jesuit priest. A few quotations from his book[3] bear upon the present discussion:

> Under the free and ingenious effort of successive intelligences, *something* (even in the absence of any measurable variation of brain or cranium) irreversibly accumulates, according to all the evidence, and is transmitted, at least collectively by means of education, down the course of the ages. The point here is that

this "something"—construction of matter or construction of beauty, systems of thought or systems of action—ends up always by translating itself into an augmentation of consciousness, and consciousness, in its turn, as we now know, is nothing less than the substance and heart of life in process of evolution. [Pp. 177–78]

The more we find of fossil human remains and the better we understand their anatomic features and their succession in geological time, the more evident it becomes, by an increasing convergence of all signs and proofs, that the "human species," however unique the position among entities that reflection gave it, did not, at the moment of its advent, make any sweeping changes in nature. Whether we consider the species in its environment, in the morphology of its stem, or in the global structure of its group, we see it emerge phyletically exactly *like any other species.* [Pp. 183–84]

So far, so good. If in the above statements there is a touch of speculation, it does not cloud the main idea. But Teilhard does not rest his case at this point; he reaches out, and in so doing, introduces a credibility gap. To illustrate:

Unique in this respect among all the energies of the universe, consciousness is a dimension to which it is inconceivable and even contradictory to ascribe a ceiling or to suppose that it can double back on itself. There are innumerable critical points on the way, but a halt or reversion is impossible, and for the simple reason that every increase of internal vision is essentially the term of a further vision which includes all the others and carries still farther on. [P. 230]

Since the effect of nuclear radiation is thoroughly dysgenic, a "halt or reversion" is by no means the impossibility Teilhard assumes it to be. Considering man's humble origin and its similarity to the origin of other species, the faith-hope that man is forever immune to a degradation of his supreme ornament, *consciousness,* takes us out of the realm of verifiable prediction. In the last pages of his book (published posthumously) Teilhard swings around, perhaps in deference to his religious order, to commonly held views. He finds for himself the unity and peace of mind he so beautifully foresees for the society of men:

Neither [science nor faith] can develop normally without the other. And the reason is simple: the same life animates both. Neither in its impetus nor its achievements can science go to its limits without being tinged with mysticism and charged with faith. Man will continue to work and to research so long as he is prompted by a passionate interest. Now this interest is entirely dependent on the conviction, strictly undemonstrable to science, that the universe has a direction and that it could— indeed, if we are faithful, it *should*—result in some sort of irreversible perfection. Hence comes belief in progress. . . . Lastly, is it not a fact, as I can warrant, that if the love of God were extinguished in the souls of the faithful, the enormous edifice of rites, of hierarchy and of doctrines that comprise the Church would instantly revert to the dust from which it rose? [P. 295]

Under Mussolini, Hitler, Franco, and Perón, the love of God was extinguished for millions of the faithful, but "the enormous edifice" survived. In a Communist society of absolute political power its survival is dubious. In a free society the church is steadily weakened by schisms and by the renouncing of rites. The erosion of religious worship on the high plane of a Teilhard de Chardin is endemic the world over. Although pessimism prevails, the problem is not one of taking sides but of finding a way to make Teilhard's remarkable vision, free from theological encumbrance, a reality in personal growth and social advancement.

God, Nature, Magic

It comes to this: God is Nature—from fugitive nuclear particles to astronomic realms beyond our ken, from the weightlessness of thought to the incredible density of a dead star. Nature's total output, including life forms on distant planets, is a construct more elegant and awe-inspiring than a belief in the supernatural. As the map is not the territory, so the belief is not the fact—except of itself as a mental phenomenon. It took two billion years for the first spark of one-celled life to appear and two billion years more for man's immediate progenitors to take form. Biologically there was no discontinuity, but culturally the emergence of man signalized a vast, unpredictable future. Language, foresight, and hindsight comprised the new, divergent elements; in an interplay between structure and function, man's cortical brain tissue took over. Henceforward all conceptions of nature (of God in nature) had to include the strictly human attributes of consciousness, history, and imagination.

Magic was the universal medium, the prepsychology. Creative power did seem to belong to another world—to enter into the human psyche rather than to emanate from it. Even today the inveterate mythmaker can scarcely credit his own mythmaking potential. What is not reserved to science will continue to be fertile ground for the wishfulness of dogma and the silliness of astrology. Imagination, a magnificent attribute of the human brain, is subject to perversion when its web-spinning, not recognized as myth, is assigned to a world of superfact and superpower. There is never a time in human affairs but what someone proclaims that the voice of God has spoken, and its commands are to be obeyed. As in parapsychology, the mechanism of this hidden channel of communion defies investigation. Rather than renounce the supernatural, orthodox theologians indulge in corkscrew logic, somehow to link human behavior to influences from afar. However defined or misdefined by the theologian, the "spirit" is in reality an expression of the vagrant thoughts and feelings of mortal man.

Orthodox religion, beset with forms and sacraments, offers few options to the seeking person. It demands subservience in principle. Having discovered The Truth, however belatedly, a sect is reluctant to risk the corrosive action of free inquiry upon its manifestations. Science takes that risk all the time, irons out its errors, and emerges triumphant. And what a triumph it is! Theologians have had to retreat before the onslaught of objective criticism. Did not early religious leaders propound and force upon others the "truths" of the origin of sun and earth and man, the "truths" of divinity, salvation, and eternal life, the "truths" about human character and conduct?

After unequal encounters extending into this century these "truths" lost their hold upon persons seeking order in the natural world.

Man's Wish for Immortality

For two and one-half millennia philosophers had remarked upon the depth of man's craving for immortality. It remained for religionists to translate this urge into fantastic accounts of life after death. The new system was pragmatically useful; it generated enormous power alike for king, priest, and medicine man.

Two factors sustained a belief in immortality. First, there was an instinctive fear of the unknown. Amidst ignorance of the nature of things on earth or in the heavens above, personification was rampant; if the gods were eternal, why not men? Death, scarcely less mysterious than birth, was a phase. Men living in "divine grace" could hardly be expected to die. The wonder is that so many pious persons, convinced of the truth of immortal bliss and of their worthiness as candidates, fought death so hard. Secondly, the belief in a life after death offered an unmatchable compensation for the hardships of this life. Eternal bliss could be gained under rules laid down by a powerful ingroup.

Having so recently come up from barbaric stages, we are only partially prepared for a civilized life. We cling to early tribal customs. Tribes felt the need for propitiation, and the business of providing it flourished during flood, famine, fire, or bloody attack. Medicine men remained active between disasters. They propounded the dismal doctrine that unless you sacrificed to the gods in good times you would be deserted in bad—and they made it stick. Without these fears arising from magic, men might have been happy more of the time; at least, they would have been spared the ravages of religious fanaticism.

We shall continue to be mystified and moved as science

pushes against the receding horizon of full comprehension. Our sense of wonder needs no reinforcement from the primitive world of the supernatural. The time has come to abandon the mythmaking that set its seal on the Middle Ages and endures to this day. All that is left to us—our total future along this line—is myth as an art form and as a key to the study of human nature. We need not bypass all forms of religion, provided the truths of science and human experience replace the "truths" of divine revelation. Science is breaking out of its shell. Behavioral science especially has something crucial to say about a world that is moving fast toward either unity or self-destruction. The atomic age has wiped out all other options. We are caught in this world, and we can count on no other.

It is always tempting to turn from a troubled earth to a shining City of God—a concept as sterile as anything imagined by Aldous Huxley. Beneath a millennial obsession with the unattainable there was indeed a moral imperative. Unfortunately it was made to serve a power structure whose Dark Ages still cast their shadow. The force designed to counteract tyranny became tyrannical itself. The humane ends of the early Christians were lost in the struggle. History is replete with examples, culminating in church alliances with brutal dictatorships. If we ask why the Jews of Nazi Germany were annihilated while most Lutherans and Catholics were safe, the answer is twofold: first, the Jews were the traditional scapegoats of Christians, and secondly, with some heroic exceptions religious leaders accepted the newly forged hyphens of Lutheran-Nazi and Catholic-Nazi. The taint is still upon us. Every school child is aware of the religious nature of the bloody conflicts in Ireland and the Middle East, but few observers mention the religious factors that played a role in pulling United States troops into Vietnam.

Split Personality

It must be admitted that the extraordinary complexity of man's brain has contributed to body-soul and here-hereafter fallacies. For example, speech is largely centered in the left cerebral hemisphere for right-handed persons and vice versa for the left-handed. However, the opposite hemisphere plays a strong nonverbal role as a source not only of inspiration but also of hallucinations, revelations, and the like. Thanks to the frontal lobes, no part of the normal brain is out of touch with the total organ, but there is a division of function. A degree of mental autonomy may strike the conscious mind as an alien penetration; this is a common affliction of the schizophrenic. Within the normal range what is subconscious or partially split off may seem to be extrasensory or perhaps supernatural. This phenomenon colors religious rites. There is a deep-seated urge to ascribe exaltation to conditions outside the human organism; nevertheless, the brain-in-action, its billions of nerve cells a resultant of evolution over millions of years—a brain irrevocably linked to its environment—is sufficiently complex to account for all its manifestations. It has to be! Knowing the source of dreams, visitations, and revelations, we accurately appraise the brain at work. As to "speaking in tongues," or conversing with the Lord, scientists will eventually reduce these phenomena to the interaction of nerve cells. More relevant to an understanding of religious aberrations will be studies of language, emotion, and personality.

Science versus Superstition

We should be on guard against superstitions that rob a person of a sense of personal and group responsibility. We should affirm the only promise of man's immortality, which is to live through descendants and the cultural record. It is time to shake loose from all dictatorship, including the dictatorship of the "soul." There are no absolute truths revealed only to a self-chosen few. Beliefs that should have been swept away by the first onslaughts of science are kept alive through habit and the residual fears of childhood. Man's best acts depend on his inner voice and his feeling for humanity. He has never been at home in the ghostly tradition, and it looks as if he never would be.

In short, if an adult believes what he was told to believe when too young to know or to care, he is set free from thought in a most thought-demanding area. One may thus achieve serenity, but the price is high. Does intellectual capitulation enhance the joy of life? It seems unlikely. In a world that has learned to place its trust in scientific method, ethereal "contacts" are suspect. The devout dogmatist must fight against a splitting of his personality. Having reserved a portion of his gray matter for irrational operations, he cannot endure the simple impact of a child's questions. Try as he may (some of my friends try very hard), he is vulnerable; the mental blocking extends osmotically to cells that otherwise are doing well. For the scholar who should not neglect anything that is relevant, this is a special hazard; he is unable to reach sound conclusions except by an absolute freedom to cut and try. Certainly in the social studies a deep-seated orthodoxy is fatal to objective findings. The scientist in any field finds it hard to be a supernaturalist. If he craves the "old-time" religion as a concession to times past, he will adhere to its forms only, avoiding its intrusion upon mature discussion. Anthropology and psychology would break the little dams he has erected against incompatibles.

True, science alone cannot supply goals for the conduct of life, for it does not provide value choices among factually equal terms. Philosophy is a sounder guide, as it was in the golden age of past civilizations. The desire to choose pure water over disease-laden water is, of course, prescientific. But science helps; it tells us what water is dangerous and how to avoid the danger. Except for their enemies, men choose life.

Science has not found it necessary to postulate any cosmic

purpose in the universe. To quote from my autobiographical sketch: [4]

> Long before I ran into the term *teleology* I rejected its implications. There was perforce a *Beginning* sensed as a dramatic event and there would be an *End* of equal proportions, but the one was preceded by infinite beginnings and the other would be followed by unending cataclysms. Through it all the tinyness of man in relation to the cosmos was clearly depicted; he could mean nothing to it, and it to him would forever be an unresolved mystery.

The earth may endure some billions of years, but the life expectancy of a complex species such as ours is much less. We shall do well to set our sights in units of decades and centuries. Science pays no regard to the effect of its findings on beliefs, however firmly held. Its whole history rests upon a discovery of the basic particles, formulas, and interactions that govern complicated structures. On the other hand, advancement in religion is balked by a reverence for false starts and past beliefs.

A Dilemma

The moving words of the late Agnes E. Meyer highlight the dilemma of the churches:

> Today the moral standards of the Churches still suffer from the fact that they date back to a pre-scientific era, while the conditions under which the clergy operate have been revolutionized by technology. The hope of the Catholic and Protestant neo-scholastics that they can recreate huge theological systems that will destroy and supersede our democratic philosophy of life, is mere wishful thinking now that the day of psychology, psychiatry, and atomic energy is at hand. It is futile to try to improve the hearts of men without regard to the new methods which science has put at our disposal for the reconstruction of human beliefs, habits and attitudes. [*Christian Register*, September 1954, p. 15]

Scientists themselves could scarcely improve upon this statement of a renowned journalist. Doubtless the Christianity of our forefathers—of our grandfathers, for that matter—provided a meaningful if not altogether happy experience. Sinners, as plentiful then as now, must have felt many a shock, especially on recapitulating their lives just prior to death. Deathbed rituals of absolution were in fashion; what self-realizing dream could surpass that one? Where, then, was the thunder on the left that caused most people to abandon the idea of absolution? It was generated by the scientific *process* as applied to astronomy, geology, and anthropology. Again and again the simplistic dilemma: If God created men "in his own image" not six thousand but more than a million years ago, *what did they look like?* There is no answer in either theology or church history. Contemporary religionists need not be enmeshed in the controversies of early theologians and scientists. Through the extension of scientific method into psychology, psychiatry, and sociology the nonscientific world is further limited. The arts and humanities remain intact, but not the nature of the stimulus or the response. Orthodox theologians spend a great deal of time vainly seeking to prove what they already believe. They are not to be solely entrusted with religious history, and their pronouncements on such concepts as *faith, symbolism,* and *God* are inferior to the analyses of our leading philosophers.

The Bible Endures

Over the country, in spotty fashion, chiefly in secondary and higher education, there will be found instances of the teaching of the Bible as literature, or perhaps as a supplement to courses in philosophy. In this way the magnificent poetry and drama of the Bible become a part of the student's intellectual experience on a par with Plato, Shakespeare, Milton, or Cervantes. The Bible as an inspirational source of literature and art is unsurpassed in the Western world. Doubtless the students who take courses in the origin and growth of Christianity should undertake parallel inquiries into Judaism, Mohammedanism, and the dominant religious beliefs of China, India, and Japan. As a safeguard against indoctrination, I feel that courses of this type should be taught by laymen. In such programs religious faiths are neither strengthened nor diminished except as the students' awareness of the evolution of religious practice may alter their views. Since a study of religious history is beyond the grasp of most elementary school pupils and may be emotionally disturbing to the parents of young children, it is best to organize it only at the high school or college level, and on an elective basis.

The Survival of the Fittest?

In the popular press the acceptance of the theory of evolution, including the effects of differential fecundity and the adaptiveness of populations to environmental change, has been overshadowed of late by the brilliant DNA–RNA findings of Watson, Crick, and their colleagues. Still, both the methodology and the results remain esoteric; they do not shock the world the way Darwin's theory did a century ago, and they are as rapidly assimilated by the clergy as by any other knowledgeable fraternity. The reason for this compliance is not hard to find. The exact way in which cells or genetic units operate does not bear upon the alleged effects of supernatural forces.

In the 1970s the mild comment of a distinguished historian of science, George Gaylord Simpson, is still relevant:

> There has been disagreement and indeed confusion through the ages regarding to whom and for what man is responsible. The lower and the higher superstitions have produced their several answers. In the post-Darwinian world another answer seems fairly clear: man is responsible to himself and for himself. "Himself" here means the whole human species, not the individual and certainly not just those of a certain color of hair or cast of

features. . . . A world in which man must rely on himself, in which he is not the darling of the gods but only another, albeit extraordinary, aspect of nature, is by no means congenial to the immature or the wishful thinkers. That is plainly a major reason why even now, a hundred years after *The Origin of Species*, most people have not really entered the world into which Darwin led—alas!—only a minority of us. Life may conceivably be happier for some people in the older worlds of superstition. It is possible that some children are made happy by a belief in Santa Claus, but adults should prefer to live in a world of reality and reason. Perhaps I should end on that note of mere preference, but it is impossible to do so. It is a characteristic of this world to which Darwin opened the door that unless *most* of us do enter it and live maturely and rationally in it, the future of mankind is dim, indeed—if there is any future. ["The World Into Which Darwin Led Us," *Science*, April 1, 1960, pp. 973–74]

It is no longer a raw question of the survival of the fittest. The issue now is *man's fitness to survive*. Thousands of species have become extinct but usually, as in the case of the dinosaur, through changed external conditions to which they could not adapt. As far as we know, man is the only species supremely cunning in the art of *self*-destruction.

The Views of Two Theologians

The distance to be traveled between the scientists and the theologians is illustrated by these excerpts from the remarks of the Reverend Hans Hoffman in a symposium sponsored by New York University: [5]

If we are right in our presupposition that religion is something that comes from beyond man and that, therefore, it can never be fully grasped by man's finite, human reason, we must accept the fact that it eludes accurate definition. Religion is each individual's conception of and relation to what he knows as the Divine. Because it is unique and personal, it defies categorization [p. 55]. . . . The special kind of confidence found through religion stems from the fact that man feels he is loved and accepted from beyond himself. Because he is first loved, undeserving as he may be, man is enabled to respond with love and thus becomes the instrument through which the creative power of love is expressed in the world [p. 57]. . . . Through the religious belief that the world is God's handiwork, the expression of God's being and intention, man can be certain that nothing in his environment exists for the specific purpose of destroying him [p. 58].

Nevertheless Dr. Hoffman, while properly noting that scientism does not contain all the answers to human problems—a truism among scientists—sounds a clear warning to religious leaders:

> A second hope that has disappointed this generation is the belief that, by adhering to the dogmatism, liturgy, and moralism of traditional religion, we will produce men who are really human and thus be able to build a new world full of better people. [Pp. 54–55]

The conference was brought to a close by Rabbi Albert A. Goldman, of Cincinnati, who stated:

> Judaism is a culture, a religion of civilization that has a sense of creativity. . . . the *becomingness* of man is what is so important to us. He is a potential, and it is in the manner in which he acts within his culture as he understands it that his potentiality can be released. Therefore, in Judaism we have not, for example, accepted some other theological concepts such as original sin. We rather see man in original tension. This is his fate. He must direct himself. [Pp. 75–76]

The Nonconformists

Considering the prevalence of mental aberration in the United States and elsewhere, we are aware that it is sometimes harder to unify personality than to give way to random mental responses. To relieve tension adults may turn to the pleasures of alcohol, for it is no stimulant but a sedative, and recovery from small dosages is rapid. On the other hand most drugs, including all opium derivatives, are deleterious and eventually stupefying. Drug addiction, like chronic alcoholism, results in organic disturbances that intensify the anxiety it was presumed to alleviate. The more bizarre the sensory effects of drugs, the greater the likelihood of damage to the nervous system. If in the endeavor to "find oneself" a person relies on chemicals, he is sure to be disappointed; they add nothing, and they take away.

Visions and dreams, together with hypnotism, hysteria, and hallucination, offer valid topics for psychological research. They are also of interest to the student of religion. Physicians sense better than the pre-Freudians the ineffable connection between the conscious and the unconscious. It is unfortunate that some priests ignore analysts and psychologists who could enhance their fitness to give advice. It is saddening, too, in the late twentieth century to note that miracle shrines such as the Grotto of Lourdes in France are made to seem more efficacious than dependable medical "miracles," which occur daily, though requiring no shrine and no supernatural power.

The manifestations claimed by contemporary cultists are reminiscent of medieval practices. An element they have in common, beyond meditation and vicarious flagellation, is hysteria. Even so, as an alternative to the taking of drugs to induce hallucinations, a turn to oriental religious fanaticism is an improvement. If we are to credit reports, what happens is a transition from suggestibility to self-hypnosis. The mind is allowed to "float," the body to assume unaccustomed postures. For persons worried about mundane affairs there is doubtless a sense of relief in this form of abandonment. That quack spiritual leaders have rushed in to supply the demand was to be expected. Religious oddity is a psychological phenomenon predictable at a time when the socioeconomic-political setup has gone awry.

Strange as these nonconformists are, seen against ordinary behavioral standards, they are usually harmless. The young people who merely dabble in occult phenomena, hoping by recourse to myth and magic to solve baffling problems, are likely to return to reason. In any event it devolves upon us all to recognize the idealism that may lie beneath the bizarre behavior of youth. The fact is that for some young men whose future is shadowed by unemployment, racial prejudice, and military service the game is not worth the candle. On the other hand, leaders in "women's liberation" are properly contemptuous of cultist escape mechanisms; they have a cause, and there is work to be done. There never has been an instant *solution* to personal problems, but in home, school, and college we can prepare youth for an instant *attack* on them.

Avant-garde Views

Since my concern in writing this chapter is to point up the reciprocal relation between religion and education, I am inserting some notes based on a survey made by Frederick Franck.[6] He interviewed thirty-seven Dutch avant-garde Roman Catholics and reported their voluntary responses in some detail. His sampling included sixteen priests together with writers, editors, and professors. All were members of the Church and desirous of remaining so. They expressed enthusiasm for the ideas and the personality of Pope John XXIII. This group departed from the traditional concept of the Church but were "willing to preserve the word *Church*, if it can be given a new content based on evangelical values and oriented to the life and value system of Jesus." They thought the concept *Church* in the institutional sense vague and at times pejorative. To quote Th. Pollman and Mrs. T. Pollman Schlichting, both teachers of literature and "active in progressive Catholic circles":

> As a revelation it [the Church] is a source of inspiration for the awareness of being responsible for one another, and of belonging together as human beings. The realization that good and evil and all in between are due to us humans offers the possibility of awareness and the capacity for a discrimination of values which is ours by birth, not administered by special injections from above. [P. 47]

Franck summarizes his interviews as follows:

> The figure of Jesus is taken with the utmost seriousness, not-withstanding, or perhaps because of the avoidance of all conventional, ecclesiastical descriptions; the person of Jesus is being de-idolized as completely as possible by peeling away all aspects of idolatry, sentimentality, superstition, popular belief, and magic. This does not result in a weakening of his meaning, but actually in a clarification of it and a liberation of his dynamic force. He is experienced existentially as the crystallization of the mystery of the truly human life and its very criterion. [Pp. 129–30]

Subsequently, on a visit to Sotto il Monte, the birthplace of Pope John XXIII, the author sought to distill some of the outcomes of his thirty-seven interviews. To quote two items, from among many that would serve:

> The emphasis on the hereafter, certainly on an anthropologically detailed hereafter, had disappeared. Life on earth-now was being affirmed, a life which only becomes fully human in growth, integration, and conscious acceptance. The guilt-machine had been stalled. Hell was either being declared empty or transferred to the earth's surface, where people were slowly becoming conscious that it is of their own making. [Pp. 274–75]
>
> People have not chosen merely between something old-fashioned and something new; they have recognized themselves and arrived at insights that cannot be reversed. All warnings from above are doomed to fail therefore; they sound increasingly pathetic and self-serving, full of ever more indigestible rhetoric. [P. 283]

One participant in Franck's survey brought the dialogue "down to earth" in this fashion:

> Questions about virgin birth, freedom of conscience, Magisterium, infallibility, etc., etc., really are of interest only to theologians and churchmen from pastor to pope, people who have been bottle-fed on these concepts and who are now trying to go through complicated acrobatics in order to be able graciously to get rid of the most embarrassing ones. Often it seems that their main concern is to attempt the rationalization of

much rather insane theology. As far as Vietnam is concerned, I should like to say to this conference that not only are the Americans misbehaving there, but that their support comes to a large extent from Catholics. Under the Diem regime the Church acted in a medieval, feudal manner. All the objections the world can voice against the Church have been, and probably still are, demonstrated in connection with Vietnam. [P. 156]

Now that the U. S. participation in the Southeast Asian war has come to an end, we may judge from news reports and commentaries that most American Catholics now share the common view of its futility and hideousness. The first to make their objections public are those who favor action, as might be expected. In this connection, some comments on radical Catholicism (as exemplified by Philip Berrigan and Daniel Berrigan) by Professor Gordon Zahn, himself a Roman Catholic, are of interest:

Even the leaders of traditional peace churches and other old-line pacifist organizations fail to take account of these deeper currents in their astonished delight over the activist Catholic resistance to war and military service. With at least equal astonishment and considerably less delight, Catholic ecclesiastics and the majority of their still predominantly conservative flocks shrink back in horror from the "excesses" perpetrated by their fellow communicants of the ultra-resistance, but they, too, miss the crucial point of it all. Most confused of all, one must assume, are political and military leaders, accustomed as they are to the unquestioning and enthusiastic support they have always received from the Roman Catholic community in time of war. These reactions all testify to the same public image of the church, an image well-earned and thoroughly validated by history. . . . But it is also true that the Catholic community in America has produced a measure of active opposition to an ongoing war that must be almost unique in the history of the modern church. Of greater significance for the future, it is an opposition that reaches beyond Vietnam as an issue to challenge and reject war and violence as means for solving any human problems, whether personal, national, or international in scope. ["The Great Catholic Upheaval," *Saturday Review*, September 11, 1971, p. 25]

These activists approach the Society of Friends in their philosophical outlook but not in their resort to illegal acts. For resisting draft laws as applied to an unjust war, the Catholic Berrigans are heroes to millions of Americans and especially to the young. Whatever the legal outcome, such men bear the stamp of martyrdom.

Following a review of the existing crisis in Christian theology, William Robert Miller arrives at this peroration:

> The point in history at which the world became so mature that it no longer needed the "god hypothesis," or at which God "died," is hard to locate with any precision. The full realization of the dawning of a secular, post-Christian era is very recent. Within this century, religion collapsed mightily in Russia, and has ebbed more gradually throughout the rest of Europe. Western-sponsored missions have been deflated throughout the world, and the places where people may be counted on to go to church are areas like the American South, Spain and South Africa. . . . The odd man out is the writer or thinker who is neither a certified Christian nor a certified atheist, but who has dared to advance his own personal religious faith, even his own personal vision of God or Jesus without benefit of church or clergy. ["Is the Church Obsolete?" *American Scholar*, Spring 1967, pp. 235–36]

For the majority of persons the end result is not protest but indifference; in the vernacular, they "couldn't care less." Those of us who do care apprehend that for want of vigilance there may come a time when powerful religious authorities will again operate against the common good.

A Famous Pronouncement

The encyclical of Pope John XXIII, *Pacem in Terris*, has aroused deep interest across the whole spectrum of religious thought; its nontheological considerations, emphasizing welfare and peace, are met with enthusiasm among people in every walk of life. In 1965 the International Convocation called by Robert M. Hutchins, president of the Center for the Study of

Democratic Institutions, presented speakers of world renown. Every speaker praised the document as a forward step in religious and public affairs. There were one or two quiet remarks from the liberal side that did not take issue with the high aims of the encyclical but rather with its specifics. Thus the late Hermann J. Muller, Nobel Prize winner in biology, stated in the convocation report, *Therefore Choose Life,*

> Humanists and many others not bound by traditional dogmas will not agree with Pope John when he attributes the existence of fellow feeling and rationality in man to the operation of supernatural causes. They will, however, agree that the germs of both fellow feeling and rationality are deeply rooted in human nature. These faculties are in the first place rooted genetically, as a result of biological evolution, because the structure and the mode of life of proto-humans and humans were unique in causing both fellow feeling and rationality to be especially conducive to survival. In the second place the cultural evolution of man laid further stress on these faculties.

Professor Muller then noted with approval Pope John's eloquent appeal to the conscience of mankind to take steps to aid the poverty-stricken and the neglected people of the world, adding:

> Departing from generalities, however, one specific feature of such aid that is an absolute essential, but that was not mentioned by Pope John, must be insisted upon. That is the imparting of information regarding the need for birth control, and regarding appropriate means of accomplishing it. This information should be accompanied by whatever technical and material assistance may be necessary in this connection. Otherwise population increase could undermine all other progress and destroy all foundations of peace.

Muller's comment was despairingly underscored at the convocation by Vijaya Lakshmi Pandit, governor of Maharashtra, India, formerly president of the United Nations General Assembly:

> Practical and revolutionary answers must be found to the menace of overpopulation. I speak of this with some feeling because in my own country, where we are trying desperately hard

to build it up to a point at which the Indian people will be able to inherit some of the things to which they are heir in a free country and in a functioning democracy, all our efforts and all the aid we receive from foreign countries are not enough to produce the results we have in mind because of the ever-growing population. (I believe, at this moment, it is at the rate of 12,000,000 a year.)

Can anyone, looking back to this convocation, escape a feeling of sadness, a sense of what might have been, on reading the closing words of Abba Eban, deputy prime minister of Israel? He said:

> The Papal message on peace on earth was governed by deep compassion for man in his vulnerability. There is also a sense, in this wondrous age, of what man can achieve in his redeeming moments of grandeur. As we look out on the human condition, our consciences cannot be clean. If we think they are clean, then it is because we do not use them enough. It is not inevitable that we march in hostile and separated hosts into the common abyss. There is another possibility—of an ordered world, illuminated by reason and governed by law. If we cannot yet touch it with our hands, let us, at least, grasp it in our vision.

In the 1970s we must again ask, as "peoples speaking to peoples," what are the *first steps* toward a lasting peace? After the crises of Southeast Asia, the Middle East, Ireland, and the ever-erupting Latin American countries, there will be a moratorium of sorts, but that outcome would not have satisfied the great heart of Pope John XXIII. Will it satisfy the Church or all churches taken together? If it does, mankind will have to look elsewhere to save its skin.

A Humanist's Conception of God

Having said so much in a negative vein, as a pendulum push against prevailing religious dogma, I should like to endorse the conception of God expounded by Professor Sidney Hook, of New York University:

God is neither a supernatural power nor a principle of immanent structure, but a symbolic term for our most inclusive moral ideals. The "divine" refers to that dimension in human life which is not reducible *merely* to the physical, the social and the psychological, although it emerges from and affects them. It is a dimension which is experienced whenever ideal ends, justice, compassion for all suffering creatures, dedication to truth, integrity, move men to change the world and themselves. This is the humanist conception of God. ["The Liberal Context," in *Religious Experience and Truth*, ed. Sidney Hook (New York University Press, 1961), p. 1]

For humanists the word *God* symbolizes the best that lies in the minds and hearts of the best of men. Over the years, having had much contact with leaders in education, government, philanthropy, and religion here and abroad, I have come to the conclusion that the designation "men of good will" overrides all other conceptions of morality.

11

CRACKS IN THE WALL OF SEPARATION

The Right to Teach

In the fifties and sixties the campaign to secure public financial aid for parochial schools and colleges gathered headway. A highly publicized statement on the teaching mission of the Church, signed by thirteen cardinals, archbishops, and bishops "in the name of the Bishops of the United States" keynoted this movement.[1] Although the right of the Roman Catholic church to teach its doctrines is unquestioned, the major part of the declaration is devoted to a defense of this right. It is, of course, a right that applies equally to all religious teaching. (The Mormons had the right to teach polygamy, but its *practice* ran into legal barriers.) A few excerpts indicate that the bishops charged non-Catholics with principles they do not affirm and practices they do not condone:

> We live in a sundered and divided world, a world harassed by conflicting voices and warring philosophies. Materialism and secularism, in particular, have made heavy inroads on the official and popular thinking of men and nations. The basic tenet of those ideologies is that man's sole concern is with the here and now, with the actual politics and economics of this world, to the exclusion, theoretical or practical, of the things of the spirit and their relegation to the realm of pure fantasy.

It is clear that by "things of the spirit" the bishops include everything except "politics and economics." To the humanist, to any liberal, the term "things of the spirit" denotes art, love, joy, compassion, and awe. These experiences transcend politics and economics as surely as any recourse to imaginary beings beyond this life. It is unreasonable to identify "secularism" with a gross and vulgar materialism. The statement moves on to a dubious premise:

> It is questioned, thus, whether she [the Church] has the right to preach her own concept of the holiness and inviolability of the marriage bond in a society which has legalized divorce and has advanced very far toward accepting it as a normal solution for marital problems of any kind. Again, there is vehement opposition raised when she states her principles on contraception. In another field it is contended that the Church is not justified in adopting measures to protect the faith of her children in a mixed society where established principles are at a discount. Her position on the moral necessity of Christian education is denounced as divisive, or, more properly, as running counter to the interests of a monopolistic statism.

Statutes operating through the pluralism of municipalities and states, supported by the vote of the people, do indeed permit divorce, birth control, and lately abortion in New York. The Roman Catholic church has fought such reforms "tooth and nail," and that is its privilege. Unhappily, Church authorities have not stopped there; they have systematically tried to force their views upon all other citizens. Moreover, while proclaiming its right to teach, the Church has attacked citizens who cherish *their* right to teach, to demonstrate, to publish. A state, or any of its political subdivisions, presumably embodies the legal wishes of its constituency; it seems odd, therefore, that a religious hierarchy whose power assuredly does *not* arise from a vote of the people should use the epithet "monopolistic statism." In the long past, and in not a few nations over the world today, the real and debilitating monopoly is found in the union of church and state, with the former aspiring to the dominant role.

To Pray or Not to Pray

At midcentury the strongest voice of Roman Catholicism on American education and public affairs was that of the late Cardinal Spellman of New York. An excerpt from a speech he made in 1962, which was printed in the *Congressional Record*, displays his attitude toward two questions, public prayer in the schools and public aid to parochial schools:

> I refer to the movement to take God out of the public school and to force the child out of the private school. You may already know of my deep concern over the recent Supreme Court decision banning the Regents' Prayer in the public schools of New York State. As you know, that prayer is a simple, short, non-denominational and voluntary acknowledgment of dependence upon God and a request for His blessing. I fully appreciate the high responsibility of the Supreme Court to guard our Constitution and the delicacy of its task. Moreover, I respect the integrity and the dedication of the men who are charged with this solemn commission. But I am convinced that in this case six Justices rendered a decision which will be harmful to America. . . . But now there is abroad in our land a new spirit which seeks to change this religious tradition of America, to place a nontraditional interpretation on the Constitution, to remove religion entirely from the public domain, and to commit our Government to the side of irreligion. This is the establishment of a new religion of secularism. This should be ruled unconstitutional.

In support of his claim, the cardinal failed to follow the reasoning of the Supreme Court, namely, that the purpose of the decision was to guard religious practice against the kind of political restraints European governments had imposed over the centuries. In the same spirit the cardinal deplored the attitude of "secularists":

> Theirs is a crusade, not for freedom of religion, but for freedom from religion. Their goal is to strip America of all her religious traditions. A classic example of their technique is the controversy over Federal aid to education. They have so purpose-

fully obscured and confused the question that millions of God-fearing Americans have been led to believe that there can be no peaceful cooperation between God and our country.

Do Catholics really believe that the verdict of the Supreme Court, gratefully received by the majority of American citizens, departs from our religious traditions? We have here a credibility gap of enormous proportions. Leaders of the Protestant denominations whose American tradition stems from the Pilgrims and the Puritans took no such stand. If the cardinal had presented a reasoned objection to the Court's majority opinion some non-Catholic sympathy might have been engendered for his point of view. However, he did not cite a single sentence from the Court's historic decision.

Now a word regarding the prayer itself. It was based on a recommendation of the New York Board of Regents, which is the highest state authority in education. The school board of New Hyde Park, New York, directed that it "be said aloud by each class in the presence of a teacher at the beginning of each school day." Its text: "Almighty God, we acknowledge our dependence on Thee, and we beg Thy blessings on us, our parents, our teachers, and our country." The New York Court of Appeals, two judges dissenting, upheld the decisions of lower courts that the use of the prayer was legal, provided pupils were not compelled to join in its recital. The high points of the 1962 decision of the United States Supreme Court are as follows:

> We think that by using its public school system to encourage recitation of the Regents' prayer, the State of New York has adopted a practice wholly inconsistent with the Establishment Clause. There can, of course, be no doubt that New York's program of daily classroom invocation of God's blessing as prescribed in the Regents' prayer is a religious activity. It is a solemn avowal of divine faith and supplication for the blessings of the Almighty. The nature of such a prayer has always been religious; none of the respondents has denied this and the trial court expressly so found.
>
> The petitioners contend among other things that the state

laws requiring or permitting use of the Regents' prayer must be struck down as a violation of the Establishment Clause because that prayer was composed by governmental officials as a part of a governmental program to further religious beliefs. For this reason, petitioners argue, the State's use of the Regents' prayer in its public school system breaches the constitutional wall of separation between Church and State. We agree with that contention since we think that the constitutional prohibition against laws respecting an establishment of religion must at least mean that in this country it is no part of the business of government to compose official prayers for any group of the American people to recite as a part of a religious program carried on by government. It is a matter of history that this very practice of establishing governmentally composed prayers for religious services was one of the reasons which caused many of our early colonists to leave England and seek religious freedom in America.

There can be no doubt that New York's state prayer program officially establishes the religious beliefs embodied in the Regents' prayer. The respondents' argument to the contrary, which is largely based upon the contention that the Regents' prayer is "nondenominational" and the fact that the program, as modified and approved by state courts, does not require all pupils to recite the prayer but permits those who wish to do so to remain silent or be excused from the room, ignores the essential nature of the program's constitutional defects.

It has been argued that to apply the Constitution in such a way as to prohibit state laws respecting an establishment of religious services in public schools is to indicate a hostility toward religion or toward prayer. Nothing, of course, could be more wrong. The history of man is inseparable from the history of religion.

It is neither sacrilegious nor antireligious to say that each separate government in this country should stay out of the business of writing or sanctioning official prayers and leave that purely religious function to the people themselves and to those the people choose to look to for religious guidance. [Engel v. Vitale, 370 U. S. 421 (1962)]

It will be recalled that in the McCollum decision (Illinois *ex rel.* McCollum v. Board of Education, 333 U. S. 203 [1948]) the Supreme Court had outlawed religious instruction in public school buildings—a decision that was followed by considerable noncompliance in various states. In this respect some religious leaders resemble Southern racial segregationists: they do not hesitate to subject the Court to ridicule if its decisions run counter to their fundamental beliefs.

As a comment on the turmoil connected with prayer in the public schools, it should be noted that public prayer received no sanction from the early Christians. As invoked by persons in power, "God's will" always seems to be a government's will, an army's will, a church's will. To carry symbolic meaning in human affairs, "God's will" should express the ideal of the greatest good of the greatest number. As such, it could be tested by man-made, man-imagined criteria. Otherwise we come close to reestablishing a cult of divine right. *Under God* and similar assertions take on relevance only by a transliteration in subvocal speech: *In the best of worlds.* Strict constructionists of the United States Constitution need have no fear; the word *God* does not appear in it. Surely this was no oversight on the part of the founding fathers.

Prayers for rain, for protection against floods, fire, or disease, for victory in war, betray the primitive ingredients in today's society. When offered by beleaguered politicians prayer is invariably suspect; public prayer is so dramatic, so righteous— and, unhappily, so often an unctuous diversion from the man-induced realities of poverty, hatred, and violence.

In politics, prayer may be a prelude to some nasty business; private prayer is a different matter. If truly private, as ordained in the Sermon on the Mount, it may, like the arts, be a source of comfort and healing power, or perhaps a sincere expression of remorse and resolve. If Christians were to follow the precepts of Jesus all prayers would be private. A public prayer is less an appeal to a Supreme Being than a call to its listeners to perform some secular act. It is really a form of public relations. After all, if God is listening, what matters the audience? But to speak in this vein is to kindle archaic fears. Ceremonial prayers, as in a baccalaureate service or the opening of a meeting, are glossed over; it is tacitly agreed that they have no religious significance whatever.

The wavering of politicians under pressure from organized groups that claim to follow God, justice, and the American dream is shown by the fact that in 1972 two hundred members of the House of Representatives signed a petition for a "Prayer Amendment" to the Constitution—this in spite of the Supreme Court's explicit rulings against any further entanglement of government and religion. The amendment would read thus: "Nothing contained in this Constitution shall abridge the right of persons lawfully assembled, in any public building which is supported in whole or in part through the expenditure of public funds, to participate in nondenominational prayer." The target, of course, is the public schools. Apart from the lack of merit and the utter untimeliness of the proposal, what congeries of scholars or religious leaders could conceivably compose a non-denominational prayer acceptable alike to Catholics, Protestants, Jews, Moslems, Unitarians, and Humanists—leaving out of consideration perhaps one hundred million Americans of "no religious affiliation"? Once more, state and local school boards would be asked to set up religious exercises! Fortunately, church leaders themselves are coming out in opposition to the proposal. More to the point, but requiring rare courage, would be the outlawing by the Congress and like bodies at the state level of the opening prayers of official sessions.

I suppose the easiest way ever devised to get on the good side of the gods—and thus be embraced after death—is to recite unsparing praises. Is it not psychological nonsense to hold that a god could be in need of praise, or of anything else from mortals? Why, then, all the insistence, through prayers and hymns, on adoration? The answer lies in the self—in man the image-maker. We cannot be neutral toward our images; they become more real than reality, with few shadings permitted. In constantly giving thanks devout persons discharge a debt that otherwise would grow to unmanageable proportions; the more frequent the payment the less its size needs to be. If the debt grew into an enormous bundle of unacknowledged favors, there might be a default on a final great act of piety! So, praise flows like a spring torrent.

The Cardinal and John Dewey

The views of the former bishop of the Pittsburgh Diocese are of interest in any discussion of public versus parochial education: [2]

> As of a couple of generations ago I might have wished we Catholics had gone, in the nineteenth century, fully into the public school system. Now I consider this would have been an unmitigated political and educational disaster. Let's face it, totalitarianism is present, seed fashion, in every purely secular government as it would be in any theocracy; the moment you say that ours is a purely secular state, at that same moment you provide a basic formula for one or another form of totalitarianism and you come perilously close to Mussolini's concept: "everything within the state, nothing outside the state." The separate school system is a major and healthy obstacle to such a situation. Many things that some of us look upon as indispensable parts of education were doomed by the educational forces that were to develop in American education. One may write all the articles and dissertations one wishes in the effort to establish that John Dewey didn't really hold what John Dewey obviously held about the nature and purpose of education and/or that his words admit of other interpretations. But the fact remains that his contentions were understood in a specific sense by universities, textbook writers, school associations, and, above all, teachers' colleges all over the land. I do not find the net result in American culture such as to make me wish we had abandoned totally our independent educational witness. [Pp. 37–38]

Presumably what John Dewey stood for, the cardinal, perhaps speaking for the ruling body of the Church, was against. It is therefore not amiss in this context to quote a paragraph of mine on Dewey's contribution to American education: [3]

> *We know, now, what Dewey helped to chase out of American schools*, not to return unless we lose our senses: mass education with almost no attention to individual differences; "book" learning as the exclusive aim of the school; intellectual orthodoxy; the teacher as autocrat; a lack of reality in content; the neglect of social behavior and inspiration; the divorce between the past

and the present; the sanctity of memory; primitive tests and measures; absurd art; a neglect of meaning; a lack of problem solving; a reliance on "mental discipline"; the view that higher education was for the socially elite; the low status of teachers; a lack of interest in world affairs; the disdain of teaching facilities; the rattletrap, firetrap, dark schoolhouses; the capture of ardent children for five or six years in a single schoolroom; the hostility toward play, teamwork, and projects. This catalogue admittedly emphasizes the dark side, but it is not much below the central tendency of schools in the 1890's, and that was when Dewey's theory, work, and example were at their best. He was busily practicing in the experimental schools of the University of Chicago what, for an additional half century, he was to preach.

I do not contend that the cardinal is opposed to all Dewey's ideas and reforms; still, like so many others, he is indiscriminate in his attack. It would be revealing if the critics of Dewey's educational concepts would submit to a twofold measure of the validity of their argument: (1) to place on the line the Dewey proposals they abhor, disagree with, partially accept, fully accept, and (2) in a correlated column of important issues state their own beliefs and practices.

The Cause Is Humanism

There is always the danger of totalitarianism in any power structure, theocratic or secular, but up to now that danger has been averted in American education not so much by the existence of independent schools as by the fact that elementary and secondary education in the United States is a responsibility of the fifty states and several thousand local school boards. The system is radically different from what is found in a church hierarchy. To a degree, parochial schools and (with some exceptions) church-controlled colleges are exactly what Cardinal Wright deplores: everything within, nothing outside. Recently, because of the far-reaching promise of Vatican II, together with the lure of public aid if a college sheds its church control, there has been some retreat from this position.

For decades there has been a torrent of abuse directed toward any activity labeled "secular." If by *secularism* we mean a resistance to church domination in civil affairs, let us have more of it. Secularism ideally calls upon every person to help counteract the defects of society—poverty, functional illiteracy, crime, ill health, environmental pollution, racial prejudice, political injustice, and war. A church that shuns these issues, whatever its "success" in the past, will lose ground. In maintaining a dichotomy between "godless" acts and acts "under God," the Roman Catholic church has made a specious choice, namely, that heresy is an evil beyond all others. To be a secularist is not thereby to dwell on the lower rungs of technology or materialism. In modern times, leaders in science, philosophy, art, and philanthropy are more often than not free from the shackling concepts of a revealed religion. On the other hand, theologians in the last century have made little contribution to the structure of thought. That life is dreary for millions of persons in this affluent nation and scarcely rewarding for many millions more has nothing to do with the clerical-secular dialogue. A liberal church or any liberating element within a traditional church that promotes the good life across all social boundaries deserves warm support. This is the converging point; it is at once secular and religious. The common cause is not *secularism*; it is *humanism*.

On Public Aid to Parochial Schools

Since 1958, laws relating to federal aid to schools (titles under the National Defense Education Act, for example) have repeatedly raised the question of public aid to parochial schools. In advance of the decisions of the United States Supreme Court in the 1970s there were, of course, barriers to such aid, especially at the state level. For a time the issue, though not resolved, was set aside in order to permit grants-in-aid to parochial schools in exclusive support of the teaching of nonreligious subjects—mathematics, science, and languages, for instance. The theory was that these subjects, even if taught in parochial schools, were free from religious content or influence. From the start, doubts were raised about the soundness of this viewpoint. It conflicted with the explicit purpose of the Roman Catholic schools, which account for over three-fourths of all nonpublic education. Thus, Pius XI's encyclical, *The Christian Education of Youth*, December 31, 1929, stated:

> For the mere fact that a school gives some religious instruction . . . does not . . . make it a fit place for Catholic students. To be this, it is necessary that all the teaching and the whole organization of the school, and its teachers, syllabus, and textbooks in every branch, be regulated by the Christian spirit.

The content of textbooks commonly used in parochial schools presents a religious matrix for such mundane subjects as arithmetic and grammar, while the teaching of biology in secondary education is overlaid with religious, nonbiological material. This state of affairs should not astonish anyone familiar with textbooks. Content is not presented in a scholastic vacuum; examples are part of the stock in trade. Moreover, teachers are free to introduce applications from their own experience; if it has been entirely in the service of a religious order, that will be the main source. In short, the teaching of biology and the social studies is usually slanted, while the teaching of history and literature affords a tempting opportunity to play up doctrinal beliefs. Although such teachings are held to be conducive to character formation, itself a proper aim of education, no significant correlation between group religious instruction and good behavior has been found. Delinquents are sometimes "refugees" from strict religious observances in childhood.

Throughout the 1960s the arguments for and against public aid to parochial schools continued unabated, with one side scarcely heeding the other. Proposals to rewrite or reinterpret state laws and local ordinances sprouted across the land. Only a comprehensive decision of the Supreme Court of the United

States would serve to clarify a situation rapidly getting out of hand. The instrument used to bail out parochial schools was the United States Elementary and Secondary Education Act of 1965. The National Education Association had been against such a move and had opposed the act. However, when the Roman Catholic hierarchy asserted its absolute hostility to any national program that excluded the parochial schools, the NEA leaders, as a matter of political expediency, abandoned their previous opposition to the legislation. That this action was repugnant to the rank and file (the teachers) of the association was revealed in the specific exclusion of aid to parochial schools in the sixth and ninth resolutions adopted by the NEA in the spring of 1970:

> The National Education Association seeks federal support of public education in line with the following principles: . . .
> (6) That legislation be consistent with the constitutional provision respecting an establishment of religion and with the tradition of separation of church and state, with no diversion of federal funds, goods, or services to nonpublic elementary and secondary schools. . . .
> (9) That where federal funds are presently provided to K-12 nonpublic schools, these funds be discontinued; however, until such funds are discontinued, these funds shall be controlled by public education agencies and be limited to tuition-free schools that meet all standards required of public schools. (This is not intended to apply to federal school lunch and milk programs.)

Doubtless it was too late to roll back any previous federal appropriations to nonpublic schools unless, as subsequently charged by the United States Commissioner of Education, the funds were misspent, but the NEA delegation was determined to call a halt to further entanglement.

The 1965 Act contemplated a reimbursement to parochial schools for "nonreligious" educational services, such as the teaching of the common school subjects. School authorities, alerted to the crisis by taxpayers and friends of the public school system, now saw more clearly than ever before the nature of the threat. Under the umbrella of "child benefit" there would be no limit to the public support of religious schools. There would emerge, in fact, two public school systems in terms of taxes, but only one in terms of local, democratic control. In school districts with a large majority of Catholic citizens, political control of both systems could be exercised by the Church. But the tide was in. One state after another, guided by politicians hungry for votes from diverse sources, responded to clerical pressure. Bills permitting direct public aid to religious enterprises, in the name of "child benefit," "purchase of services," "tuition vouchers to parents" and other euphemisms flooded the state legislatures.

President Nixon gave covert support to the movement and in 1971 hinted at some loosening of national restrictions on such aid. Apart from the putative political advantage, there was the question of finance: if parochial schools were forced to close, local school boards would have to build new facilities and hire additional teachers. Lost sight of in this argument was the fact that every state and municipality is jointly obligated by law to provide for the education of *all* the school-age children. Although church authorities have long encouraged parents to put up with the extra charge for parochial education, they now view with alarm the transfer of this cost to a much larger financial constituency. Actually, the economic argument against such an outcome is a smokescreen. Taxpayers who grudgingly pay taxes to support education—the nation's biggest bargain—uncomplainingly pay out big sums to make sure that the family is not deprived of commercial television. (A cynic once remarked, "If public schooling could be designated a *luxury*—like smoking, drinking, cosmetics, TV, movies, gambling, or sports—there would be no trouble in finding the money.")

Shared Time; Released Time; Voucher Plans

Attempts to exalt democracy and its attendant value systems to the status of a *legal religion* serve only to make a mockery of the law. Since every American would then have at least one religion—and all church members, two—the intent of this obfuscation is to push denominational religions under the tent of public aid. Public education in the United States is compulsory in an age bracket prescribed by state laws; it is inconsistent with the insertion of any religious belief or practice. Religious instruction on time released from the school's program is also indefensible. The school's day is already short. Religious instruction should be offered only beyond school time and away from school grounds. Churches have in their membership lists a ready means of child identification. Religious leaders who fight to retain "released time" reveal a lack of faith in the pulling power of their own offerings. Also, "shared time" opens a channel of public aid for parochial instruction—an entanglement of government and religion.

There is indeed something hypocritical about granting released time from a public school classroom in order to transport pupils perhaps one hour a week to a church or church school for special religious instruction. The objections to this practice have been well documented: a weekly disruption of the school's program, an embarrassment and a deprivation to those who remain in class, a divisive social situation, and the like—all annoying but not the main issue. The absurdity lies in the assumption that teachers of religion must rely upon school attendance records to gather in their young flock. It is not a matter of time. In effect the church is claiming that, given several free child-hours every day, plus a two-day weekend, plus a three-month annual vacation, there is no time available for religious instruction. The truth lies elsewhere. What the church wants, and often gets, is a double sanction for the practice of religion: (1) a latching on to the public school enterprise, and (2) an implicit endorsement of religious instruction as an ingredient of public schooling.

The so-called "voucher" plan is designed to permit parents to send their children to *any* school, public or private or parochial, at a cost not exceeding the prior per-pupil cost. In theory the implications are foreboding; in practice, the first victim would be the public school. No amount of shuffling of a deck of cards will give *all* the players a better hand or any player a guarantee of winning. Whatever is wrong with the schools would remain unchanged by a voucher system, but a chaotic factor would be introduced.

Many Devices, One Aim

Voucher plans, direct payments to parents, tax rebates, and the like are all designed to secure public funds in aid of church-controlled education—to set up through public aid a second, presumably equal system of schools, at first predominantly Roman Catholic but eventually appealing to the latent parochial drives of other denominations. The often expressed idea that individual parents would thus attain a greater voice in the conduct and character of their children's education is a will-o'-the-wisp: religious denominations strong enough to establish schools do not bend their ways to a free choice of beliefs on the part of a parish, let alone its individual members. Nor can the question of national divisiveness be set aside as inconsequential. Even the relatively innocuous aid for transportation to parochial schools stirs up discontent. In my four years as commissioner of education of the State of New York, the failure of school boards to provide free transportation for parochial students, as they were required to do by a state law, outnumbered all their other delinquencies put together. A standard complaint was the expense of transporting a few children in the neighborhood of a public school to a distant Catholic school.

In any event, aid given only for secular purposes would not bail out the parochial schools now experiencing a drastic reduction in income; at best it would buy time in which a more lenient Supreme Court, beguiled by the sophisms of "free parental choice," "educational economy," or "double taxation" might succumb to the frantic drive to bolster the teaching of religion by a flow of public funds. We should know by now that *any* dual system of education is more expensive in the aggregate than a common system with the pluralism that stems from the states' control of education. Therefore, if we are to have a dual system, which I favor, persons who sincerely regard the nonpublic form as superior should be prepared to meet the extra expense. The issue is clean-cut with respect to independent higher education. Is there any educator today who openly regards the maintenance of a costly independent assemblage of colleges as "double taxation"? I think not.

In a factual article,[4] the former chancellor of the University of Massachusetts, reported on a symposium on Catholic education held in Washington in 1967. The data he cited depict the magnitude of the involvement: over 14,000 Catholic schools, consisting of 10,750 elementary schools, 2,400 high schools, 325 colleges, 450 seminaries, 250 schools for atypical children. Altogether he listed two hundred thousand teachers and over four million students. The combined student body below the college level comprised about half the Catholic school-age population. Many of these schools and colleges lack sufficient funds. In fact, a number of church-controlled schools close each year. This is the background against which is held the never-ending debate on public aid to religious institutions.

The truth is that a carefully staged progressive transfer of all four million elementary and secondary students from Catholic to public education, if deemed desirable, would not add greatly to the total cost of education in the United States. Such a move would call for *noblesse oblige* on the part of public school authorities and a guarantee, backed by federal funds, that they would imaginatively plan and fully support a superior educational program for one and all.

Whatever happens, let us put an end to the use of the term "burden," as applied to the cost of public education. Consider the bargain contained in a contract to educate a child at a cost of five or six dollars a day for 180 days, a pledge that may start in the nursery school and continue through high school. That is not where the taxpayer's "burden" lies; it is made to seem so only through a dependence on local taxes. State aid with a comprehensive tax base and national aid with its access to the income tax offer the chief hope for the future. This explains why church authorities rarely seek an increase in local taxes as a source of parochial aid. Their leaders, hoping to circumvent stringent state laws and Supreme Court decisions, may again launch a frontal assault upon the principle of the separation of church and state. Education in the United States will then witness a season of bitter dispute along religious lines comparable to the conditions that drove so many Europeans to America in the first place.

The argument that a failure to divert public funds to parochial schools results in "double taxation" is incurably fallacious. Parents, strongly encouraged by bishops and local priests, *elect* to pay the additional cost of their children's parochial education. Parents of children in expensive independent schools pay the tuition in the belief that such education is superior. Our most prestigious schools and colleges are open to students of any faith or of no faith. Since copious scholarship funds are usually available, the benefits of this plan, both to the individual student and to society, are manifest. Catholic, Jewish, and Protestant parents could send their children to public schools for all the common subjects and extracurricular activities, reserving to their respective denominations only the religious instruction they cherish for themselves and their offspring. The two differentiated parts of education, common and sectarian, would be kept in separate domains.

A Cloud on the Horizon

In the literature not much attention is paid to the long-range effect that massive public support for denominational schools would entail. If the Catholics had won this bitter fight, they would not have been alone for long. Every denomination and sect, starting with those already maintaining private schools, would be eligible for support on some pro rata basis. In the decades ahead, a multitude of Protestant and Jewish schools, split a hundred different ways, might surpass not only the Catholic school enrollment but that of the public schools as well. A tripartite system sustained since colonial days, comprising free public education, voluntary independent education, and voluntary parochial education, would have gone down the drain and with it one of the pillars of our free society. In a nation already torn by domestic strife and foreign entanglement, such an outcome should be a cause for dismay.

However, it makes sense to place nonpublic education from nursery school to college in the two categories of *independent* and *parochial,* reserving to the former the privilege of seeking public aid at state and national levels. Such aid would be granted—or withheld—in a frame of reference free from the religious entanglements prohibited by law. Under the heading of "entanglement" there is one more irrational situation that should be cleared up. I refer to an irregularity in the collection of taxes on corporate earnings. Some churches have enormous holdings in profit-producing enterprises unrelated to direct religious services; unlike similar enterprises of independent colleges and universities, they are tax exempt. In short, spaghetti profits for the independent university that owns the factory, *taxable*; liquor profits for the church that owns the distilleries, *nontaxable!* In recent years fly-by-night religious cults have been taking advantage of such tax loopholes to reap a rich harvest through tax exemption. Unless the courts step in, the lease-back of tax-free profits will emerge as a nationwide scandal.

The Separation of Church and School?

With respect to any reduction in parochial or independent schooling, there need be little wastage in a progressive transfer of property to public use. Good school buildings would be in demand; obsolete ones should be demolished anyway. A church, on relinquishing the costly business of secular instruction, could set up in its place lively centers of social interaction and recreation. Most urban populations lack these opportunities.

Will religious leaders—the Roman Catholic leaders in particular—finally abandon their efforts to secure tax funds in support of sectarian schools? Let us sincerely hope so. Once the wall is breached, the political pressure for increasing support eventually without limit would be hard to resist. The unhappy experience of the Netherlands is testimony to that. There we find what most Americans regard as intolerable: a freezing of the social order into three segments, Protestant, Catholic, and the uncommitted, with little interplay among them. In a pluralistic society like ours, politics and religion already make a bad mixture; given a large-scale competition for public funds, the mixture would become explosive. The damage would be twofold. Horace Mann's prophetic vision of a common school for all children would be endangered. Furthermore, the right of a parochial school system *to pay its own way and therefore go its own way* would be in limbo. Critics who despise the "godless" public school are silent about this prospect of an invasion of parochial affairs by public servants who would demand an accounting for every tax dollar spent.

Regardless of tradition, change is in the air. I doubt whether economic factors are the sole cause of the recent decline in parochial school enrollments. As the issue of church and state is resolved, there may be a drift toward the separation of church and *school*. The move would be accelerated if there were to be no formal religious instruction before the age of fourteen. As of yore, religious devotions involving the whole family would then predominate.

In my opinion the strength of an independent school system rests upon its *independence*. Voluntaryism has led to the maintenance of some of our finest educational institutions, from the elementary school to the university. Having served in public education for a quarter of a century and in private education for sixteen years, I for one am heartily in favor of this academic duality; the two systems have much to learn from each other.

The Dilemma in Higher Education

Now and then a certain amount of sophistry creeps into the church-state argument. Consider this bold statement: "If one is convinced that higher education ought to be essentially state-operated on the model of the California or Illinois or New York systems, then there is no rationale for Catholic colleges, or indeed, for any other private schools." [5]

Having worked in all three of the state systems mentioned, and noting that higher education is for the most part publicly supported, I am puzzled by Greeley's cynicism. Should California desert Stanford and the California Institute of Technology? Should the citizens of Illinois abandon Knox College and the University of Chicago? Should New Yorkers say farewell to Syracuse, Rochester, Columbia, Fordham, New York University, and a hundred others? Any such approach is unrealistic. What we have and should keep is a dual system of higher education—really a triple system if church-controlled institutions are placed in a separate category. This diversity is invaluable. It helps to deter a corrupt government from taking over, let us say in the fashion that Perón, through his obnoxious "interveners," took over the universities of Argentina. We know, too, what happened in Japan and Germany prior to World War II: not a single university remained free, though fortunately some dissident professors and priests escaped.

If we can trust history to repeat itself, a parallel but less dangerous dilemma confronts American institutions today. There is safety in state control, for it is pluralistic. But if a private university's income from national—that is to say, military—grants exceeds a certain critical mass, its independence is thereby threatened. Liberal arts colleges in which research support is negligible constitute a line of defense against this outcome. In theory, a church-related institution is the most effective of all barriers against governmental interference, for the parent church can take a stand against oppressive edicts. However, it does not work out that way. Intertwined with government on great political issues, the church may abdicate its moral leadership. In the person of a Joseph McCarthy, the country faced a religious-political cartel of menacing proportions. Happily President Kennedy brought about cooperation between the two worlds through a far-reaching program of human advancement.

The combined strength of the private colleges and universities is a counterpoise to the massive structure of public higher education. A crucial factor is the voluntary nature of their financial support. There are those who look upon all private education as elitist, undemocratic, discriminatory. To them, the future of higher education in the United States is to be found in such gigantic operations as the City University of New York (180,000 students), the State University of New York (300,000 students), and, of course, the California system of higher education. However, excellence is not a monopoly of either the big or the little, nor is it a monopoly of public or private auspices. That is not the issue. The issue, as mentioned above, is to preserve the right and the intention to maintain institutions of higher education by voluntary contributions and tuition without governmental interference—an issue eloquently set forth by Daniel Webster in the *Dartmouth College* case.[6]

Jewish Spokesmen

Having presented to some degree the views on church and state of Protestants, Catholics, and deists, I should like to insert a few paragraphs by two Jewish authorities. Philip Jacobson states, in an article entitled "Jewish Viewpoint on Church-State-School Relations":

> The religious school is an adjunct of the church, serving sectarian ends. Indeed, religious education is the foremost responsibility of the church. . . . Jews are for religion and the unrestricted right to practice it according to the dictates of conscience. They are for free institutions of religion, completely independent of the state and truly voluntary in character. They

desire a basically moral society; in the current phraseology, they are for moral and spiritual values. They are for a society in which the rights of the individual are paramount. They are for an educated citizenry steeped in the best democratic traditions. They are for free, secular public schools. They see them as the finest expression of American democracy. [*School and Society*, May 20, 1961, p. 242]

However, a humane religious scholar, Louis Finkelstein, gets into logical difficulties when he discusses the place of religion in publicly supported education. To quote Rabbi Finkelstein:

> Our colleges, of course, are the seats of great spiritual confusion. Teaching religion is not permitted in any of the tax supported institutions, although apparently teaching non-religion *is* permitted. So a biologist can say that he does not believe in God or that he thinks man is an "accident." But if a religious person said that biology cannot be understood without reference to a wise Creator, he might be fired for trying to "indoctrinate" his pupils. [*American Character*, Center for the Study of Democratic Institutions (1962), p. 178]

In making this statement Rabbi Finkelstein had forgotten that Protestant, Catholic, and Jewish professors have taught religion since the 1920s in the School of Religion at the State-supported University of Iowa. One professorship not set up there, or elsewhere as far as I know, was that of atheism or agnosticism. More important is the rabbi's identification of the secular with the nonreligious. A professor teaching chemistry, biology, or engineering is not teaching "nonreligion"; he is teaching subjects whose principles, findings, and conclusions do not depend upon religious beliefs. I doubt whether a teacher would be fired for a reference to a "wise Creator" without which biology could not be understood, but I should enjoy eavesdropping on his responses to the questions of alert students. The truth is that for centuries, culminating in the struggle against Darwinism, the Christian churches stood on the side of biological darkness and deception.

A State Court Decision: Oregon

Up to the 1960s state constitutions and state courts were more effective than the Supreme Court in preserving the principle of separation of church and state. Thus, early in the decade, some state courts took a dim view of the idea that public aid to parochial schools was not aid to a religion but simply a "child benefit." In 1961 the Supreme Court of Oregon reached this conclusion:

> The difficulty with this [child benefit] theory is . . . that . . . unless it is qualified in some way it can be used to justify the expenditure of public funds for every educational purpose, because all educational aids are of benefit to the pupil. The expenditure of public funds for textbooks supplied to pupils of parochial schools is clearly identified with the educational process, and does not warrant the assumption made in the Everson case that the expenditure is for the general welfare thus justifying the use of the state's police power. We attach no significance to the fact that the books are loaned to the pupil or school rather than given outright; in either event a substantial benefit is conferred upon the recipient. . . . Instruction in the public schools is available to all. Catholic schools operate only because Catholic parents feel that the precepts of their faith should be integrated into the teaching of secular subjects. Those who do not share in the faith need not share in the cost of nurturing it. [Dickman v. School District No. 62-C, Oregon City, of Clackamas County, Oregon, 366 P.2d 533 (1961)]

An Outstanding Supreme Court Decision: Rhode Island and Pennsylvania

It is now time to salvage out of the flood of newspaper reports and magazine condensations the historic decision of the Supreme Court on aid to parochial schools in Rhode Island and Pennsylvania. The following are key excerpts from the eight-to-one decision:

> These two appeals raise questions as to Pennsylvania and Rhode Island statutes providing state aid to church-related ele-

mentary and secondary schools. Both statutes are challenged as violative of the establishment and free exercise clauses of the First Amendment and the due-process clause of the Fourteenth Amendment.

Pennsylvania has adopted a statutory program that provides financial support to nonpublic elementary and secondary schools by way of reimbursement for the cost of teachers' salaries, textbooks and instructional materials in specified secular subjects.

Rhode Island has adopted a statute under which the state pays directly to teachers in nonpublic elementary schools a supplement of fifteen percent of their annual salary. Under each statute, state aid has been given to church-related educational institutions as well as other private schools. We hold that both statutes are unconstitutional.

The District Court concluded that the act violated the establishment clause, holding that it fostered "excessive entanglement" between government and religion. In addition two judges thought that the act had the impermissible effect of giving "significant aid to a religious enterprise." We affirm.

Pennsylvania has adopted a program which has some but not all of the features of the Rhode Island program. The Pennsylvania Nonpublic Elementary and Secondary Education Act was passed in 1968 in response to a crisis that the Pennsylvania Legislature found existed in the state's nonpublic schools due to rapidly rising costs.

The statute affirmatively reflects the legislative conclusion that the state's educational goals could appropriately be fulfilled by government support of "those purely secular educational objectives achieved through nonpublic education."

The statute authorizes appellee State Superintendent of Public Instruction to "purchase" specified secular education services from nonpublic schools. Under the "contracts" authorized by the statute, the state directly reimburses nonpublic schools solely for their actual expenditures for teachers' salaries, textbooks, and instructional materials.

The act went into effect on June 19, 1968, and the first reimbursement payments to schools were made on September 2, 1969. It appears that some $5-million has been expended annually under the act. The state has now entered into contracts with some 1,181 nonpublic elementary and secondary schools with a student population of some 535,215 pupils—more than twenty percent of the total number of students in the state.

More than ninety-six percent of these pupils attend church-related schools, and most of these schools are affiliated with the Roman Catholic Church.

The Court granted Pennsylvania's motion to dismiss the complaint for failure to state a claim for relief. It held that the act violated neither the establishment nor the free exercise clauses, Chief Judge Hastie dissenting. We reverse.

In Everson v. Board of Education, 330 U. S. 1 (1947), this Court upheld a state statute which reimbursed the parents of parochial school children for bus transportation expenses. There Mr. Justice Black, writing for the majority, suggested that the decision carried to "the verge" of forbidden territory under the religion clauses.

Our prior holdings do not call for total separation between church and state; total separation is not possible in an absolute sense. Fire-inspections, buildings and zoning regulations, and state requirements under compulsory school attendance laws are examples of necessary and permissible contacts.

In order to determine whether the government entanglement with religion is excessive, we must examine the character and purposes of the institutions which are benefited, the nature of the aid that the state provides, and the resulting relationships between the Government and the religious authority. Here we find that both statutes foster an impermissible degree of entanglement.

The District Court concluded that the parochial schools constituted "an integral part of the religious mission of the Catholic church." The various characteristics of the schools make them "a powerful vehicle for transmitting the Catholic faith to the next generation."

The substantial religious character of these church-related schools gives rise to entangling church-state relationships.

We cannot ignore the danger that a teacher under religious control and discipline poses to the separation of the religious from the purely secular aspects of pre-college education.

The Pennsylvania statute also provides state aid to church-related schools for teachers' salaries. The complaint describes an education system that is very similar to the one existing in Rhode Island.

We noted earlier, the very restrictions and surveillance necessary to insure that teachers play a strictly nonideological role give rise to entanglements between church and state.

The Pennsylvania statute, moreover, has the further defect of providing state financial aid directly to the church-related school.

The Constitution decrees that religion must be a private matter for the individual, the family, and the institutions of private choice, and that while some involvement and entanglement is inevitable, lines must be drawn. [Lemon v. Kurtzman, 403 U. S. 62 (1971)]

Justice Brennan's Opinion

At the same time the Court, by a vote of five to four, upheld the federal aid for church-related colleges and universities under Title I of the Higher Education Facilities Act of 1963,[7] which provides construction grants "for buildings and facilities used exclusively for secular educational purposes." Associate Justice Brennan, a Roman Catholic, held that all three laws were unconstitutional, stating that Catholic teachers would surrender "their right to teach religious courses" or to invest "secular" courses with religious implications. A further dissent was recorded by Justices Douglas, Black, and Marshall to the decision on Title I (the federal program in aid to college construction). Certainly the judicial standing of these four dissenters should give second thoughts to any college administrator tempted to stretch this privilege to the slightest degree.

The reactions of church and parochial school authorities to the decision on elementary and secondary education are a matter of record. If the public pronouncements of Cardinal Cooke of New York are typical, they add up to a bitter denunciation. It would be helpful to both sides—to the parents, teachers, and students involved—if bold steps could now be taken to strengthen both public and parochial education as separate enterprises. As concerned people ponder these decisions and their underlying philosophy, like Justice Brennan they may conclude that the cause of religion, no less than the cause of education, has won a momentous victory.

Continuing Efforts

It is certain that some persons—college students, for example —are in process of clarifying their views on religious matters. External influences cannot be expected to do more than confirm or antagonize their interior dialogue and personal experience. Beyond words there is belief; beyond belief there is faith. What counts is behavior, but behavior is an end product of the mental act.

Having identified *good* behavior (credit Confucius, Moses, Aristotle, Jesus, Mohammed, Spinoza, Mill, Emerson, James, Dewey, and others) and *bad* behavior (credit the same sources), we are comforted to note that the moral life of religious leaders parallels that of the nonreligious. The publicity given to the nasty fight between Irish Catholics and Irish Protestants underscores the rarity of overt religious confrontation in today's world; there, too, the issues carry strong political overtones. While the vast revolutions in Russia and China substituted new idols for old, what counted most was the change in economics, politics, and the social structure. Were the United States to be subjected to a measure of control by a powerful clerical hierarchy, Catholic or Protestant, we should take alarm. We have evidence of the social backwardness inherent in such capitulation. (Pockets of clerical domination can be found in numerous cities and a few states.) Our courts have done well to hold the religious zealot within bounds; they are the best safeguard we have for the preservation of a pluralistic, democratic society.

It is apparent that a report on the status of public aid to parochial schools will be obsolete by the time it is published, *except as it indicates a trend.* And there is indeed a trend, if not a strong movement. To quote Stephen Arons, of the Harvard Center of Law and Education:

> In the past two years—overnight as legislatures count time— at least six states have passed laws providing substantial general aid to private schools, and similar bills are pending in half a

dozen other states. This new concern by state legislatures for
nonpublic education is a response to a well-organized Catholic
lobby and to simple arithmetic. By supporting in part the education of children in nonpublic schools, nine-tenths of which
are operated by the Roman Catholic Church, they can avoid
supporting in full the education of the same children in public
schools. . . . Aside from preserving the existing private schools,
the effect of these laws will likely be to preserve or make worse
the already intolerable inequities and inadequacies of public
education. ["The Joker in Private School Aid," *Saturday Review,*
January 16, 1971, p. 45]

There is hope that further Supreme Court decisions will slow
up, if not reverse, this trend.

Further Supreme Court Decisions: Ohio and New York

It is reassuring to note that the Supreme Court shows no
signs of wavering. In October 1972, by a vote of eight to one,[8]
it confirmed a ruling by a Federal District Court that the
1970 Ohio law enabling parents of students in private and
parochial schools to receive tuition grants was unconstitutional,
a violation of the principle of separation of church and state.
In the words of the Court, "one may not do by indirection
what is forbidden directly." Nevertheless, novel forms of "indirection" are sure to be given a trial run the country over,
wherever Church authorities refuse to accept either of the two
permissible options: (1) to support a parochial school entirely
by private means, as in the past; or (2) to transfer the students
to a public school system. Yet it is apparent that only these
options are within the intent of the Constitution and, further,
that they still reflect the will of the people.

On June 25, 1973, the Supreme Court invalidated four New
York programs that the governor and the legislature had supported. By a vote of six to three it declared unconstitutional
statutory provisions affording (1) grants to parochial schools
for maintenance and repair, and aid to the parents of dependent children in non public schools in the form of (2) tuition

reimbursement or (3) tax relief. It was held that maintenance aid "advances religion in that it subsidizes directly the religious activities of sectarian elementary and secondary schools." The proposal partially to reimburse tuition payments to parents of parochial school pupils would produce financial aid to schools unqualified to receive such support. In general the Court ruled against "an eroding of the limitations of the establishment clause now firmly implanted." Also, by a vote of eight to one, the Court decided that the New York plan to provide (4) aid to schools in order to meet the costs of record keeping was unconstitutional.[9]

The cumulative effect of closely reasoned decisions handed down by both state and federal courts should discourage further attempts to entangle religion and government, but the pressure is still on. As in many other crucial decisions involving the success of democracy in America, the watchword is again *vigilance.*

12

SCIENCE AND TECHNOLOGY
IN THE SERVICE OF MAN

In times past education was an indistinguishable part of the environment. The elders in tribal communities taught the young, and the young taught each other, in accordance with tradition as modified by the demands of the moment. The keynote of all instruction was action—action in response to survival needs. Beneath our layers of civilization early precepts are laid down in neural tracts and infant behavior. Educational experience, which begins at birth, culminates in the mind as consequence.

On the Future of Man

Now that mindless nature has produced a mind in man, it is of interest to speculate about the next stages. They may be of two kinds and sharply differentiated. The first is along the lines of further natural selection—a slow process but to be speeded up if scientists learn how to produce viable mutations. Of course an artificial hastening as a by-product of atomic war may be as destructive to the race as the immediate loss of life. What other prospects are there? Well, human beings may lose a few familiar accessories—the vermiform appendix, tonsils, teeth, hair, nails, and toes, for example—but new fashions in anatomy will compensate. The second stage is the

245

possibility of new sensitive zones in response to common physical stimuli such as magnetism or irradiation, together with a higher sensory acuity for sound, smell, and light. What use the cerebral cortex makes of these impressions will determine the true limit of evolution.

The penultimate paragraph of my book on intelligence reads as follows: [1]

> Man is the only earthly animal that poses the riddle of its own existence. This is the supreme abstraction: out of the seething cauldron of forces and materials over the ages, how has life come to be, and with it that form of life at first guided by, and now subservient to, the cerebral cortex? The building of a bridge from the inorganic to the organic waits upon man's ingenuity in abstraction and experimentation; it is of one piece with what the biochemical scientist has already accomplished. In nature this is an old thing accomplished many times and perhaps contemporaneously.

Sir Julian Huxley soon raised objections to the conclusion stated above: there is no room on earth for natural life to be formed *de novo*. Existing forms of life to an infinitesimal degree have preempted all space and all conditions conducive to life. Therefore, the scientist "creating" life—probably as a by-product of certain biochemical experiments—will have to do so in a medium from which all existing life has been precluded. The nonliving ingredients must come together under forces and conditions that will start a living cell on its way and carry on from that point solely through interaction with nonliving matter. All this will be accomplished and perhaps in the near future. Education can do little about these matters except to prepare scientists to arrange for the first appearance of life and its mutations. Education concentrates on man as a social being whose hazards and opportunities alike are determined by social structures. Through this intellectual power to change social structures in the direction of conscious aims there is placed in our hands the ability to reshape ideas and events. Science has arrived late, and social science is in its infancy. Had science flourished ten thousand years ago, as it might well have done, we should not be weighed down with mythologies that get in the way of human progress. Of course we might have long since been exterminated. The one article of faith of twentieth-century man is this: we are wedded to science and technology, and there is no turning back. We may destroy ourselves, but we will not voluntarily return to caves or primitive social conditions. Social evolution invents its own forms of progress or deterioration; for us, the tragedy would not be to go simple, for we *are* complex; it would be to go mad. A stopped watch is no mere heap of metal; a stopped city is no fresh-starting tribal compound.

Geological studies indicate that the earth has existed for more than four billion years. In a peculiar way this finding seems to bring us comfort. We continue to push back the date for the origin of life and of the human race. We have had a most impressive past, from the standpoint of evolution, and we long entertained the hope of a respectable future. But, as Molière's physician said, we have changed all that. We are not worried about how long the earth will continue to revolve. What we fear is much closer to home: a nuclear holocaust. Already several nations are physically in a position to bring this about. The restraint is not in technology but in practical politics, rooted in the certainty of reprisal. The danger everywhere acknowledged is that another Hitler will use atomic weapons to satisfy his paranoiac ambitions.

The Task of the Social Scientist

The fortuitous success of physical scientists in relating to this problem of survival should lead social scientists to make survival *their* all-absorbing study. Willy-nilly, these may be the decades of the social studies, envisaged as an interlocking network of anthropology, psychology, and psychiatry; of economics, sociology, and ecology; of philosophy, history, and political science. These sciences should serve as the structural elements for every high school and college student and—let us face it—as an advanced seminar for legislators and public administrators. Physical science as a part of liberal education is also to be included and must be available in depth for students of scientific bent. But social and physical sciences cannot by themselves be expected to maintain happiness in human affairs. They must be supported and enlivened by the arts and the humanities; however deeply rooted in past events or allied to imagination, humanistic studies are relevant to the unresolved issues of our time. Evolution, whether biological or cultural, involves change—perhaps improvement of a sort and up to a point. In this sense, a "new" man emerges, and the hope is that he will seek social structures and forms of government compatible with advances in art, ethics, and peaceful cooperation. Since gene changes are uncertain, it is necessary to rely upon education and experience—the classic race "between education and disaster." The unity already achieved in scientific circles, across all linguistic and political barriers, gives promise that it can be approached in human relations. As a step toward such an idea we can at least shed our debilitating superstitions and seek to rid national governments of their fears, deceits, and hatreds.

We cannot expect that a social millennium will follow our best efforts, only a greater likelihood that more children will achieve the good life, however defined. No single generation can be faulted for falling short of its high expectations, but it can be and surely will be condemned in history if it fails to analyze existing conditions, to sense their trend, and in some discernible fashion to move ahead. The secret element in social evolution, as in the biological, is to make sure that the good outweighs the bad. For a million years man has maintained a generally favorable balance, but he is not immune to the troubles that precede and foretell degradation. His unique superiority is to be found in the quality of his cerebral cortex—the seat of learning and the target of the educational process.

Our civilization rests on science and its technological outcomes, but we have not as yet developed social agencies capable of managing what is produced—managing, that is, in terms
of the total effect on the welfare of the human race. There
has always been a disjunction between spectacular breakthroughs in technology and the availability of socioeconomic
counterparts. As a rule the wreckers get there first and seize
upon some nasty uses for ships, explosives, motor vehicles,
planes, and nuclear energy. The demand of the times, and
henceforth of *all* times, is to help our social sciences and
social instruments to catch up.

The New Place of Science

Thoughtful Americans are not hardened in a traditional
culture or religion, nor are they satisfied with the easy victories
they have won in technology and business enterprise. They
are intellectually and spiritually hungry. They ask, *Who am I,
and where do I fit in? What are the supreme values for our
time, and what are their manifestations in daily life? How
can a third world war be avoided?* Science cannot give the
answers, though only a culture rooted in science is able to
cope with such questions. We can no longer be prescientific;
we can only be for or against science. There is nothing inherently small or mean about science, and in the twentieth
century to hold back science in order to serve the supernatural
is to degrade the human condition. Applied science helps to
supply our basic needs for food, clothing, shelter, transportation, and communication. It contributes mightily to health
and to the means of spreading knowledge. Today's students
are clear-minded about the neutrality of science; they sense
its power. However, enthusiasm is reserved for the peaceful
utilization of power, especially atomic power.

The race is not between science and humanity; it is between
the brutal and the humane in a world society. Man in a certain mood is a thinker. A succession of scientists has discovered

worlds within worlds, bequeathing a new freedom of thought to succeeding generations. To say that technical procedures retarded the creative search elsewhere is to miss the point. Did the astronomical data of the Egyptians, Greeks, or Incas spoil the work of their artists and priests? Not at all. A temple oriented to the stars, its architecture set in geometric principles, seemed better to them, as it does to us, than one lacking such logic. Workers in the arts and humanities absorb whatever science offers and go beyond, following their own imaginings.

Contrary to popular opinion, the American people are not immersed in science. The testimony rolls in from secondary and higher education, from business, industry, and agriculture, that most persons shy away from abstract symbols, hypotheses, and experiments—from the close reasoning and detachment that scientific analysis demands. Americans really adore machines—those glamorous by-products of science that work for us, compounding manpower at the push of a button. We sing the praises of anything that reduces drudgery. Gadgets, no delvers into the secrets of nature, with no insistence that you look under the hood or behind the panel, in and of themselves are neutral. To eliminate mechanical aids to comfort would be foolish; there would be small satisfaction in a return to the primitive. The thing to do is to take technology in stride while emphasizing the rewards of living derived from nontechnical sources. Nothing can be subtracted from the truths of science, but much can be added to them. We can not keep science in a compartment all its own; such confinement is inconceivable in a fast-moving world. An essential characteristic of truth in science is that it cannot be absolute. One way to test the truth of any statement is to test the method of its discovery and demonstration. Method counts, for otherwise we are hopelessly dependent upon authority. Untested doctrine is selective with respect to the items reported upon, thereby falsely supporting itself. Unlike scientific discoveries in physics, astronomy, or biology, dogma cannot be modified as knowledge advances; it can only be reasserted or dropped. Dogmas are not truths, however much of truth is contained in them; they serve a cause and are independent of demonstrable fact or law.

Persons who identify science with materialism do not understand science. Science is only a way of arriving at answers to questions—questions asked, as far as possible, in a language that is universal. Scientific results may affect values, but they are not the values themselves. The least to be expected in science is zealous objective endeavor. The physical scientist has no interest in tyranny except to avoid it and to fight it if necessary.

Science is an ideal milieu for thought, since the questions asked are asked of nature itself. We proceed in thought from a prepared position: the unknown is approached through the known. The first steps deal with simple measurements based upon the ability to count, to weigh, and to compare. Finally the search extends into the nucleus of the atom, the constituents of a cell, and out into galactic space. It boils down to this: in science the facts and their interrelationships must prevail, and the way of ascertaining and testing the facts, itself open to error, must be described with scrupulous care.

Science does not, *ipso facto*, contribute to the humanities, but the potential is there. A student in science must undergo a rigid discipline; even a narrow branch of it is vast and ever-expanding. Except in the way new discoveries are made—as in genes, X-rays, DNA, lasers, and the like—the pursuit of science does not call for great imagination. There is much past knowledge to be assimilated, and little attention is paid to social or artistic implications. I have myself witnessed indifference on the part of technical students to the so-called "soft" subjects of literature, history, and the arts. In fact, universities long catered to such prejudices, the first breakaway being undertaken by the Massachusetts Institute of Technology. Why, then, is it consistent to maintain that science is properly a central ingredient of the humane attitude? The answer lies in a new approach to the teaching of science for nonscience majors—and for beginners in science as well. It is to emphasize the process of discovery and verification as against a huge pileup of facts, and further, to stress what finally emerges in terms of its impact upon a culture pattern. Darwin's discovery of the place of natural selection in evolution and Einstein's derivation of the mass-energy formula are illustrative. The infiltration of general science is conducive to the growth of the humanities. It will add strength to our cultural institutions, at long last shaking them loose from the lingering mental defects of the Dark Ages.

Science and Liberal Education

As they must do in later life, students need to live in two intellectual worlds, the general and the special. Every student needs to enter the wide world of the arts and letters and human affairs, for otherwise preoccupation with the technical demands of the special world that centers around his vocational pursuits will keep him narrow. He will be expected to make important choices in the context of liberal education. No lawyer, the concerned citizen votes on legal and political issues; no physician, he decides questions of public and private health; no psychologist, he faces complex issues in family life; no artist, he quietly responds to artistic works in a half-dozen mediums. In the workaday world there is time for all this.

This is not to say that liberal education should measure out the same ingredients to everyone. Students pointing toward an active amateur role in politics or social welfare may abridge the time given to the arts. Still, an unreasonable neglect of the arts will impoverish them as activists. Beyond the common aspirations for a good life, however defined, is an unconscious craving for something personal. The world needs this variation; it is a hedge against uniformity and a computerized social structure. In a well-knit society the principles and ideals held in common are essential but few in number; further choices are praiseworthy, provided that indulgence in them brings no harm to others. Overriding all, prostituting science and technology, its leaders deaf to all supplication, is the nasty business of war. The great religions pay only lip service to this issue; by a persistent otherworldliness they sugarcoat its horror. It is as if the noble aims that justify religion—peace and humane progress—are too much for it.

I do not disparage those who follow science as a career or an avocation. Except by fanatic religionists, scientists have been greatly honored, even revered, often at the top of the intellectual ladder. Their contribution to medicine, agriculture, and technology is immeasurable. They are supreme in disciphering nature's secrets. Their faults as scientists lie in the company they keep. On being inducted into technical applications, especially by the military, scientists reveal no special grasp of psychological, social, or political realities; the absolute objectivity they try for in scientific pursuits is not transferable to the world of affairs. Scientists and technicians can be found who will work for anybody, regardless of human values. True, many have elected not to do so, as in the talented group that fled to the United States from Germany and Italy. The unpardonable act of the dictator was to interfere with their scientific work and, through racial hatred, to threaten their lives. Without this colossal political error more scientists would have stayed in their native lands, not contentedly, to be sure, but willing to carry on.

Science Has Limited Liability

Today the *savoir-faire* that science and technology so generously impart is our chief cause of worry. It seems trite if not rude to say it again, but the overwhelming fact of life today is the threat of instant global destruction. This power, seemingly immune to treaties or traditions, is wielded ever so dangerously by just a few men at the top. Ill will among nations springs from fears deeply embedded in persons. Groups of persons acting as one through the ties of geography, nationality, or religion react to fear and frustration the way the individual

does. This is the demagogue's source of power; this is the road
to Armageddon.

One of the masters that science is serving, however un-
willingly, is war technology. In a free society there are not,
and there must not be, any controls on scientific endeavor,
but the risk is always there. To quote from my Cubberley
Lecture: [2]

> The freedom the scientist demands in order to be productive
> and original is no inalienable right, for the simple reason that
> it cannot stand alone. He needs funds, books, laboratories, and
> assistants; he needs a free press. Very likely he will return all
> expenditures a hundredfold, but the question is, *to whom?*
> Hitler had his scientists. Some remained out of politics and
> asked only to be let alone. They were not let alone; they were
> forced into political action. They lost their freedom. Soon they
> lost everything that makes a man either scientific or decent.
> [P. 27]
> Unhappily science will grow more deadly. In this war we have
> learned the fine art of destroying cities above ground. The
> countermeasure, which is supposed to neutralize the latest
> method of military attack, is in itself monstrous—a life under-
> ground. Man is driven into the caves from which he emerged
> only a few thousand years ago, and he no longer feels at home
> there. [P. 28]
> Now it can be argued that technology really has had nothing
> to do with world wreckage. The scientist likes to feel that way
> about it. He knows that research will continue despite all
> charters, treaties, and covenants. It will be as hard to control as
> thought itself, for it *is* a form of thought. The scientist is
> discovering new pathways to danger and death. The same meth-
> ods that grow crops, develop machinery, feed children, and
> multiply incredibly our control over disease can be devoted to
> the best means of destruction. [Pp. 28–29]

Yet science as such is not the real villain:

> Except in methodology, physical science (not the individual
> scientist, of course) cannot be said to have any preference as
> between beauty and ugliness, noise or silence, sin or virtue. It
> undergirds homely or handsome buildings but never the poor
> design. It is the greatest noise producer in the world and the

greatest silencer. If your good health is a virtue, science will contribute to it with amazing effectiveness; if your enemy's ill health is an equal virtue, science is quick to burn him, poison him, or blow him to bits. In a gentler mood, as it were, science will discover strange things in a cup of water, leaving for the humanist, the moralist, or the educator the delightful task of making cleanliness a virtue. Is it reasonable for anyone to get angry at so obedient a servant? [P. 35]

The pursuit of science generates its own incentives and detaches itself from any ill effects; the latter are regarded as abuses not of science but of technology and the social structure.

Technology as a Force

Clearly technology is more than a handmaiden to which scientists may give much or little, not caring how their discoveries may be utilized. There is a reverse action. Applied technical knowledge constitutes a driving force for further work in pure science, and it procures the big appropriations. Governments are given to this preference. On a small scale, those of us familiar with university operations are accustomed to this "inversion" of values. The system is not wholly unfruitful. Since the days of Pasteur we have known that great discoveries may result from the need to solve practical problems. The pitiable effects of polio on children gave a tremendous push to the search for a successful vaccine. Salk, Sabin, and their colleagues became leaders in both medicine and social progress. Of late the public is aware of the fact that cancer will not be controlled, much less cured, until fundamental research is further advanced. In spite of their persistent efforts to deceive, the promoters of shortcut "cures" and mystical treatments for cancer are finally exposed. In one notorious midwestern case, the alleged drug was not only useless; it did not even exist!

Basic nuclear research has followed a different pattern. Its very success has introduced the greatest threat to human sur-

vival the world has ever known. The technology that under-
pins national defense has crept in as master. It will not be
displaced until global security is established by either the
United Nations or a successor organization. The dilemma is
that science, having lost a measure of its freedom of discovery
and reportage on this frontier, has found no way of reasserting
itself as an independent intellectual operation. Its every move
in this field is assessed in nationalistic terms. Until notable
political reforms are undertaken, is there anything more to
add to the billion-word pileup on the issue of nuclear strike
forces? Perhaps a few words that bear upon the future of
education will not be amiss. Throughout the early history of
warfare it was hard to kill a man except through starvation
or disease. The fighting arm tired; the fighter began to think
of home. Killing was a person-to-person affair utilizing crude
weapons. Artillery and the machine gun modified but did not
eliminate this hand-to-hand feature of combat. But in 1945 the
dropping of the first atomic bomb rendered warfare on a large
scale obsolete and unthinkable; no nation could afford to win
that way. One need not be privy to confidential reports to
sense that the next war, if it comes, will be an undeclared
rocket war, signed, sealed, and delivered from isolated bases.
The first target (will there be any others?) will not be an
army or navy, for the military elements are dispersed, nor the
hidden, well-protected rocket silos. It will be the densely populated cities. The certain victims will be all the men, women,
and children living within a circular probable error of the
point of impact of a thermonuclear bomb. In this frame of
reference, the total population of Boston, Providence, Hart-
ford, New Haven, New York, Philadelphia, Baltimore, Washington, and Richmond, with their suburbs, could succumb to
the dozen or so bombs in a first strike. Try as we may, in
imitation of Hermann Kahn, we cannot exaggerate the horror
of that event. The delicate equilibrium of our world can be
upset by a single unbalanced mind at the controls. This is the
deadly issue that should deposit its imprint in the forebrain

of every teacher and student, not to make other learning seem pointless but to improve the chance that it will mean anything at all.

Aggression Is Not Instinctive

Few sociologists or psychologists today would link war with any putative aggressive instinct in the individual. War is a phenomenon of the social structure. As such it is most likely to break out when, for reasons of pride, glory, or greed, a people has allotted fateful decisions to a leader or clique epitomizing these perilous traits. For some, up to now, war has been a safe and profitable venture; for them it permits an assumption of power unheard of in times of peace. War is an emotional experience so powerfully channeled through slogans and symbols of solidarity as to blot out all thoughts of defeat. However, none of these hitherto effective means of recruitment and sacrifice characterized our Vietnam generation; by the hundreds of thousands American young men sullenly submitted, left the country, or deserted. In such a war before, during, or after the fighting there is no sense of glory, no intimation of victory, no pride of service to one's country, no welcoming parade at home. The individual acts of bravery, as numerous as in any other war, are committed in self-defense or to help one's comrades. The shame of indiscriminate killing has spread to all walks of American life. The alleged high aim of the venture, to ensure a democratic regime in Vietnam, was a grim joke; it was on a par with the previous war cry, "Unleash Chiang Kai-shek on the mainland of China."

So, the question remains: When shall we cease to blame war on something embedded in the human nervous system and therefore inevitable? When shall we turn to the background causes, which reside in the weakness of social and political structures under stress? For man, the sabertooth is a collective phenomenon beyond sorcery or genetic controls. Its nature is a fit study in education.

The Zoo Story

Beyond all learning that feeds upon itself lies the wisdom that embraces learning but moves on, at some point, toward action and decision. It is then that we approach the ideal of the well-rounded person. A scholar may live exclusively among his books, far away in time and space, but if he teaches or writes, his influence will be felt. Other persons, a far more numerous company, shun books and inhabit only the narrow span of their daily contacts; they revel in chores, games, gossip, and spectatorship. In our affluent society of the upper quartile, these dull experiences that stay dull through repetition have replaced the fatigue of the overworked day laborer of other times. It is a poor exchange, but it springs in part from poor education. The schools of the future will do well to cherish both the thought and the deed.

As René Dubos has said, all mankind lives in a zoo of its own making and has not yet learned to do so peaceably. He adds: [3]

> We cannot escape from the zoos we have created for ourselves and return to wilderness, but we can improve on societies and make them better suited to our unchangeable biological nature. I do not have much faith in the nineteenth-century version of the perfectibility of man, but I believe deeply in the perfectibility of human institutions.

In spite of recurrent breakdowns in the control of violence, Dubos's faith in the improvement of institutions gains wide support. On the whole, new laws are better than those they supplant. Efforts to establish the machinery of peace among nations are no longer regarded as visionary but engage serious attention at the highest diplomatic levels. Interlaced, interlocking groups, devoid of religious fanaticism—that ancient breeder of hate—should be able to discover values that transcend national boundaries. Violence would still spring from individual frustration and alienation, but it would, so to speak, take retail forms. It is no accident that violence is so often a characteristic of newly emerging or developing nations to which everything foreign is a target for attack.

To achieve peace we cannot depend upon species evolution, which is too slow, nor, as I see it, upon the advent of utopian arrangements. We must rather depend upon the rise of a school of social scientists and activists whose leaders, ahead of their time, will inform and guide a new brand of world politics. To keep ahead in this endeavor is to forestall the next nuclear blast. Once more, as with ecology and population control, we are brought around to the utter necessity of placing *humanity* at the heart center of every social reform. All else is supportive only.

Ecology, Science, and Education

The concept of *ecology*, having entered into common speech, is destined to be not only a permanent adornment of the language but also a constant reminder of the limited resources of the planet in contrast to unlimited growth in population. Through a complex network of energy exchanges, every environmental condition has the *potentiality* of harmfully affecting the human race. The statement holds for diverse physical and organic effects: air pollution (which reduces sunlight and sends poison into our lungs), water pollution (which reduces the supply of proteins), cumulative radioactive impacts (received directly or in a food-chain reaction), and depletion of essential mineral resources. There must be added as a part of the environment certain deleterious social conditions such as crime, poverty, and the spread of disease.

Clearly *ecology* denotes much more than the old-fashioned term *conservation*, although the conservationists were on the right track. We owe to the heroic work of a Gifford Pinchot or a John Muir the preservation of some of our unique spots of natural beauty, and to the Audubon Society and the Sierra Club, among others, a heightened awareness of natural treasures. The conservationists emphasized the affective, artistic, soul-nourishing attributes of nature. Today's ecologists stoutly defend conservation in principle and practice, but at the same time they bring in the competing factor of survival at an acceptable cultural level.

In the future no educational curriculum will lack some reference to ecology. Educationally it is important to keep in mind that the solution of an ecological problem depends upon a mastery of biology, technology, economics, and politics by their respective adherents. We are faced with a moral decision. If we recklessly consume the life-supporting elements of the earth and exhaust its supply of culture-supporting substances, the earth will eventually consume us.

For students whose mathematics from junior high school onward was directed toward statistical problems, ecology offers fascinating materials. Statistical computations are essential if one is to understand the interplay of agriculture, forestry, mining, industrial production, and the recycling of waste products, along with consumer demands and recreational habits. The postindustrial revolution whose advance waves we are now experiencing may really be more of a reform movement; it may emphasize the deployment of science and technology on behalf of the *person* and of all peoples in a humane society. The process will not reduce the scope or the necessity of science, but it will bear down heavily on the production of *things.* Since science, technology, and the social studies will team up to provide the underpinning for ecology, it follows that every high school and college curriculum should offer the student a fair start along these lines. Education can alert students to the whole complex weave of relevant factors. Objective information, careful analysis, and a weighing of the values embedded in the available options will guard students against foolish decisions. Still, there are "supervalues" that do not emerge from a computer or get listed on opinion polls— for example, the preservation of Yosemite, the Grand Canyon, and Yellowstone Park. Any departures from measures designed to protect such natural wonders should require the same consensus as an amendment to the United States Constitution.

An Ecological Dilemma

The long-range impact of gloomy ecological predictions has been obscured by a local—that is, a nonuniversal—success in the technology of food production and the exploitation of new sources of fuels. In the United States cereal crops are produced so efficiently and in such abundance that we create a "surplus," and the market drops. This concept of surplus is artificial and deplorable in a world state of undernutrition and starvation; it is inaccurate even as applied to the total American population. Corn may be priced too low for the farmer's liking, but beef and pork are generally priced beyond the reach of some millions of people. Private organizations such as the Ford Foundation and the Rockefeller Foundation have sensed this dilemma more quickly than the federal government. They have gone as far as their relatively limited resources will permit along four helpful lines:

(1) Applying basic research and technology to the upgrading of agricultural production.
(2) Increasing the effectiveness of food preparation, storage, and distribution.
(3) Altering food habits in order to conserve nutritional values.
(4) Assisting in programs of population control.

It may be said that if a kind of prudence can be exercised, henceforth applying to densely populated nations the indices of birth rate that obtain in the United States and western Europe, the specter of famine can be held off and the peaceful uses of power vastly increased. Following the expert prediction of Glenn T. Seaborg, formerly chairman of the Atomic Energy Commission, by the year 2000 the United States will produce seven hundred and fifty million kilowatts of nuclear-generated power, or one-half the world's production, all of this, we may hope, with a complete absence of harmful radiation.

Athelstan Spilhaus, of the American Association for the Advancement of Science, succinctly depicts the industrial side of the ecological movement:

> In the next industrial revolution, there must be a loop back from the user to the factory, which industry must close. If American industrial genius can mass-assemble and mass-distribute, why cannot the same genius mass-collect, mass-disassemble, and massively reuse the materials? If American industry should take upon itself the task of closing this loop, then its original design of the articles would include features facilitating their return and remaking. If, on the other hand, we continue to have the private sector make things, and the public sector dispose of them, designs for reuse will not easily come about. We industrial revolutionaries must plan to move more and more into the fields of human service, and not leave such concerns to the so-called public sector. We have seen our food supply grow to abundance in the United States, with fewer and fewer people needed to grow it. We are seeing the automation of factories, with an abundance of "things" provided by fewer and fewer people. On the other hand, we have a shortage of human services and a shortage of people providing these services. It follows quite simply that, if private enterprise is not to dwindle, while the public sector grows to be an all-embracing octopus, then private enterprise must go into the fields of human service. The next industrial revolution is on our doorstep. Let us be the revolutionaries who shape it, rather than have it happen—and shape us. ["The Next Industrial Revolution," *Science*, March 27, 1970, p. 1673]

As to the future of science and its relation to human welfare, it is appropriate to cite the opinion of the former president of the National Academy of Science, Dr. Frederick Seitz:

> I would like to emphasize again that our well-being is now so completely dependent upon science and science-based technology that it would be virtually impossible for us to abandon our present pattern for gaining new and useful knowledge. Any such rejection of science would be followed by a rapid retrogression in our way of life. To focus on specific issues, we are already beginning to face some of the consequences of the inevitable exhaustion of nonrenewable natural resources, such as

rare metals and fossil fuels. The search for new supplies and reasonable substitutes will inevitably require extensive research. Still further, I see no possible letup in the need for biological research related to medicine, if we continue to value low infant mortality and general freedom from disease. ["Science and Modern Man," *American Scientist*, Autumn 1966, p. 241]

Of equal interest is the view of a leading historian, Lynn White, Jr.:

Scientists must become increasingly aware of the complexity and intimacy of science's relationships to its total context. The modern tendency to regard science as somehow apart from, or even dominant over, the main human currents that surround it is dangerous to its continuance, and can be harmful even to progress within science. . . . The continuation of civilization as we know it depends on science, and the continuance of science would seem to depend on our ability to examine this sphere of human activity objectively and relate it to its human context. Those responsible for the statesmanship of science must develop a scientific understanding of science itself. [*Science, Scientists, and Politics*, Center for the Study of Democratic Institutions, September 1963]

In the same paper White points out that the Roman Empire, like early Christianity, ignored science. The Romans declined, but Christianity moved into the modern world by following the dictum of St. Francis of Assisi that things and events in the natural world were intrinsically important. If in the future the public became convinced that the destructiveness of the science-technology pairing was incurable, a massive opposition to science could usher in a second "Dark Age." The principal safeguard against this outcome is education.

Some Practical Considerations

What are the limits to ecological improvement? Where does the curve turn? For one thing, any attempt to correct early mistakes by evil means would only intensify the trouble.

We cannot accept infanticide; we cannot withhold food, shelter, and medical care if it is in our power to give aid. We do not condone either suicide or euthanasia for the "surplus" aged. The extermination of peoples by military means has not lost in horror by repetition. All we can do is to control two major factors: (1) The percentage of population increase in crowded countries; (2) The depletion of natural resources in the service of unreasonable consumer demands. In the United States, fewer large families, yes, but on a voluntary basis. The mother with a large family on welfare, lacking a "breadwinner," is a case in point: no compulsory sterilization or abortion, but arrangements to bring back a potential wage earner and to secure proper care for the children. The idea is to gain time during which a suitable program of rehabilitation can be carried out.

For ecology as a whole there will remain the conflict between what is scarce (restful, refreshing, inspiring) in nature and what each family regards as the minimal essentials for decent living. The proliferation of devices and mechanical services of every description, usually served by fuel and electricity, together with the failure to recycle materials and objects, pollutes land, air, and water. It takes mechanical energy to slow down or reverse the trend. Standards of living will vary widely over the world and will retain a factor of difference at home. Where anything of value is in short supply, it will of necessity be unevenly distributed. The social aim, which is being slowly realized, is to reduce the dispersion and skewness in the distribution of goods and services so that the poor lead a satisfying life to which the wealthy, by law, make a progressive, tax-based contribution. A concurrent aim is, through public education and recreational plans, to offer wide opportunities that are independent of economic differentials. The hope is that the quality of life can be enhanced without recourse to radical socialism, which exacts heavy payments along lines repugnant to our ideals of a free society.

The question comes down to this: What population, what

group above all others, is to be charged with the guilt of spoiling the natural environment? Nobody sets out to achieve unsightly, unhealthy effects; they are by-products of other needs considered, up to a point, as basic to human advancement. We have reserved the right to have large families, to rear them in densely crowded cities, to supply each person with a plethora of goods characterized by built-in obsolescence. The denuded forest, the putrid waterway, the city's dirty streets and smoky skies, its square miles of slums, garbage heaps, and abandoned-car lots are painfully in evidence. Not the least blight is one rarely touched upon by people who identify skeletons with the "last resting place of the soul," namely, the sprawling cemeteries filled with abandoned gravestones. They already disfigure large urban areas and threaten to vulgarize our most beautiful rural areas. Even in death, social distinction and a mortgage on property! This alternative will come to pass: well-kept garden parks and stately groves where at public expense the ashes of all, high or low, will be consigned to the earth. There the bereaved will come to mourn or memorialize, if they so desire, in an atmosphere of quiet loveliness.

In today's world the ability to produce *things* has outrun all the criteria of social value. Economic demand is both cause and effect. What is made has to be sold, so the truism runs; accordingly, demand receives enormous artificial stimulation. A partial listing of the categories of individual consumer demand for manufactured items in the United States might include these:

—Factory-built housing, furniture, and fixtures; tools; utensils.
—Electronic devices.
—Processed foods, beverages, tobacco, and their containers.
—Clothing; cosmetics; ornaments.
—Automobiles; other motorized vehicles and implements.
—Refined fuel and fuel conveyors.
—Printed matter, photography, and their attendant supplies.
—Toys, games, and sports equipment.

The demand from a group, agency, or corporation includes in addition rails, rolling stock, roads, planes, computers, laboratory and office equipment, and machines of many different kinds. How much of this is necessity and how much is luxury I leave for the social scientists of tomorrow. We have lived in and through this period of object-affluence so long that the most we can hope for by way of economy or ecology is a deceleration in the rate of obsolescence and waste.

Humanists and ecologists cannot save us from the dehumanizing forces inherent in uncontrolled technology. To be effective they must be backed up by an informed, dedicated group of citizens who confront the zeal for financial gain with the political power of aroused voters. The battle lines are not rigidly drawn. It is easy to be against cutting down the trees or polluting the waters, but the demand for wooden houses remains, and the market for household and industrial products is insatiable. However, in a free enterprise system there is predicated some reasonable restraint upon profit making so as to ensure the protection of more satisfying values. As the taxpayer-consumer demonstrates a willingness to pay the price, we approach the ancient ideal of combining self-interest and social benefit.

NOTES — INDEX

NOTES

Chapter 1 John Dewey and American Education

1. John Dewey, *Democracy and Education* (Macmillan Co., The Free Press, 1961), p. 151.
2. John Dewey, *Logic: The Theory of Inquiry* (Henry Holt and Co., 1938), p. 8.
3. Ibid., pp. 43–44.
4. George D. Stoddard, *The Meaning of Intelligence* (Macmillan Co., 1943), p. 475.
5. George R. Geiger, *John Dewey in Perspective* (Oxford University Press, 1958), p. 233.

Chapter 2 Theories and Principles of Learning

1. B. F. Skinner, *Beyond Freedom and Dignity* (Alfred A. Knopf, 1971), p. 185.
2. Jerome S. Bruner, "Nature and Uses of Immaturity," *American Psychologist*, August 1972, p. 687.
3. From *The Language and Thought of the Child*, in 1923, to *The Psychology of the Child*, with Barbel Inhelder, in 1969.
4. Alfred J. Marrow, *The Practical Theorist—The Life and Work of Kurt Lewin* (Basic Books, 1969), p. 232.

Chapter 3 Intelligence and the Learning Process

1. Translated from Alfred Binet, *Les Idées Modernes sur les Enfants* (Flammarion, Paris, 1911), pp. 156–57.
2. George D. Stoddard, "On the Meaning of Intelligence," in *Conference on Testing Problems*, Educational Testing Service, October 30, 1965, p. 4.
3. David Krech, "Psychoneurobiochemeducation," *Phi Delta Kappan*, March 1969, pp. 372, 373.

4. Stoddard, "On the Meaning of Intelligence," pp. 6, 7.
5. Ibid., p. 8.
6. George D. Stoddard, Chm. *Intelligence: Its Nature and Nurture: Comparative and Critical Exposition*, pt. 1, and *Original Studies and Experiments*, pt. 2 (Public School Publishing Co., 1940).
7. Arthur R. Jensen, How Much Can We Boost I.Q. and Scholastic Achievement," *Harvard Educational Review*, Winter 1969.
8. Theodosius Dobzhansky, "Genetics and the Diversity of Behavior," *American Psychologist*, June 1972, p. 530.
9. George D. Stoddard, *The Meaning of Intelligence* (Macmillan Co., 1943), p. 4.

Chapter 4   The Art of Teaching

1. The basic reference for the origin and development of this plan is George D. Stoddard, *The Dual Progress Plan* (Harper & Row, 1961).
2. In Clarence W. Hunnicutt, ed., *Education 2000 A.D.* (Syracuse University Press, 1956), pp. 141–64.
3. "Mathematics Education," *Sixty-ninth Yearbook of the National Society for the Study of Education*, Edward G. Bogle, ed. (University of Chicago Press, 1970), pt. 1, p. 22.
4. Morris Kline, "The Ancients versus the Moderns, a New Battle of the Books," *Mathematics Teacher* 51 (October 1958): 418–27.
5. Stoddard, *The Dual Progress Plan*, pp. 16–17.
6. Glen Heathers, *Organizing Schools through the Dual Progress Plan* (Danville, Ill.: Interstate Printers and Publishers, Inc., 1967), p. v.
7. A helpful comparison of such plans will be found in Judson T. Shaplin and Henry F. Olds, Jr., eds., *Team Teaching* (Harper & Row, 1964).

Chapter 5   Some Thorny Issues

1. Serrano v. Priest, 487 P.2d 1241 (1971).

Chapter 6   Secondary Education and Tertiary Education

1. "On the Mathematics Curriculum," *American Mathematical Monthly*, March 1962, pp. 189–93.
2. *The Arts in Secondary Education*, United States Department of

Health, Education, and Welfare, Office of Education (November 1970) pp. 18–35.
3. George D. Stoddard, *Tertiary Education* (Harvard University Press, 1944), p. 18.
4. Geoffrey Crowther, *15 to 18* (Her Majesty's Stationery Office, 1959).
5. Geoffrey Crowther, "English and American Education," *Atlantic*, August 1960, pp. 37–42.

Chapter 7   Inside the American University

1. James B. Conant, *The Education of American Teachers* (McGraw-Hill, 1963), p. 7.
2. George D. Stoddard, On the Education of Women (Macmillan Co., 1950), pp. 60–61.

Chapter 9   The Winds of Change

1. George D. Stoddard, "A New Design for the College of Liberal Arts and Sciences," *School and Society* 93, no. 2261 (May 1, 1965): 265–67.
2. Herman R. Allen, *Open Door to Learning* (University of Illinois Press, 1962).
3. *Journal of Higher Education*, February 1969, pp. 135–44.
4. "Open Admissions and Programing for the Disadvantaged," *Journal of Higher Education*, November 1971, pp. 629–47.

Chapter 10   Science, Philosophy, and Religion

1. Julian Huxley, "The Coming New Religion of Humanism," *Humanist*, January–February 1962, p. 4.
2. Ibid., p. 6.
3. Pierre Tielhard de Chardin, *The Phenomenon of Man* (Harper and Brothers, 1958), pp. 177–78, 183–84, 230, 295.
4. George D. Stoddard, in "Leaders in American Education," Robert T. Havighurst, ed., *Seventieth Yearbook of the National Society for the Study of Education* (University of Chicago Press, 1971), pt. 2, pp. 333–34.
5. Harvey J. Tompkins, ed., *Religion, Science, and Mental Health* (New York University Press, 1959), pp. 54–55, 57–58, 75–76.
6. Frederick Franck, *Exploding Church* (Delacorte Press, 1968), pp. 47, 129–30, 156, 274–75, 283.

Chapter 11 Cracks in the Wall of Separation

1. According to the *New York Times* of November 16, 1958, the statement was reported at the annual meeting of the Catholic Bishops of the United States at Washington, D.C., on November 15, 1958, and was signed by Cardinal Spellman, Cardinal McIntyre, and eleven others.
2. John J. Cardinal Wright, *American Character*, Center for the Study of Democratic Institutions, Fund for the Republic (January 1963), pp. 37–38.
3. George D. Stoddard, *The Dual Progress Plan* (Harper & Row, 1961), p. 45.
4. Francis L. Broderick, "Washington Symposium on Catholic Education," *Educational Forum*, March 1969, p. 293.
5. Andrew M. Greeley, *From Backwater to Mainstream* (McGraw-Hill, 1969), p. 158.
6. The Trustees of Dartmouth College v. Woodward, 4 Wheaton 518 (1819).
7. Tilton v. Richardson, 403 U. S. 672 (1971).
8. Essex v. Wolman, 409 U. S. 808 (1972).
9. The Committee for Public Education and Religious Liberty v. Nyquist, 410 U. S. 907 (1973).

Chapter 12 Science and Technology in the Service of Man

1. George D. Stoddard, *The Meaning of Intelligence* (Macmillan Co., 1943), pp. 480–81.
2. George D. Stoddard, *Frontiers in Education* (Stanford University Press, 1945), pp. 27–29.
3. René Dubos, "The Despairing Optimist," *American Scholar*, Autumn 1971, p. 572.

INDEX